KU-532-018

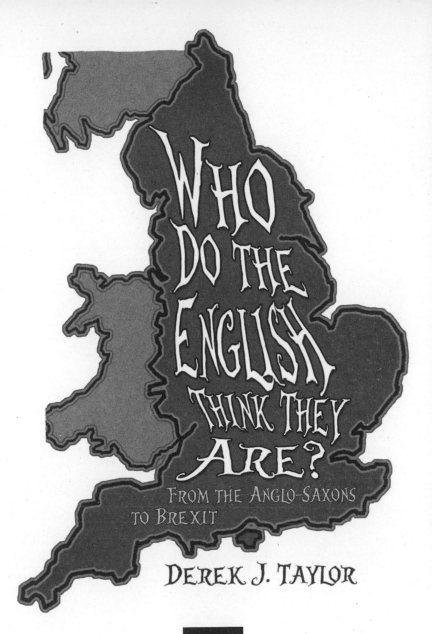

WHO DO THE ENGLISH THINK THEY ARE?

FROM THE ANGLO-SAXONS TO BREXIT

DEREK J. TAYLOR

The History Press

To Maggie, Dan, Jo and Nathan

By the same author:
A Horse in the Bathroom
Magna Carta in 20 Places

First published 2017

The History Press
The Mill, Brimscombe Port
Stroud, Gloucestershire, GL5 2QG
www.thehistorypress.co.uk

© Derek J. Taylor, 2017

The right of Derek J. Taylor, to be identified as the Author
of this work has been asserted in accordance with the
Copyright, Designs and Patents Act 1988.

All rights reserved. No part of this book may be reprinted
or reproduced or utilised in any form or by any electronic,
mechanical or other means, now known or hereafter invented,
including photocopying and recording, or in any information
storage or retrieval system, without the permission in writing
from the Publishers.

British Library Cataloguing in Publication Data.
A catalogue record for this book is available from the British Library.

ISBN 978 0 7509 7739 5

Typesetting and origination by The History Press
Printed and bound in Malta by Melita Press

CONTENTS

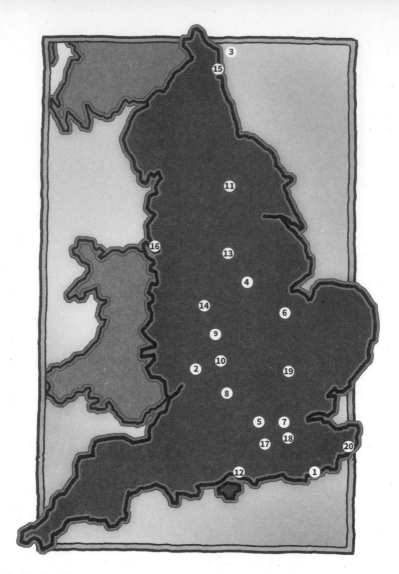

1   Hastings, Sussex.
2   Deerhurst, Gloucestershire.
3   Farne Islands, Northumberland.
4   The Trip to Jerusalem, Nottingham.
5   Runnymede, Surrey.
6   Longthorpe, Cambridgeshire.
7   House of Commons, Westminster.
8   Oxford.
9   Stratford-upon-Avon, Warwickshire.
10 Stow-on-the-Wold, Gloucestershire.

11 Newby Hall, North Yorkshire.
12 HMS *Victory*, Portsmouth.
13 Barrow Hill Roundhouse, Derbyshire.
14 The Back to Backs, Birmingham.
15 Bamburgh Castle, Northumberland.
16 Liverpool Docks.
17 Epsom Downs Racecourse, Surrey.
18 Imperial War Museum, Lambeth.
19 Duxford, Cambridgeshire.
20 Dover, Kent.

1

Hastings, Sussex

....

No Jackboots, Please. We're English

....

The English never know when they are beaten

Spanish saying

'Listen mate,' says the Saxon soldier, hitching up his sword belt. 'Never mind about the result on the battlefield. What counts is inside here.' And he gives a thump on his chain mail where it covers his heart. 'Inside here, mate,' he repeats with a glare, 'we English win every year.' He's not joking.

I've just arrived at the spot near the south coast of England where Duke William of Normandy defeated King Harold's Saxon army at the Battle of Hastings in 1066. Today is the anniversary of the battle, and our Saxon soldier is one of several thousand individuals who come here every year on this day, dressed in cross-gartered leggings, hand-stitched leather boots, chain mail, shining helmets and armed with spears, swords and battleaxes, just as their ancestors did 950 years ago. He's a battle re-enactor. And thousands more of us on this sunny day have turned up to watch them fight it out.

Meanwhile, before the mayhem starts, the mood on the vast field below the walls of Battle Abbey is both festive and feverish. There are kids chasing each other, brandishing brightly coloured plastic weaponry. There are parents yelling at them not to get lost, and come and get a burger, and yes, I mean now! And mingling among those of us in jeans, T-shirts and trainers or similar twenty-first-century kit, adults in medieval dress are trying with self-conscious nonchalance to look as though it's perfectly normal on a Saturday morning in a field in East Sussex to be dressed like an extra from *Lord of the Rings*.

This is not just a blokeish pursuit. I can see around me plenty of female camp followers as well, mostly in long brown frocks made from rough cloth and wearing white pointed hats with silky material swirling around their shoulders. There's one here now, hanging on the arm of our Saxon soldier.

What I'd said to him – after a pleasant and informative conversation about the handiness of the short-sword hanging from his waist – was, 'Good luck this afternoon in the battle,' and I'd added with a stagey wink, 'You never know, maybe this'll be your year to beat the Normans.' Not a side-splitter, I realise, as Saxon jokes go. But his answer is collectable. 'In here,' (he taps his heart) 'we English always win.' – such a poetic sentiment from a man dressed as an old-time thug. It tells of his pride in his country, a nation somehow able to snatch glory from the humiliation of defeat. So, waiting till he and his damsel have strode on so I won't offend him further, I pull out a notebook and biro to scribble down a couple of lines about the encounter.

A panel from the Bayeux Tapestry, dating from the 1070s. The idea that Harold was hit in the eye by an arrow is probably a myth, started later by the Normans who wanted to portray his death as God's judgement on an illegitimate ruler. Then in the eighteenth century, during overenthusiastic restoration of the tapestry, an arrow was added where there may not have been one originally.

I've come here today not just for the entertainment. I'm on a quest for first-hand evidence that might help unravel a puzzle. Who, exactly, do the English think they are? Where do they come from? What is it in their history that makes them so ... English? And what does being English mean? To find answers, we're going to travel through time and space. We'll explore twenty places that have played a role throughout history in forming the national identity of the English. Our journey will take us from an Anglo-Saxon church to a Second World War airbase, from a Northumbrian island to the White Cliffs of Dover, and in between we'll be visiting a pub, a racecourse, a slum, a mansion, a battle-ship and many more places, criss-crossing England through 1,600 years. And at the end of our journey, we'll ask the unthinkable: does the whole idea of English national identity still have mean-ing in the twenty-first century? Or have European federalism, globalised commerce and mass migration rendered it obsolete?

***

So why have we come first to Hastings? The reason is simple. The battle fought here in 1066 was the most important turn-ing point in English history. Once the Norman duke, William the Conqueror, had triumphed and been crowned King of England, no jackbooted army of occupation ever goose-stepped through the land. In almost a millennium since that battle on the south coast, England has never again been successfully invaded. Napoleon, Hitler and others have tried. None managed it. That doesn't mean the English have been free from any outside influ-ence for all those centuries – far from it. As we shall see on our journey, many encounters – both peaceful and warring – with others beyond our shores have all helped mould the English character. Nevertheless, the fact that the country has seen off every foreign attempt to seize the country by force for the last nine and a half centuries has had two effects. It has reinforced the sense of an unchallenged English national identity, and it has established the notion (in English minds, at least) that the English are a free and independent people. The English have a political and social history that goes back in an unbroken line further than that of any other race on earth.

Thus, the Battle of Hastings – defeat as it was for the English – has become a symbol of the nation's independence. And so here we are today on the anniversary of the battle, along with many thousands of our fellow countrymen, for whom Hastings means… well, that's one of the things we're here to find out.

***

The re-enactment itself is due to start at 3 p.m., so there's time to interview a few subjects first. One of the attractions is a medieval market. Apart from half a dozen food stalls, each with a line of hungry visitors, and one tent selling gifts, as well as the sort of armaments with which the small children are bashing each other, the rest of the tented shops cater for the Saxon re-enactor's yearning for authenticity. Some sell pointed helmets and heavy belts. Some have got smocks, headscarves and medieval shoes for sale. Others advertise eleventh-century cooking equipment. And another has an array of standards and pennants as used by Aethelwold, Eadwig and other pre-Conquest monarchs.

A man in a green smock is hammering away over a glowing forge, pausing occasionally to explain to a small crowd how you make chain mail. A young woman, whom he refers to as 'Lady Matilda', is passing among us. Folded across her arms is a complete coat made of little iron rings interlocked like a loose-knit sweater.

'How heavy is it?' I ask her.

'Over 40 pounds,' she replies.

'Good heavens!' I say. 'I wouldn't want to be wearing that while I was trying to run away!'

'You would if they caught you,' she says with a grin. 'Here, hold it.' And she drapes it across my wrists.

'Bloody Hell!' I exclaim, staggering for a moment as my arms sag under the weight.

Further on is an axe shop. The salesman is a young guy who, above the usual chain mail, leather and scabbard, sports a thick growth of facial and head hair at odds with the youthful features they frame. I pick up one of the axes. There are a dozen of them hanging on a rail, each with a black blade and a wooden handle as long as your arm.

'How much?' I ask.

'Sixty-five quid,' he replies.

'Sixty-five quid!' I exclaim. 'Crikey, it's expensive, this re-enacting game.'

'Yes,' he says. 'You can spend hundreds on the right costumes and equipment.' I raise my eyebrows in a quizzical expression. 'Everything – weapons, clothing – has got to look authentic. We'd be letting the side down if we turned out with some tatty old plastic sword and a polyester T-shirt.'

I nod. 'So, when you say "letting the side down", you mean your fellow re-enactors?'

'Yes. And the country. England,' his voice now slightly raised in irritation at my ignorance, and perhaps at my lack of patriotism.

I feel the need to be defensive. Running my finger down the axe-blade, I remark, 'Not very historically sharp, is it?'

'Well, we're not so authentic that we want to actually kill each other,' he smiles.

'So how *do* you avoid people getting hurt in the battles?'

'We train,' he says, 'at weekends. You're not allowed to take part in a battle till you've been on a course.'

'A course? You mean with professional combat instructors?'

He nods. 'And,' he adds, pausing for emphasis, 'we have a health and safety officer.'

At that moment, a giant thug of a man arrives at my side. He's tooled up like a Saxon gangster, smoke drifting from his nose, a cigarette cupped in his hand. Even I am not foolish enough to point out to him that he's infringing the central rule on anachronistic behaviour.

***

It's time to grab a sandwich and a good place to see the battle. There's half an hour to go. Most visitors have been cannier than me. They bagged their spots an hour or more ago on the grassy slope above the roped-off part of the field where the big event is going to happen. The spectators are clearing the picnic remains off their blankets and adjusting their collapsible chairs. Kids are managing – as only kids can – to run about, trip over and eat ice creams all at the same time. I'm relegated to a back row, where I need to stand to get a decent view.

Before us, on the other side of the rope barrier, a man in knitted tie and corduroy jacket (the universal uniform of male history teachers) is walking up and down with a microphone, delivering a lesson on the background and origins of the Battle of Hastings. Creditable as this is, no one's listening. They're all gossiping or playing about. It's just a background drone, like the TV on in the corner during the day.

After twenty-five minutes of this, the mood suddenly shifts. A mob of men – at a rough count about a thousand – in pointed helmets, carrying swords and shields, trudge into view on the right-hand side of the field, and the lecturer promptly switches roles to commentator, ups the tempo of his monologue and shouts through his mic, 'Let's have a big cheer, ladies and gentlemen, for Harold – and – the – Saxon – ARMY!' Everyone around me bawls their heads off.

Two tall young men come and stand directly in front of me so I can't see.

'Excuse me, guys,' I say.

The nearer one turns to me, 'I do apologise, sir. Please forgive us,' his excessive politeness making me wonder if he's being sarcastic. But then, as they both move to one side, he continues, 'We had not realised already that you your view we are blocking.'

'No problem,' I say. 'Where are you from?'

'Germany,' he replies. 'We are both in London University.'

'Ah, I see. From Saxony, by any chance?'

'Ahh, a very good joke,' he replies. 'But no, we do not live in northern Germany. But my friend here and I are from Bavaria. It is very nice there.' And he launches into a detailed, if fractured, account of Bavarian Christmas street markets.

Soon, the Saxon soldiers start to chant something with three syllables which is difficult to make out through the description of Alpine Weihnachtsfest infiltrating my left ear. 'Excuse me a sec.,' I say to the student, who bows politely, and I make out the words, 'God-win-son. God-win-son. God-win-son.'

The announcer explains. 'The Saxon troops are chanting the name of their king, Harold Godwinson.

Then the chant changes to what sounds like, 'Oot! Oot! Oot!' (I've yet to meet anyone who knows what that means.)

At this point, the enemy arrive, about a thousand foot soldiers clomping in from the far left. They line up 200 yards from the Saxons, then fire off a few arrows that curl high into the air before making a miserable touchdown in no-man's-land. 'Let's give a big hand now, everybody, for – William – and – the – NORMANS!'

Once the crowd has stopped booing, I turn to the student, who's now busy videoing the whole thing on his phone, and ask, 'Do you have anything like this in Germany?'

'Once I was in a restaurant in Bavaria,' he replies, 'where two men dressed up like soldiers of Frederick the Great and demonstrated to the customers their swords.'

'And that's it?'

'Yes, that is the only re-enactment I have seen in Germany.'

I look around for more interviewees. A few yards behind me, three men in red tracksuit tops are standing to attention. Each is holding a pole 9 or 10ft tall from which flutters a red flag with a white lion on it. I trot over to talk to them. As I get close, I see written on their chests, 'English Community Group (Leicester).'

'Hello there,' I say, trying to sound as matey as possible. One of them nods, so he's the one I address. 'I'm curious about ...' – I pointedly study the words on his jacket – '... the English Community Group.'

'(Leicester),' he adds.

'Forgive me, I've not heard of it before.'

He relaxes his shoulders and stands easy. 'We exist to politely represent the interests of the English community in Leicester and Leicestershire,' he says.

'Oh,' I say. '"Politely"?'

'That's right, we're not the BNP.'

'A-ha. I see. So why is the Battle of Hastings important to you?'

'We're dedicated to giving back to the English their unique identity and culture,' he recites, 'with a particular focus on our Anglo-Saxon tribal roots.'

'Oh,' I say, and I'm just about to point out to him – politely – that the Anglo-Saxon's tribal roots were in Germany and Denmark, and that the words 'community' and 'group' both came into English from Old French, when he continues, 'And another thing: we're actually anti-racist. We're challenging institutionalised Anglophobia in Leicester.'

'Discrimination against whites?'

'Discrimination against Anglo-Saxons.'

At this point, there must be an incident on the battlefield, because the cheering starts again, and the Anglophiles (Leicester) begin a co-ordinated, 'Oot! Oot! Oot! Oot!'

I nod my thanks and drift back. Our commentator is now urging us on. 'C'mon, ladies and gentlemen, let's hear it for the English,' he shouts, adding in exasperation when he doesn't get the required excited response, 'These men are fighting for your freedom!' Is he from Leicester, I find myself wondering.

But he has no need to fret. The two armies stamp towards each other, banging their lances and swords against their shields, and shouting unintelligible eleventh-century oaths. You can almost hear the collective lips of the crowd smacking at the prospect of blood and mayhem. Near me, a young woman with black hair and a lip ring is jumping up and down on tiptoes, as the gap between the mighty forces of King Harold and Duke William of Normandy narrows to a broadsword's length. 'We hear the terrible noise of battle,' according to the commentary, 'as bones crack and men die bloody deaths!'

The crowd in front of me crane their necks for a glimpse of the cracking and dying. This sort of thing goes on for about ten minutes. The commentator then sorts out any confusion in our minds: 'The English are winning. The Normans still can't break the English lines! Let's hear it for the English!' (Scattered 'Oots', off left.)

'Oh no, ladies and gentlemen!' the dread words then come over the loudspeaker. 'Oh no, who do we have here with an arrow in his eye? It's King Harold. He's fallen. He's been killed!' The spectators in front of me rise as one from their foldable chairs to try and glimpse the appalling fatal injury, thus blotting out my own view. 'The news of Harold's death spreads through the English lines,' continues the commentary. 'The English spirit is sapped' – this in a tone of desperate sadness – 'and the Normans are emboldened by this terrible tragedy for England.' As the crowd before me sink back into their downcast seats, I see the melee start to nudge back towards the Saxon camp. Then the retreating soldiers turn and break into a stumble, leaving behind half a dozen corpses.

The action's over, and the field is occupied by the victorious cavalry, who are galumphing about like Labradors on a beach. A mounted knight in a bright red smock comes close to us, waving his sword in the air. 'Vive le duc Guillaume! Victoire!' he shouts. We hiss him and whistle.

It's then I catch sight of the Saxon soldier I'd first interviewed. He's standing just the other side of the rope barrier with the blade of his short-sword hanging forlorn below his limp arm. He waves two fingers at the triumphant Norman, and calls out, 'You wait. We'll see you later at Agincourt!' I can't tell if he's joking or not.

* * *

So what does all this tell us about who the English think they are? Clearly, a mild brand of nationalism has been on offer at Hastings today, and we've drunk it in. The crowd may not by and large have listened much to the commentator's warm-up routine, explaining events that led to the battle. But he did establish his credentials as a historian, someone who is well informed. So his remarks, when he started to get us excited about the re-enactment, were likely to carry weight. And his words were telling. He presented the show not as a fight between two ancient tribes. Instead he talks about it as a battle which the crowd can get involved with, a tussle between traditional rivals, the English and the French. He urged the crowd, 'C'mon, ladies and gentlemen, let's hear it for the English. These men are fighting for your freedom!' It's ridiculous, but the thousands of English spectators at Hastings today loved it and cheered. We all knew – or thought we did – that if it hadn't been for one unlucky arrow in the king's eye, the English would have won. And of course, in at least some of our hearts, we did.

On the face of it, our Saxon soldier's heart-tapping remark is illogical: 'The result on the battlefield doesn't matter. In here, mate, we always win.' The bare truth is that if you lose on the battlefield, you're likely to be invaded, possibly killed and probably oppressed by a victorious enemy. So in what sense do you win? The suggestion must be that the English always behave nobly and heroically even when they've got their backs to the wall, staring death or defeat in the face. It's a belief that was held by Victorian soldiers at the time of the Empire, as we shall discover later on our journey. And for our Saxon soldier, being a re-enactor at Hastings enables him to be a part of a long and glorious English tradition, even if just for the afternoon.

Of course, some of us here today took it more seriously than others. The adherents of the English Community Group (Leicester) seem to be revering the Anglo-Saxons as the purest example of Englishness, and so regarding all later generations as some sort of corruption. If nothing else, it goes to show that English national identity is not always about rational argument, it can be about emotion. In this case, about ignoring the far-reaching influence of the Normans and their successors on English history, culture and language, as well the myriad of other developments over the past 950 years that have shaped and changed the English and made them what they are today. The English Community Group (Leicester) are drawing strength from what they regard as some long-lost golden age in England.

These chaps standing to attention beneath their fluttering white lion standards, are of course a tiny minority of the English. But what the English Community Group's members do have in common with many more of their fellow countrymen is a strong feeling that it's something in our history that makes us who we are.

Social psychologists argue that national identity – that is, the particular values that a national group holds dear and the traditions they have of behaving in a certain way – derive from that nation's history. Psychologists believe that distinctive groups of people have what's called a 'collective memory' of their past. In other words, there'll be a popular idea about what it is in the nation's history that's important. If, for instance, one group of people celebrate those of their ancestors who travelled the globe buying and sell-ing goods, they'll say, 'We are a great trading nation.' Or other folk might choose to remember their ancestors' struggle against oppression, and then they might say, 'We value our freedom. We're prepared to die defending it.' And these selected bits of history then get reinforced in the popular mind. To quote the psychologists again, they are 'memorialised.' That might mean they're celebrated at mass events – like battle re-enactments for instance, or armistice ceremonies. Or else, a nation's key achievements in history are 'memorialised' in the places where they happened: at historic sites that people can visit, cherish, feel proud of and sometimes volunteer to look after. And this is why we're going to investigate English national identity by visiting twenty places that tell the story of how the English came to have certain values and why they behave as they do.

It's a story full of mystery. The English – as you'd expect from a race 1,600 years in the making – are a complex lot. They've often behaved in contradictory ways. So for instance, the English place the highest value on their democracy but took centuries to give everyone the vote. They've been seen as tolerant, even though at times in their history they've persecuted minorities. They've loved political stability yet have fought among themselves. They've been eccentric and funny on the one hand, conformist and straight-laced on the other. They've revered the rule of law, but put a military dictator's statue outside Parliament. They've fought like lions in wartime, while making hatred of war respectable. The English have managed to be both self-centred and outward-looking, puritanical and permissive, arrogant and benevolent. And for much of their story, the English have been divided by a snobbish class system yet united against all foes. Bewildered? Don't worry. We'll sort it all out on our journey.

But we have to watch out. As on any adventurous exploration, it's easy to get lost. Before us is a crossroads, with signs pointing one way to 'Englishness' and the other to 'Britishness'. You may indeed be asking: 'Why isn't this book called, *Who Do the British Think They Are?*' After all, no one has a passport that says, 'Nationality; English.' As we shall see on our journey, not only the English, but foreigners too, in recent centuries have often got the words 'English' and 'British' mixed up. They say 'English' when they mean 'British,' and 'British' when they mean 'English.' Why they do that is one of the puzzles we'll be unpicking, and incidentally learning a lot about the English in the process.

The fact is that Britain is a ragbag, and a comparatively recent ragbag at that. The Scots were a separate nation until 300 years ago and, of course, are more and more asserting their independence. They sometimes dismiss the English as 'Sassenachs', which, as any dialectician will tell you, means 'Saxons'. The Welsh are understandably proud of their own language, culture and history. And Northern Ireland or Ulster, depending on your politico-cultural standpoint, has existed as a province of the United Kingdom for only a century, and its citizens are still sometimes divided as to which side of the Irish Sea their loyalties lie. The Scottish, Welsh and Northern Irish/Ulster folk can all claim they've got their own identities. It's true that the English have often been subject to many of the same influences as the other UK home nations. But the reaction of the English to those influences has not always been the same. The Brexit vote is an obvious example. The English are part of Britain, but still often see themselves as a separate group with their own values and their own way of doing things. So there'll be no confusion for us. Our journey is along the road signposted 'English.'

***

So we'd better get moving. Where did the story of the English begin? Our Hastings re-enactors were right – the Anglo-Saxons were English, the first to call themselves that. So who were they? And do they have anything much to do with the English today and their sense of who they are? To find out, we're going to visit a skyscraper. A medieval skyscraper. And if you think that's improbable, you are – like me – in for a surprise.

2

DEERHURST, GLOUCESTERSHIRE

....

ARE THE ENGLISH BASTARDS?

....

NO, THEY ARE NOT ANGLES, BUT ANGELS

POPE GREGORY I (540-604)

So here I am, parked up by the church gate and biting my bottom lip. It's the view across the huge graveyard that's giving me doubts. I can't take my eyes off the side of the church. It's such a disappointment. Don't get me wrong – it's impressive. *Too* impressive. I've come to the village of Deerhurst in Gloucestershire to investigate the Anglo-Saxons, and to see in what way, if at all, these first English had any influence on the national identity of those who live in this land today. The church here is said to be one of the best preserved Anglo-Saxon buildings in England. Its architecture and art claim to be among the finest expressions of Anglo-Saxon culture from more than 1,200 years ago – a primitive age in the construction industry.

But by a quick calculation, I'd say the edifice before me now is the height of a seven-storey building, way beyond the capabilities of eighth-century stonemasons. It looks as though it dates from much later. Maybe the guidebooks are exaggerating and there's only the odd bit of stonework at knee-level that's actually Anglo-Saxon. Or could the explanation be that Deerhurst has got two places of worship, and I've come to the wrong one? That must be it. I know the original church was part of a priory. I probably took a wrong turn, back on the outskirts of the village, where it said:

Left, 'To church and chapel.' Right, 'To Priory Farm B&B.' 'Left' looked a cert. But maybe I should have gone right. The remains of the Saxon church could be somewhere that way, near Priory Farm.

And then there's the church gate itself. It's like no church gate I've ever seen. It's a shoulder-high sheet of heavy, grey steel and looks more like a barrier that could be electronically slammed against suicide bombers, than the welcoming gateway to a tranquil country churchyard. Then I realise: it's a floodgate. And this makes me even more convinced I've come to the wrong place. The idea that eighth-century workmen could not only erect a seven-storey building, but do it on marshy land that's prone to flooding ... well, it's ridiculous.

I decide to have a closer look anyway, just to be sure, and head down the path through the graveyard, tutting all the way at life's irritating confusions. The first thing that catches my eye inside the door at the west end of the building, is a stone carving above the inner doorway. It's a fresh orangey yellow, with simple lines. Looks very modernist. The kind of sculpture Anthony Gormley is famous for. All very well in its place. Probably the idea of some vicar here who thinks he's being 'with it'.

'Hello there. Can I help?' I hear a voice behind me, and turn. It's a woman, neatly dressed in long black cardigan and grey flared skirt.

'Lovely church,' I reply. 'I'm just having a browse.' Having a browse! Where do I think I am? Marks & Spencers?

'I see you're admiring our carving of the Virgin and Child,' she says. 'The Christ child is represented as still in the womb.'

'Hmm,' I say, and, not wishing to be rude, add in an encouraging voice, 'So who's the artist?'

'Wouldn't it be wonderful to know?' she replies. 'I suppose some Saxon mason with a talent.'

I'm stunned, and repeat with a disbelieving frown, 'It's Saxon?' She nods, and I take a closer look. 'Crumbs!' (You'll notice that in my concern to be respectful of the sacred surroundings, I've resorted to Enid Blyton type expletives) 'I thought ...'

'I know. Incredible isn't it? There's been scientific analysis carried out, and we now know that originally it would have been brightly coloured. There are tiny remnants of red paint.'

So this is my first mistake. But, sometimes, it's a delight to be wrong. And I'm starting to wonder what else I've not understood.

'Has the sculpture been moved … from … from …?' I stutter.

'I don't believe so,' she interrupts.

'So parts of this church *are* Saxon, then?'

'Goodness, yes,' she says. 'Come outside and I'll show you.' We go back along the path and she points upwards. 'See the herringbone pattern…' – this is at the top of the outside wall of the nave – '… that's Saxon.'

'But that's twenty-odd metres high! How could they do that in, what? … AD 790?' I shake my head in wonder at all the benefits of modern structural engineering they lacked back then, from mechanised diggers, steel joists, giant cranes and reinforced concrete to stress-test computer programs, not to mention hi-viz jackets and safety helmets. 'By the standards back then,' I remark, 'building this place must have been on a par with putting up a hundred-storey skyscraper today!'

My guide smiles with pride. And I tick off Mistake No. 2.

'I know, it's amazing,' she says. 'And what's more, this is a flood plain. The river's just over the other side of that field, so they had to put in foundations that would cope with marshy ground as well. We got terrible floods here in 2007.'

By now I'm prepared, and I just nod as though I knew that all along, though clocking Mistake No. 3 in my head. I'd better go for the fourth error of the day.

'And one other question,' I say. 'Where was the original priory?'

'Why, right here,' she says, and leads me back along the outer stonework of the church, and directs me to look over a 4ft-high wall. It's an unexpected sight. Tacked onto the back of the church is a long, two-storey house with Tudor windows. Its garden – complete with shrubs and a lawn dotted with kid's trikes and a couple of tents – is set against the church wall. 'This was the cloister from the ninth century on,' says my guide. 'And the house was part of the monastery. It's now Priory Farm.'

'Priory Farm, as in Priory Farm B&B?' I ask. She nods. 'But the sign back down the road pointed in the opposite direction,' I complain.

'That's winding country lanes for you,' she says with a smile. I cover my embarrassment with a quick fig leaf of theatrical laughter.

We introduce ourselves. Alice, it turns out, is a local historian. 'Actually, I'm meeting some pilgrims from Liverpool arriving any minute. Perhaps you'll excuse me. There are a couple of things I need to get ready.' I thank her and off she goes.

***

So who were the people who built this magnificent structure? Should we call them English? Or Saxon? Or Anglo-Saxon? Or what? And regardless of what name we choose to give them, do they have any connection with English people today, other than the fact that they back then, like some of us now, lived and prayed in this Gloucestershire village?

The Anglo-Saxons (lets stick with that title for a minute) had arrived here over 300 years before the heroic foundations for this church were dug. In the early fifth century, the Romans packed their baggage trains and, after their 400-year occupation of this land, left for ever. They deserted the country to go and defend their empire against the assaults of the Goths and other people branded by the Romans 'barbarians.'

The ancient Britons, now without a Roman army to see off attacks from neighbouring tribes of Scots and Picts, decided to call in military help from Continental Europe. And in answer to that plea, in the year 449 on a beach near Ramsgate in Kent, three long, open-topped rowing boats arrived – according to legend – under the command of two brothers, Hengist and Horsa. They were followed by many similar groups who beached their boats on these shores and set off inland armed with spears, short swords and shields. No one was recording at the time exactly where they'd come from, or at least no such contemporary writings have survived. The best we can do, in terms of the written word, is 300 years later, when the chronicler-monk, Bede, put pen to parchment. He wrote: 'Those who came over were of the three most powerful nations of Germany – Saxons, Angles and Jutes.'

The Saxons and the Angles came – roughly speaking – from an area now part of northern Germany, and the Jutes from Jutland in northern Denmark. The ancient Britons may have regretted invit-

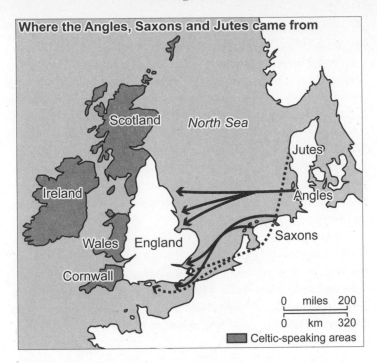

Where the Angles, Saxons and Jutes came from

Scotland

North Sea

Jutes

Ireland

Angles

Wales England

Saxons

Cornwall

| 0 | miles | 200 |
| 0 | km | 320 |

Celtic-speaking areas

Neat lines on a map belie a complex pattern of invasions and peaceful migration by many different groups during the fifth century.

ing them over. As more and more Germanic tribespeople arrived from the east, they turned their weapons against the Britons themselves. Year by year, the newcomers gained the upper hand. They weren't just soldiers, they were farmers too, and they settled further and further to the west. By the time Bede was writing, their descendants ruled the whole land.

It's significant that Bede calls his chronicle, *A History of the English People*. And once he reaches the final paragraphs of his work, he no longer uses the word 'people'. Instead he refers to the 'English *nation*.' A leading twentieth-century historian of the Anglo-Saxon period, Patrick Wormald, wrote that Bede had a decisive role in 'defining English national identity'.

Bede of course was Christian. Hengist, Horsa and those first migrants were not. The Angles, Saxons and Jutes worshipped the ancient Norse gods. Their ghosts are with us still. In place names like Wednesbury in the West Midlands, meaning fortress of the chief god Woden, or Thanet in Kent, the clearing of Thunor, god of thunder. And today, though we've stopped worshipping the old gods, we still recite their names every day of the week. Well, almost every day. Tuesday is Tiw's day, Tiw being a one-handed Anglo-Saxon god who was renowned for his skills in single combat. Wednesday belongs to Woden himself, and Thursday to Thunor. Woden's wife Frig gave her name to Friday. The Anglo-Saxons also worshipped the sun and the moon, hence Sunday and Monday. Only Saturday was left as a reminder of the Romans and their god Saturn.

But within 150 years, the terrifying warrior gods of the first Anglo-Saxons came under attack. It was a war they would lose. In the year 597, a 43-year-old unarmed Italian arrived on the south coast and started to talk about there being only one god, who had a son. St Augustine established his base at Canterbury, and, remarkably, within seventy years Anglo-Saxon England was converted, more or less, to Christianity.

The Anglo-Saxons had brought with them a rich artistic culture. In 1939, in a field just east of the little Suffolk town of Woodbridge, archaeologists uncovered the remains of a small ship that had lain buried in the earth for thirteen and a half centuries. The excavation of the Sutton Hoo ship and of several burial chambers nearby brought to light some beautiful and historically important objects, now housed in the British Museum. They included a fearsome metal helmet with mask covering the face, decorated swords, various buckles and shoulder clasps fashioned with densely interwoven patterning in gold with inset garnets, ornate belts, and a shield adorned with a bird of prey and a flying dragon, and much, much more. The archaeologist and art historian, David M. Wilson has said that the metal artefacts found in the Sutton Hoo graves were 'work of the highest quality, not only in English but in European terms'. Their conversion to Christianity saw the Anglo-Saxons' artistry and skill thrust upwards in a new direction. They built churches, some of the most magnificent structures in Europe since the collapse of the Roman Empire. And still, today, in over 430 villages and towns across England, you can find a church with substantial parts – walls, columns, window slits, archways, carvings and other stone decorations – just as they were when the Anglo-Saxon masons fashioned them. St Mary's, Deerhurst is one of the finest such structures.

***

As I enter the nave, I find myself among one or two other visitors. There's a middle-aged couple in shorts and hiking boots. He's taking photos, while she's being pulled along by a panting West Highland terrier.

'Terrific church,' I say, hoping to follow up with something a bit more penetrating.

They both nod with 'Lovely,' and, 'Magnificent, isn't it?'

'I'm a stranger here myself,' I say. 'May I ask what's special for you about the place.'

'I wanted to photograph the font,' says the man, pointing to what looks like a huge, stone handleless teacup standing just inside the door. 'It's the oldest one in England,' he adds.

'Really?' and I stare at it in admiration. Its decoration is a maze of spirals with delicate leaves that scroll around its lip and base.

'I don't know if you've come across this design before,' says the woman, 'but the Saxons, and the Celts before them, believed that the Devil travels only in straight lines, so a wiggly decoration like this was supposed to stop Satan entering the baptised baby.'

I step forward, the pattern tempting me to feel its smooth contours. That's what I do, and with a shiver realise that my fingers are following the same grooves and bumps that the nameless Saxon mason chipped out from a single piece of stone – maybe right here where I am now – 1,200 years ago.

'Amazing, huh?' says the man. 'We're talking fifty generations back when this was first made.'

'Are Saxon churches a special interest of yours?' I ask, glancing at both of them, to encourage a joint answer.

'Not necessarily Saxon,' she replies. 'We always try to include a couple of old churches on our walks.'

'You never quite know what fantastic surprises you're going to find,' her partner adds. 'Maybe some beautiful piece of wooden carving 800 years old, or a little window where lepers had to watch mass being said, or a dark underground vault where monks hid during the Reformation.'

'Hmm, I know what you mean,' I say.

'We're so lucky in this country,' says the woman. 'So many beautiful old churches.'

The man laughs. 'Who'd want to go the Spain or France or wherever, when you've got all this ...' he looks up at the soaring nave above our heads, '... right here on our doorsteps?'

We all smile our agreement and part.

The nave must be over 15m up to its roof. But I am a little disappointed. It's light and airy. The Anglo-Saxons didn't do light and airy. In the eighth century it would have been dark and stuffy, the only sunlight flickering in through a couple of little triangular holes close to the roof. It's been changed recently. 'Recently', that is, in Deerhurst terms. We've got to blame the abbots of nearby Tewkesbury, who a mere 500 years ago had four huge, square Perpendicular windows knocked through into each side wall.

Alice spots me frowning up at the mid-morning sunshine. I explain my desire for more Saxon gloom, and she suggests, 'Pop round to Odda's Chapel. I'm going to be giving a little chat to the pilgrims in about ten minutes. You'd be welcome to sit in. Just time for you to go and have a look.'

She explains that Odda's Chapel was built 200 years later than the church, then at some point it disappeared, and was thought to have been knocked down. But in 1865 the vicar of Deerhurst, one George Butterworth, pieced together some clues and realised that the kitchen and main bedroom of a nearby home were actually the chancel and nave of a Saxon chapel. It had been built by Earl Odda to commemorate his dead brother. The Reverend Butterworth set to work and restored it as close as he could to what it would have been like in the eleventh century.

My route takes me along the graveyard path, and through a second floodgate. As I round the corner, an extraordinary vision hits my eyes. It's an oak-framed Tudor house – all white plaster and black criss-crossed beams, like Shakespeare's birthplace. But the odd thing is that stuck onto its end, like a snail eating an ice cream, is what looks like a dour grey-stone barn. A small metal sign tells me this is Odda's Chapel. I pass through its gaping door-hole, and all is murky and glum. As it would have been back in Odda's day. No light, no pews. I suck in its mysterious misery for a few minutes, so I can return to the nave of the main church with renewed and darkened Saxon eyes.

Back outside St Mary's, a jumble of pilgrims awaits. When I hear that word, 'pilgrims', I think of the Nuns' Priest and the Wife of Bath roistering down to Canterbury, or of tiringly joyful young backpackers foot-slogging through Northern Spain to Santiago de Compestela. These Liverpool pilgrims are retirees in blue anoraks and have come in a coach.

We all go and sit in the front pews, me screwing up my eyes to peer at the best-preserved double-headed, Saxon window opening in England. Compared with the huge sixteenth-century perpendicular windows along the side of the nave, it is tiny. But the neatness and simplicity of its shape suggests a strength and a modesty lacking in their big younger brothers. Alice welcomes the Liverpudlians, then says, 'And today we also have with us a special gentlemen, Mr Jepherson, who just happens to be here visiting with his wife. It was his great-grandfather who rediscovered our wonderful font!' He nods in acknowledgement from a pew across the aisle.

What does she mean, 'rediscovered'? But there's no chance yet to ask Mr Jepherson, because Alice is explaining about the painted Saxon beast heads carved from stone by the entrance door. They've got snarling nostrils and eyes that spear you to the spot: works of art in any age. But what have they got to do with Christianity, I wonder. Of course, the early churchmen were clever enough to add a sly suggestion of the old-fashioned paganism to make the new-fangled religion more swallowable by the illiterate common folk.

At last, we break up and I go and introduce myself to the Jephersons – his name's Ken. What's his connection exactly with the font?

'Well,' he replies, 'I was born in Deerhurst; we live in York now and we're just down on holiday in the Cotswolds. And the story in the family was that my great-grandfather ...'

How St Mary's, Deerhurst, would have looked in Saxon times. Note the tiny slits to let in light and the balcony where the monks would display holy relics to villagers and pilgrims on feast days. (By kind permission of ©Maggie Kneen)

'It was on your mother's side, wasn't it?' his wife interrupts.

'That's right,' he says. 'It was around the turn of the last century, and apparently he found the font on one of the farms nearby.' He pauses for effect. 'It was being used as a pig trough.'

I give a gasp of disbelief. 'But you know this is the oldest known Saxon font in the country,' I say, 'and it's the finest too.'

Alice has joined us and says, 'Fantastic, isn't it? It was probably ripped out either during the Reformation or by Cromwell and the Puritans. But they left the base in position, so after Mr Jepherson's ancestor rediscovered it, it was put back exactly where it had been twelve hundred years ago.'

'And I was baptised in it,' says Ken.

Who wouldn't be proud? I thank him and his wife.

As the pilgrims head for the door and back to their bus, I find myself standing next to Alice. They thank her and shake her hand. Several of them thank *me* and shake *my* hand. For a moment or two, I feel Deerhurst is *my* church. Which, of course, it is.

***

Churches are unique. The extraordinary thing about St Mary's, Deerhurst – like all medieval churches – is that it's still today used for the same purpose as it was over 1,200 years ago when it was built. If the words 'living history' have any meaning, it's to describe medieval churches. A parish church is not a museum, nor a castle that's open to the public '10 till 6 (excl. Weds)': It's a working building that tells us about our history. In England, 40 million visits a year are paid to churches by people for that very purpose: not to worship, nor see a friend wed or buried, but to admire the beauty and marvel at the history of the country reflected in these places. There's even a phrase for it nowadays. It's called 'church tourism'. Deerhurst and its like are the perfect example of how we – in the words of the social psychologists – 'memorialise our past', and thereby create a collective memory, what makes a national identity.

That memory, however, does not always square with the way historians see things.

We often think of the Angles, the Saxons and the Jutes – perhaps in a story started by Bede – as national armies who systematically drove all the ancient Celtic Britons west until they were confined to the Welsh mountains, the Lake District and Cornwall. It's a version that sees the English born of pure Anglo Saxon blood (the Jutes get lost in this account).

Historians today see it differently. For a start, the invaders would have arrived in small parties, and probably wouldn't have identified themselves as Angles, Saxons or Jutes. They would have been more likely to see themselves as followers of Aethelulf, Stithwulf or whoever. So the town of Reading for example is where the people led by Read (the red one) settled.

Even the names, Angle, Saxon and Jute, probably didn't indicate distinct tribes. The Jutes, for instance, didn't come directly from Jutland, but had been wandering around coastal areas to the south for several generations, intermarrying and picking up local religious and cultural customs – so much so that some historians think they shouldn't be separately considered at all. And then there were the Saxons. The word needn't have had anything to do with a race of people. It described men who carried a particular kind of short sword in battle, called a *saex*. That meant, for example, that an Angle who armed himself with a *saex* was a Saxon.

But perhaps most startling is what recent research has revealed about the ancient Britons, those people whom – legend has it – the Anglo-Saxons drove out, to the last Celtic family, and replaced in what became England. The arrival of DNA analysis has revealed what one scientist has called a 'truly stunning' picture of who the ancient ancestors of the English were. Researchers from Oxford University have investigated the genomes of 2,000 white English people whose four grandparents were all born in the same area of England. The scientists also conducted a similar survey of 6,000 people from western Continental Europe. Then they compared the two. The results surprised everyone, geneticists and historians. By far the biggest grouping of English people – an astonishing 45 per cent – had a bloodline going back not to the Anglo-Saxons but to France. 'Ah,' you might say, 'that must be the Normans.' But it's not. It mainly represents people who migrated from the Continent to England even before the Romans, sometime after the last Ice Age, 10,000 years ago. So, if 45 per cent of modern English DNA is French, how much is Anglo-Saxon, i.e. English? The answer is a less impressive 20 per cent. So how did that come about?

Once the small bands of Anglo-Saxons arrived, it's likely there was no one pattern to what happened next. Undoubtedly, in some places, a victorious troop of Anglo-Saxons would have chased away the defeated Britons and their families. But elsewhere, the natives stayed on, often moving to the safety of a nearby hill. It's true that some ancient Britons did flee to Wales and the far southwest, though probably not a majority. More stayed, accepting – perhaps reluctantly – the rule of their new masters. Then, as the generations passed, they would intermarry and merge until it was impossible to recognise anymore who was descended from the ancient Britons and who from the Anglo-Saxons. So the English nation had a muddled birth. We can't be quite sure who its parents were. The English are not thoroughbreds. They're not pure Anglo-Saxons – and they weren't so even back in the early Middle Ages.

But this leaves another puzzle. Given that so many of the Celtic ancient Britons stayed on, you would expect that the old

Celtic language would have been absorbed at least in part by the conquering Anglo-Saxons. That's what often happens in such circumstances. But this time it didn't. The Celtic language seems to have been all but wiped out in what became England. Modern English can count on one hand the number of words that came from Celtic, and even they are not in daily use. There's 'dun' meaning grey-brown, 'crag' for a rocky point, 'broc' for badger – and that's about it. There's no satisfactory answer to this conundrum.

What makes it even more puzzling is that Celtic words have survived in hundreds of England's place names. For instance, Leeds, Avon, Arden are pure Celtic, while many towns, villages, cities and counties can trace at least part of their names back to the ancient Britons. *Man*chester for instance, from the Celtic *mam*, a breast-like hill. Lincoln, from *lin*, a lake. Berkshire, from *bearroc*, a hilly place. And over 200 small towns and villages in the south of England, from Combe Bottom in Surrey to Compton Basset in Wiltshire, are still celebrating their Celtic origins in a valley or *combe*. However, we shouldn't run away with the idea that all these places somehow remained islands of Celtic life in an Anglo-Saxon sea. More likely, the Anglo-Saxon rulers just found it too much trouble to change some of the old names. So they stuck.

The Anglo-Saxon language, on the other hand has come down to us today with great force. It's arguably the most powerful current that's flowed down the ages through the English language. Many thousands of words that we commonly use today have their origins in the Old English of the Anglo-Saxons. Here's a selection: *above, baby, crash, dog, eat, fly, goal, hat, indeed, jaw, kidney, lick, moon, narrow, ought, plight, quake, rake, shop, tide, up, vixen, woman, you*. And many Anglo-Saxon place names too have come down to us. Anywhere with *-ford* in it, meaning a shallow river crossing, like Stamford or Chelmsford. Or *-ham*, meaning in Anglo-Saxon a village, revealing the humble beginnings of Birmingham. *-hurst*, as in our own Deerhurst, is a wooded hill. Henley's *-ley* is a forest clearing. *-mer* in Cromer is a lake. And those who have been bored waiting for their flight at Stansted airport may not be surprised that it means 'stony place' in Anglo-Saxon.

The Saxons also identified themselves in the wider land they occupied. Essex being East Saxons; Sussex, denoting the South Saxons; Wessex, the West Saxons; and Middlesex – you get the idea.

And this brings us to where the terms 'England' and 'English' came from. You'll have noticed that in the county names above the 'a' morphs into an 'e'. It's Essex not Essax. So English comes from the Angles. Why, we may wonder, the Angles rather than the Saxons? After all, we talk about Saxon churches, not Angle churches. No one's quite sure, but one theory is that in order to make a distinction between the two sorts of Saxons – those that had stayed in Germany, and those that had migrated across the sea – the latter were referred to by Latin writers as the Angli Saxones, that is the English Saxons – the Saxons who associated with the Angles during the great migration to these shores, as opposed to the Old Saxons who had remained in Germany. Our influential friend, Bede, writing in the eighth century, abbreviated it sometimes, and talked just about the 'Englisc' (the 'a' now having started to mutate to 'e'), clearly referring to the inhabitants of the whole country.

The nation itself had to wait rather longer for its name. Not till the eleventh century, 600 years after Hengist, Horsa and the first Anglo-Saxons had arrived, did chroniclers start to write of 'Engla lande' or sometimes 'Engolond' or 'Ingland'. And it was another 300 years before these variations sorted themselves out to become England. The world should be thankful that the country took its name from the Angles and not the Saxons. If it had been the other way around – and given the 'a' to 'e' shifts in Essex and Sussex – the land of Shakespeare and Queen Victoria might have been called Sexland. And what would that have done for English (Sexish?) national identity?

***

So, were the battle re-enactors of Hastings exaggerating when they felt themselves to be Anglo-Saxon?

It was not unreasonable to make the words 'Anglo-Saxon' and 'English' interchangeable. The English didn't exist when Hengist and Horsa first turned up. But by the time the Normans took over, 600 years later, the two Anglo-Saxon brothers' successors were commonly called English. So, what have the English today inherited from the Anglo-Saxons?

If we limited our question, 'Who do the English think they are?' to the television search for blood ancestors, the answer has to be: we're not very Anglo-Saxon. At most, only one fifth of our DNA can be traced back to our first forebears. The English are more Celtic than Anglo-Saxon when it comes to ancestry.

But, if we're talking about the English language, then the English today owe a lot to the people who built Deerhurst church. And, what's more, the heart of our language is Anglo-Saxon, still today. Then there are those 430 Saxon churches. They're part of England's heritage: beautiful survivals from a history that the people of England feel are special to them.

And that word 'feel' is significant. When the historian Patrick Wormald talks of the Anglo-Saxon historian Bede as playing a decisive 'role in defining English national identity,' I believe he means that if we *feel* the Saxons helped make us who we are, then – like the battle re-enactors of Hastings – we behave accordingly. That's national identity.

***

Deerhurst, as well as being the tangible root of English national identity, was the scene of a crucial event in the Anglo-Saxon story. It's where, in the year 1016, two warring leaders, King Cnut and Edmond Ironside met to negotiate a peace deal. They agreed to carve up the country between them. Cnut would take the north and Edmund the south. But within a year, Edmund was dead – by one account he was murdered while on the privy, and died of multiple stab wounds delivered by an agent of Cnut. Cnut thereby became king of the whole country. Edmund was English, an Anglo-Saxon, and his people were now the subjects of a foreign invader. Cnut was a Viking. To find out what the Vikings did for the English, we're going to a remote set of islands off the northeast coast of England. It's where violence and beauty have often met, and – as I'm about to see for myself – blood is still being spilled here.

3

FARNE ISLANDS, NORTHUMBERLAND

THE VIKINGS GIVE US DIRT, EGGS AND FOG

THE HARROWING INROADS OF HEATHEN
MEN MADE LAMENTABLE HAVOC
IN THE CHURCH OF GOD IN HOLY
ISLAND BY RAPINE AND SLAUGHTER.

ANGLO-SAXON CHRONICLE (AD 793)

A thin, sharp light picks out the boats bobbing in the wind below the harbour wall. And when the clouds suddenly roll back to reveal a dramatic sunset over the black profile of a distant castle to the north, it feels as if we might be in the land of the midnight sun.

I've been joined by my old school friend, Geoff who'll be my guide, not – as you might imagine from this description – in Norway but in Northumberland. He knows the area well. We're staying in the small fishing port of Seahouses. And even though the countryside between here and the frontier of the Roman Empire, Hadrian's Wall, 50 miles south, has the required number of green fields, hedges, parish churches and village pubs to qualify it as English homeland, Seahouses has a remote feel to it.

We've booked a boat trip out to one of the Farne Islands a few miles to the east and, soon after breakfast next morning, we find ourselves among some sixty fellow voyagers, all trying not to poke our neighbours with our camera cases or rucksacks while we squash together on wooden seats in a converted fishing vessel. We hit choppy water passing through the harbour gate and we're all wearing clip-on smiles. 'In the event of an emergency,' announces our skipper over the loudspeaker, 'ye orl follow me into the life-boat.' How we laugh.

But we've no need to fret. The weather is glorious. We're heading for Inner Farne, which is where the seventh-century Anglo-Saxon hermit St Cuthbert ended his days. The boat's steady dip and rise through the waves soon becomes soporific in the sunshine, and I muse on how life here for the saint must have been full of the direst extremes. On a warm spring day like now, it would have been a taste of heaven-to-come. But when the freezing gales lashed in off the North Sea, as they frequently do, life on the Farne Islands would have been a very hell. I suppose though this could have been the attraction of the place for Cuthbert. He apparently liked to say his prayers standing up to his waist in the icy North Sea, so these balmy, sunny days must have been a nightmare for him.

As well as being home to one of the Anglo-Saxons' most revered saints, the Farne Islands were the scene of a terrifying turning point in the history of the English. In the year 793, there was a sudden and unforeseen outbreak here of mass murder combined with large-scale theft, arson, destruction and desecration, carried out by a band of well-armed and mercilessly brutal foreigners. What happened was significant because it was only the first of many such violent attacks to hit wide areas of England over the next hundred or more years. The Vikings had arrived. And the English were to lose much more than a handful of tiny, remote islands. Within 250 years, these Scandinavian invaders would control the whole country.

The question for us is this. Were the Vikings no more than a violent interruption to the growth of the English race born of the Anglo-Saxons? Or were the Vikings, their culture and their language absorbed, so that the English of today can claim they're part Viking? We've come to the Farne Islands to find out.

***

Our boat begins to rock and sway as the skipper slows the engine to manoeuvre into a craggy inlet. The rocky cliff before us, at every point, up, down and along its length, is pitted with narrow ledges, and every ledge is crammed with shrieking sea-birds. Guillemots. Millions of them, squabbling and flapping. The skipper explains that they don't build nests, but lay their eggs straight onto the tiny rock ledges. Guillemot eggs are pear-shaped, so they don't roll off but simply spin. There's not a square foot of grey cliff face that doesn't have rivulets of white slimy guillemot droppings dripping down it. The stench sticks in our noses.

As we move away, two gannets – bigger than swans – cruise overhead, while puffins streak by like insects which might fall from the sky if their too-small wings paused for a moment. Our boat's engines idle again, and as we bob helplessly, the nearby rocks suddenly swell and lurch as though they're alive. Once we get closer, I see they *are* alive, or rather scores of seals are. At a distance, their grey skins had merged with their stony home. Each animal is so fat that it can only shift and roll its blubbery mass by jerking its head. Our skipper tells us they're Atlantic grey seals, and there are between 3 and 4,000 of them on the Farnes. As our boat drifts in closer to them, the animals set up a mournful howl, like the sound of wolves circling a camp at night.

Ten minutes later, our boat is manoeuvring alongside the little jetty on Inner Farne. The crew, i.e. a burly, tattooed bruiser in a singlet, leaps ashore with surprising agility, secures the mooring rope, holds out a helpful hand, and instructs us in the sweet tones of a primary school teacher, 'Be very careful, my dears. There you go, all safe.'

As Geoff and I stretch our legs on the small concrete pier, we can see, a couple of hundred yards away, the small stone chapel that marks the spot where Cuthbert lived and in the year 687 died. Between us and it, a pathway is roped off from the surrounding heathland.

'Ah, look,' says Geoff. 'See those birds flying everywhere? They're arctic terns. They must be nesting on the ground all around here.' And off we set, Geoff in front and me a couple of steps behind. We're among the first off the boat, and it's only when I glance back at our fellow trippers getting themselves ready on the jetty that I notice them all doing something that we have not done. They're donning thick woolly caps and wide-brimmed outback hats. Some are pulling hoods up, and others look like they're practising crouching under umbrellas, which seems strange, given that by now there's not a cloud in the sky. I'm puzzled. And before I can turn back to face the path up towards Cuthbert's chapel, I hear from that direction a squawk followed by, 'Get out, you little bastard! Get off!'

It's Geoff. He's being attacked.

Now I hesitate to say, 'He's being attacked by a bird,' because you wouldn't take it seriously. But this is serious. An arctic tern is hovering just inches over his head. It's screeching like a tortured pig, and it keeps hammering down with all its weight, beak first, onto the top of his head. Geoff, of course, is not standing there idly letting the creature have its evil way. He's ducking and weaving, and jerking his arms about in an attempt to keep it at bay. But to no avail. The bird's beak is constantly open, forming two red needles that it manages to keep jabbing, between Geoff's parries, to reach its target, i.e. his head. It's like a scene from the Alfred Hitchcock movie *The Birds*, and I'm expecting any moment to see Geoff fall to the ground and be set upon by a flock of these monstrous creatures till their bloodlust is satisfied by a tasty elevenses treat of his eyeballs.

And I can't go to help him either, because the moment I step onto the roped-off path, another of these little harpies goes for me as well. I hear a shriek, and just manage to get my hiking stick above my head and start twisting it about, like a stricken helicopter's rotor blade. But this is only a part-deterrent. The bird screeches even louder. And, though I'm relieved that it appears unable to get past my whirling cudgel without risking a clout round its black feathered ears, I soon find it has another shot in its revolting little locker. I feel a warm splat on my forehead. Yes, I'm afraid so.

I catch a glimpse of Geoff, a few yards ahead. He's crouching, dodging about, and hitting out to try and drive his opponent off, all the while hurling a torrent of unimaginative curses at it.

Without the benefit of a defensive weapon, like mine, he's in trouble. He seems to bounce against a woman coming in the opposite direction. Her head is sensibly swathed in a hood beneath an overlarge cowboy hat that looks like it once belonged to a sloppy plasterer. But she's not looking where she's going because she's attempting to take a photograph of her avian assailant with, for some unfathomable reason, a very long lens. And every time she raises her head to line up the shot, the tern, which is screeching just inches away, seizes its opportunity and makes a dart, either hitting her hat brim or else her camera, which is the only thing between her and permanent blindness in one eye.

When she and Geoff bump, I could swear I hear a 'Sorry!' in between a 'Shit!' and a 'Bastard!' It's difficult to tell exactly, what with the noise of the birds, the swishing of my pole and the inevitable mental confusion which my own rising panic engenders. For a moment, it looks as though the two birds – Geoff's and the one attacking the camera woman – crash wings. They shriek at each other then shoot apart, each ready to defend its corner against an enemy more cunning and deadly than any earthbound human.

It all takes only a second, but Geoff, seeing his assailant distracted, seizes his chance. He legs it, his head shrunk as far into his shoulders as is possible without actually dislocating his neck. And he might have made it. He has only a couple of metres to go to the finishing line (the open gateway where the roped-off path merges into a small yard outside Cuthbert's chapel), when a different bird dives at him without the usual shrieking and splatting preliminaries. It scores an immediate hit somewhere just above Geoff's right temple – or that's what I guess from my position several yards behind. I too now have broken into a stumbling trot to try to reach safety before the tern that's on my case figures out all it has to do is come at me from the side, below the helicopter hiking pole, in order to deck me.

Geoff ducks his way through the gate and into the supposed sanctuary of holy ground. His opponent continues to harass him, though admittedly in a more half-hearted, mainly verbal fashion now. By the time I reach him, an armistice has been signed. The tern has retired to celebrate victory. Geoff is left to tend his wounds, viz a trickle of deep red blood which is seeping down his face from his hairline to his chin. He keeps repeating some unrepeatable oaths.

A warden – not a day over 19 years old, I'd say – in an RSPB T-shirt and regulation white-spattered hat, admonishes him, 'Don't wave your arms about, Sir. You'll harm the birds.' Before either of us can think of a suitably cutting response to do with health and safety or adequate warning signs, the chap has marched off down the pathway, head erect, chatting to a fellow warden and paying no more attention to the tern zipping around his ears than if it were a cabbage-white butterfly that had lost its way.

After an hour spent in the peace of Inner Farne, recovering from our beating, we prepare to run the gauntlet back. But I'm happy to report that human ingenuity now triumphs over animal brutishness. Geoff's wearing a thick fleece, I a red anorak – neither, though, with a hood. So we each grasp the back collars of our respective garments and pull them up and forwards over our heads, till we look like not-very-convincing headless ghosts in an amateur dramatics production of *The Return of Anne Boleyn*. And off we set at a sharp pace down the roped pathway. The ruse doesn't stop the shrieking, splatting or stabbing, but does prevent further bloodshed.

***

Next morning, we head for Lindisfarne, also known as 'Holy Island', the largest isle in the group and the precise scene of the first known Viking attack on England. Lindisfarne was also the site of another landmark in our investigation. Here in the early eighth century, a monk called Eadrith wrote out on parchment the four gospels of the New Testament. But he didn't simply copy out the words. He illustrated the text with an array of vivid colours and swirling designs. It must have been a life's work. Someone has counted how many tiny dots went to make up a single initial letter: 10,600. But what makes the Lindisfarne Gospels even more significant for us is that 200 years after Eadrith died another nameless monk added between each Latin line a translation in Old English – that is, the language of the Anglo-Saxons. What was to develop into the language you're reading now on this page had become official. You can admire the original Gospels today in the British Library in London. The Library's curator notes the Gospels' 'importance in the growth of English national identity'.

To reach Lindisfarne, Geoff and I must across a 2-mile-long causeway that disappears beneath the sea twice a day at high tide. That will leave us with five or six hours on the island before we'll have to scoot back or get marooned. Now, I'd imagined that this causeway would be a stone and rubble spit, built up several feet higher than the exposed seabed. But I'm wrong. As Geoff steers the car onto it, I see the comforting sight of a narrow tarmac road, like any minor road in England, complete with broken white line down the middle. Less reassuring is that it's on the same level as the surrounding sand, ribbonned with sea-weed and long briny puddles, though I do take comfort from the immediate absence of any actual wavy ocean, which we can just make out on the horizon off to left and right.

It's apparently a common occurrence for drivers to cut their return crossing a bit too tight as the tide comes in. They observe the inch-deep water lapping at the side of the road, and set off, without realising that here, as on any such flat surface of sand, the tide rushes in at a frightening speed. Many a driver – probably from the mollycoddled south of England – is then surprised to find the car's steering wheel doesn't work as they float off into the North Sea. There has long been a debate hereabouts as to whether a barrier should be erected at each end of the causeway, to be opened only when it's safe to cross. But the locals always oppose the idea. After all, there's not a lot to make you laugh up here on a cold Friday night.

Geoff and I make it across, park and set off. But to reach the precise spot where the Vikings wreaked their havoc we find that, having braved the causeway, we now have to pass through a couple of streets' worth of pebble-dash bungalows that look as though they've been transplanted from suburban Swindon or Halifax. There is nothing wrong with such places; it's just that we're supposed to be stepping back into the pages of history. The only notable feature here is a giant shoebox-shaped block of dirty concrete, lurking among waist-high weeds. Just in case anyone might mistake it for a Renaissance chapel or a Georgian orangery, a large sign on it says PUBLIC CONVENIENCES.

Then, suddenly, it's as though we've passed through a magic mirror. The retirees' affordable residences are gone, and we find ourselves amid what must surely be one of the most romantic ruins anywhere in England. We're surrounded by soft rose-coloured stone walls rising in smooth columns that guide the eye to delicate arches, half-circled by weather-worn dogtooth carvings. And, as if to provide an artistic contrast, here and there the rounded pink masonry is shattered and punctured in jagged lines. And you can't help but peer up in wonder at the thin arc of stones vaulting across the blue sky from one fractured wall to the next. It's not the wreckage of something that was once more beautiful. It's as though what went before was just the preliminary stage. And the irregular walls and precarious spans of soft stone we see now are the finished product, a giant artistic installation chiselled down and sculptured from rawer material.

You may think this is an overly romantic assessment. But go to Lindisfarne and see for yourself. And anyway, I'm in good company. If you were a romantic aesthete back in the late eighteenth

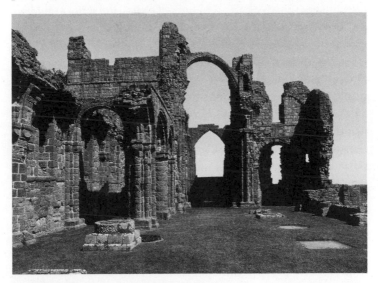

Lindisfarne Abbey could claim to be the most romantic ruin in England.

and early nineteenth centuries, fond of melancholic, remote, fallen
beauty, then here, among the remains of Lindisfarne Priory with
its distant view of the island's crag-top castle, is just the sort of
place where you'd tell your friends you wanted to meet your
lonely, tragic end. English landscape artists flocked here to capture
Lindisfarne's sad beauty from every possible, well-composed angle,
usually with the odd cow grazing where the altar once stood, or
an occasional farmhand leaning against a broken pillar, oblivious
to the magnificence around him. Turner came to Lindisfarne in
1829 and painted a violent storm lashing the island, while men
and women struggle ashore beneath the indifferent, eternal gaze
of the tumbled-down priory.

St Cuthbert was in charge here at the priory during the seventh century, before he decided that it was all too civilised and
took himself away, alone, to Inner Farne, where we were yesterday.
The sandstone ruins are the remains of the twelfth-century building. And the half-destroyed state they're in now is the result of
Henry VIII's decision to close down the country's monasteries in
the sixteenth century.

Geoff and I are not alone here today. In amongst the Women's
Institute bus tours, two-by-two lines of chattering school children
and the occasional earnest chap in a reversed baseball cap with
strings of cameras around his neck, we come across Carol. Carol
is an English Heritage guide and is the sort of person you'd want
to teach your kids history. Her every word exudes excitement. 'It
would have been an incredibly busy place in the Middle Ages,' she
tells us. 'Full of tourists, of course!' She's smiling. 'I always think
that the origin of tourism was the pilgrimage. Not much different
from today really. People travelled to a site like this from all over the
north of England. And what did they find here, as well the shrine
to St Cuthbert? Gift shops. Or the fourteenth-century equivalent,
anyway. People trying to sell you religious relics.'

Geoff and I both laugh. Carol's one of those rare people that
knows the truth is often funny.

'And what sort of visitors come here now?' I ask.

'Well, there are still some pilgrims, of course,' she replies. 'But
I'd say it's more people who're interested in the history of the

place. I mean, just look around you …' She points up at the arch leaping across the sky 80ft above us. 'You couldn't help but be stirred by the history of something so beautiful, now, could you? And then of course we get lots of school groups. The Vikings,' she explains, 'are on the national curriculum, so of course this a great place to bring school parties.' She nods over to her right, where a troop of about thirty what look like 8-year-olds, are sitting on a convenient grassy bank, from which, with quiet concentration – well, quietish - they keep glancing up then down then up again as, with pencils and rubbers, they copy the broken lines of the priory ruins. 'Excuse me,' she says, 'I must just go and see if they've got everything they need.'

***

It's not known precisely where the Vikings beached their longships and rushed ashore to catch their victims before they could flee. But given that the priory is on the south-east tip of the island, the best guess is that they came around the headland and into the bay that lies next to it, a shelter from North Sea gales.

It's only a short step from the remains of the old priory clois-ters to where the waters of the bay splash and rattle the pebbly strand. That's where Geoff and I head off to now, across a tufted meadow dotted with yellow wildflowers. The sea itself is almost as flat as the surrounding low fields. Half a dozen small fishing boats are anchored a few yards away from the water's edge. On a concrete yard to our right, a single-masted sailing boat sits on blocks, waiting for someone to repaint its hull. All around us are chaotic piles of rope-framed, sea-bleached boxes ready to trap unwary lobsters and crabs. And there are three or four sheds. Not sheds like the one in your garden; these are made from old boats turned upside down and sawn in two, with faded rotting doors fitted on the end, each decorated with a rusty padlock and a horseshoe for luck. Even the odd plastic box stuffed under their hulls-turned-eves can't spoil the simple pleasure of admir-ing their curved roofs. Across the bay, a mound of rock is topped off with Lindisfarne's homely little castle.

We don't have much detail of the Viking's attack. The *Anglo-Saxon Chronicle* suggests that it wasn't quite as unexpected as we might imagine, though you have to believe in omens to go along with that. In its entry for the year 793, the *Chronicle* speaks of:

> dreadful fore-warnings over the land of the Northumbrians, terrifying the people most woefully: these were immense sheets of light rushing through the air, and whirlwinds, and fiery drag-ons flying across the firmament. These tremendous tokens were soon followed by a great famine.

These events, according to the chronicler were the indications that something even worse was about to happen:

> and not long after, on the sixth day before the ides of January ... the harrowing inroads of heathen men made lamentable havoc in the church of God in Holy Island [i.e. Lindisfarne], by rapine and slaughter.

The monks were either murdered where they no doubt knelt to pray for their lives, or else were taken away as slaves, while the priory was put to the torch and its treasures plundered. And it wasn't just the holy men of Lindisfarne who suffered. This was an extensive religious institution, and the monks would be depend-ent on the ordinary folk who lived round about to act as servants and help provide them with food. So families of men, women and children would also have found themselves victims of these 'heathen men' and their 'rapine and slaughter.'

Those who survived the attack struggled to understand how God could allow this to happen. The explanation was damning. One of the leading ecclesiastical scholars of Europe, Alcuin of York, wrote a letter, shortly after the devastating raid, to the Bishop of Lindisfarne. Alcuin didn't, as you might expect, offer his sympathies to those who had suffered and managed to survive. Instead he said it was all their fault, and what's more they should stop whining and stand up for themselves. That's the sense of his letter. His actual words were:

> Never before has such an atrocity been seen ... Either this is the beginning of greater tribulation, or else the sins of the inhabit-

ants have called it upon themselves. Truly it has not happened
by chance, but it is a sign that it was well merited by someone.
But now, you who are left, stand manfully, fight bravely, defend
the camp of God.

And just in case the bishop, the monks of Lindisfarne and the
people of Northumbria didn't get the message, Alcuin spelt it out:

> Consider carefully, brothers, and examine diligently, lest per-
> chance this unaccustomed and un-heard of evil was merited by
> some unheard-of evil practice … Consider the dress, the way of
> wearing the hair, the luxurious habits of the princes and people.

We may think it harsh that a decadent haircut or two should be
punished with a massacre of innocents. Alcuin did not.

The raid on Lindisfarne was no random event. The Vikings
had chosen it because of the treasures it held – gold, silver and
jewel-encrusted chalices, crucifixes and other altar adornments.
The raid set a pattern. Over the next few years, other monasteries
in similar exposed spots also suffered bloody hit-and-run assaults.
Those who carried out the first attack on Lindisfarne were almost
certainly from the area of modern-day Denmark. And in the years
ahead, the raiders regardless of where in Scandinavia they came
from, were given the catch-all name 'Danes'. By the middle of the
ninth century, these 'heathen men' were venturing further afield.
Their targets were the south coast, from Cornwall to the Thames
Estuary and London itself. And at first, they didn't settle nor move
far inland.

All that changed, however, in 865 when not just a handful of
raiding longships arrived but a Danish army landed in East Anglia.
We shouldn't imagine battalions of well-disciplined soldiers. This
army was probably no more than 500 to 1,000 men, led by the
intriguingly named Ivar the Boneless and his two brothers. Within
a year they'd reached York and, aided by the arrival of more of their
fellow tribesmen, they conquered wide areas of the north-east.
Now they started to set up home. One chronicler wrote that they
'were engaged in ploughing and making a living for themselves.'

And it wasn't just the Danes. At about the same time, Norwegians came ashore in the western Isles of Scotland then headed south, and were soon in north-west England and present-day Yorkshire. But the Scandinavian invaders didn't have it all their own way. The English King Alfred, in 878 inflicted a defeat on them at the Battle of Ethandun in Wiltshire. The Danish leader, Guthrum, agreed to abandon the old Norse gods and convert to Christianity. But whatever the heavenly achievements of the victory, the facts on earth were less glorious. A subsequent peace deal between the two men still left England a divided land. Alfred and the English were to control Wessex (an area roughly south of the Thames) and Mercia (the West Midlands as far as Cheshire). But Alfred had to recognise that the Vikings now ruled in East Anglia, the East Midlands and the north, an area to be called the Danelaw, just that, where Danish, Viking, law applied.

The next 150 years saw power in England ebb and flow between the English and the Danes. Then, in 1016, the chain of events that had begun 200 years earlier with the Viking raid on Lindisfarne reached a climax. Following the peace treaty we spoke of at Deerhurst, the Danish leader Cnut became king of all England. The Vikings ruled. Cnut's reign, however, was a far cry from the anarchic violence of the early Vikings. It's true he immediately set about eliminating any Anglo-Saxon rivals. But this was more a case of well-targeted political assassinations than random mass slaughter. And in some ways Cnut saw himself as more English than Scandinavian. He adopted what had become a highly efficient administrative system developed by the Anglo-Saxons, and to accentuate the continuity of his kingship he married Emma, the widow of one of his Anglo-Saxon predecessors, King Aethelred II.

The end of the Danish dynasty on the English throne came without bloodshed. Cnut's successor, his son, Hardicnut invited a leading member of the Anglo-Saxon nobility to his court. And when in 1042 Hardicnut was suddenly taken ill at a wedding feast and died, that same English nobleman was on hand to claim the throne as Edward the Confessor.

That was the finish of over 250 years of Viking interference in English history. But is 'interference' the right word? Were the

The ghosts of the Danelaw are still with us today: 2,000 of its towns and villages have Viking names.

Vikings, the Danes, the Norwegians, the Scandinavians or how-ever we call them simply bloodthirsty attackers? Or did they have an impact on the growth of English national identity? Was their culture, their language, their blood absorbed?

***

Perhaps the most startling Viking impact on English identity comes from the buildings they left behind. Startling, because there aren't any. Not one. It's true that archaeologists have detected the foundations of two Viking farm buildings in a remote field on the Isle of Man, and of course in the middle of York there's a splendid museum, the Yorvik Centre, standing at the spot where the remains of timber buildings from the Viking age were discovered in the soil beneath a sweet factory. And that's it. Unlike the Anglo-Saxons from the same period, the Vikings left us no grand churches nor fortified walls to admire today. It seems they built largely in wood, which of course tends to rot, burn or collapse within a historically short time frame.

But have the Vikings come down to us in a different way? Has their bloodline reached us? After all, the Danelaw – the area they controlled – covered a vast area, not to mention that in the eleventh century under King Cnut and his son, England was actually a Danish country. And what about the Vikings' reputation not only for plundering but for raping? We might at least expect that many of us today have Viking ancestry, the result of such violent couplings.

There had been no way to find an answer until the DNA survey we looked at on our last stop, at Deerhurst. That showed 20 per cent of our bloodline has come from the Anglo-Saxons. So how much do we owe to the Vikings? The survey revealed that in northern England, where Viking influence was strongest for the longest period, only a meagre 4 per cent of our DNA comes from those Scandinavian invaders.

Why? It's partly because, relative to the population at that time, very few Vikings arrived on England's shores. And it's also probably because they didn't intermarry much with the local population. While there would always be exceptions, in most villages and towns where the Vikings settled, they became a sort of dominant elite, an aristocratic minority who didn't mix with the Anglo-Saxons.

The low DNA count has also led to speculation among historians that the Vikings didn't do quite as much raping as their reputation has suggested. And this has been borne out by the discovery in Scandinavia of the skeletons of women and infants in the remains of longships. It seems the Vikings brought wives and children with them. Perhaps the invaders were loyal family men, and not as sex-mad as we picture them.

The Vikings have been cast as the bogeymen of England's story. And like all bogeymen, every manner of evil has been attributed to them. Like the Devil himself, they've grown horns. But the image of the screaming Viking warrior in a helmet decked with two long twisting horns is nonsense. Think about it. In battle, such an awkward piece of headgear would be easy to knock off, and even if it stayed in place the unwieldy projections on your head would be just as likely to poke out a comrade's eye as that of an enemy; as you prepared to repel boarders on your long-boat, 12in curved spikes poking up would forever be getting snagged in the rigging. So no horns. But we shouldn't go to the other – peace-loving – extreme either. In order to dominate a much larger population with their small numbers, the Vikings must have merited their general reputation for ferocity, whether or not that included much raping. And dominate, they clearly did.

Over 2,000 villages and towns where they settled have still today kept their Viking names. As you might expect, this is particularly so in the more northern part of England. Any place name ending in -*by*, meaning town or farmstead, is Viking, as in Grims*by* and Rug*by*. There are over 600 of them. And incidentally, when we talk today of '*by*-laws', to denote local as opposed to national laws, we're using the language of the Vikings. Other Old Norse place name endings give clues to their origins. So -*thorpe* indicated a village for the Vikings, as in Scun*thorpe* or Clee*thorpes*. Cross*thwaite* and Brai*thwaite* were established in *thwaites* or clearings. The -*toft* in Lowes*toft* was a Viking homestead.

And what about the language spoken by the Vikings? Does English today have any roots in Old Norse? It was after all the language used by those in power, by kings of England in the mid-eleventh century, and by local rulers especially in the north for longer periods. The answer is surprising. Judged purely by numbers, the Viking influence on modern English is thin. Only 400 to 500 words at most are recognised as derived from Old Norse. That compares with many thousands from the Anglo-Saxons. However, just as a thousand and more years ago, a few Vikings exercised power disproportionate to their numbers, so do their words today. There may not be many Old Norse terms used in modern standard

English, but they are among the commonest ones. There's barely a sentence we utter that doesn't echo back to the Danish invaders. Some of the verbs we bandy about every minute of the day are Viking: *get, want, take, seem* for instance. Nouns such as *anger, bond, cake, dirt, egg, fog, kid, leg, neck, skill, smile, window* were all given to us by the Vikings. Then there are useful little syllables like *both* and *till*, not to mention *they, them* and *their.*

Linguists also point out that many more Old Norse words have survived in local dialects. I can vouch for this myself. I grew up in the Erewash Valley on the border between Nottinghamshire and Derbyshire. There were seven coal pits around our town, and the old miners often spoke in a way that folk a mere 10 miles away could find hard to grasp, like this (the words in bold are a legacy of the way the Vikings spoke).

> Miner 1: Ey up sorrey. It's **silin'** it dairn, entit? (Hello friend. It's raining hard, isn't it?)
>
> Miner 2: Aye. Way **mun** goo in doars. (Yes. We must go inside)
>
> Miner 1: 'Ay a **gleg** at that'n. (Have a glance at that person).
>
> Miner 2: **Ow** wi't **skep**? (She – i.e., the woman – with the basket?)
>
> Miner 1: Aye, **ow** goo'in dairn't motha **geet**. (Yes, she who's going down the main street)
>
> Miner 2: **Ow's scraitin'**, ent'er? (She's weeping, isn't she?)
>
> Miner 1: **Nay. Lig** 'er bay. (No. Leave her be.)

Pronunciation, of course, also plays a role in making local dialects like this so different from Standard English, especially changes in vowel sounds. 'Geet', for instance, is the Erewash Valley pronunciation of 'gate', the name for many streets in York and other Danelaw cities.

We know a little about Viking pronunciation, because sometimes the same word ended up being spelt differently in the north from the south, the spelling reflecting the difference in pronunciation. The Viking word usually has a hard 'k' or 'sk' sound compared with a softer 'sh' or 'ch' in the Anglo-Saxon area where Viking influence was weaker. 'Keswick' (cheese farm) in Viking land is just a different way of pronouncing 'Chiswick' to the south. And often the meanings split in two as well, though not so radically we can't recognise the link. So 'ship' and 'skip' in modern English refer to things roughly the same shape. Then there's 'skirt' and 'shirt', which should tell us something about changes in dress fashion as the two words went their separate ways. And often the Viking form of a word has survived alongside the Old English one and kept a similar meaning. You can find 'shrubs' on 'scrub'-land and hardly notice. And a 'shoal' of fish is not much different from a 'school' of whales. 'Kirk' in Viking Scotland is 'church' further south, but the sort of building is the same. And in Lincolnshire, we can choose whether to say 'dike' or 'ditch' for a trench, though in Holland – for reasons I can't understand – a dike is an embankment to keep water out, not something full of it.

***

So when we ask 'Who do the English think they are?' perhaps more of the answer is 'Viking' than we might have thought. It's true that very few of us can claim those Scandinavian invaders as our great-great-great-etc.-grandparents. And they left behind no buildings which the English can – in the jargon of the social psychologists – 'memorialise' and absorb into our national identity. On the other hand, the language of the Vikings, Old Norse, is there in the everyday words we use – perhaps more so in the way we chat to each other than in formal documents we read or write. And if the north or east of the country are where we live or choose to visit, we'll know of places which the Vikings named.

Despite these facts, the popular notion persists that the Viking invaders were just a violent interruption in our history. And it's often perceptions, not facts, that mould our understanding of who we are, and where we came from. But this is changing. Let's not forget those school children at Lindisfarne. The Vikings are on the national curriculum. A more balanced assessment of them and their role in English history is being absorbed by a new generation.

***

The very last Viking to invade England in fact hit these shores in 1066, only weeks before the Battle of Hastings. He was Harald Hardrada, who landed with a Norwegian army. The Saxon King,

Harold, rushed north and defeated him. But Hardrada and his Vikings had – unwittingly – delivered a fatal blow to the Anglo-Saxons. Within days of his victory, King Harold heard that another enemy had arrived in the south of England, the Normans. It could be argued that if Harold's troops had not been exhausted from the battle with the Norwegians, he might have managed to see off the Normans at the Battle of Hastings. But as it was, William the Conqueror earned his title, Harold was killed, and the English came under the influence of an invader whose successors were to change the country and its people forever.

To find out more, we're going to an example of perhaps the most English of institutions. A pub. This one is where the first Normans quenched their thirsts. And it's a pub like no other pub you'll find anywhere. You have to sit in a cave to drink your pint.

4

The Trip to Jerusalem, Nottingham

England, the Normans' backyard

I attacked the English of the Northern Shires like a lion. I ordered their houses and corn, with all their belongings, to be burnt without exception.

William the Conqueror (1028–87), according to the chronicler-monk, Orderic Vitalis.

Nottingham. I know about Nottingham. The very name has a special ring for me. If anyone mentions the city, or if there's an item about it on the news, ancient memories stir in my soul.

I was born 7 miles to the west of the city and went to grammar school here. It's where we used to shop for anything the local Co-op didn't stock, i.e. Eagle annuals, Meccano sets, cricket bats, that kind of essential stuff. And as a teenager I lived it up here on Saturday nights. This often involved trying to meet girls at the Rainbow Rooms, where a shouted conversation during a clumsy jive usually led to nothing more than a glazed stare following a suggestion we might meet again. More successful romantic encounters were to be had at the Elite Cinema, where you arranged to meet your date inside, thereby avoiding the embarrassment of revealing you didn't have enough money to buy her ticket as well as your own.

I said 'I know about Nottingham', but as the car now crawls along Maid Marion Way and Greyfriar Gate, I soon realise I should say, 'I once knew about Nottingham.' A four-lane highway has obliterated the old coffee bar and the school uniform shop. And the towering windowless walls of a nuclear power station – oh, my mistake, it's the back of something called 'Broad Marsh Shopping Centre' – have replaced … well, I don't know what used to be here. I've no idea where I am.

Suddenly I see a blue 'P' sign and wrench the car over into as dreary a multi-story as you could dread to find anywhere in the world. I dump the vehicle and burrow my way out to the street. There's a clutch of fag-smoking bus drivers on the pavement. They should be able to direct me.

'Excuse me,' I say. 'I'm looking for Brew House Yard.'

They all look blank. Then the woman in the group finishes a sip from her steaming plastic cup and says, 'Breu 'Aas Yaaad, dukk?'

I nod. You can tell how long I've been away, because I've forgotten we're all ducks in Nottingham. And then there's that peculiar way people here have of pronouncing words like 'through' and 'two' and 'brew.' They rhyme with a female sheep, *ewe*, and are squeezed even more. It's not unlike how the queen talks, though the rest of the city's syllables are the give-away that the place isn't brimming with royalty. Here's what I mean:

Received pronunciation, like David Dimbleby: 'Broo House Yard, d'k.'
The queen: 'Breu Hice Yod, dak.'
Nottingham citizens: 'Breu 'Aas Yaaad, dukk.'

The bus drivers compare notes, then one of them declares, 'It's where Trip t' Jerusalem is, innit?'

I nod with added vigour.

'Raa–ait, dukk,' says the woman again, 'Gu dahn Carrington Street, tairn raa–ait int' Canal Street, then upp Castle Street an' yer in Breu 'Aas Yaaad.'

It's a mark of how localised are the many varieties of English pronunciation that the sound of most of these words bears little relation to how the old miners of my birthplace would utter them just 7 miles west.

I thank the good bus conductors of Nottingham, giving a thumbs-up in case they have trouble understanding me. They're right, The Trip to Jerusalem is where I'm headed. It's a pub I used to drink in back when I wasn't quite old enough to do so legally. My old school friend, Geoff, whom I'm meeting again today, had been a fellow lawbreaker there.

But The Trip to Jerusalem isn't just a haunt of my youth, it's a piece of English national identity. In one sense you could say that about all pubs, because the pub is a peculiarly English institution. Any English person who has travelled abroad will know that a bar is not the same. A bar in Italy, for example, or America is like a shop that happens to sell alcoholic beverages (ughh!) that you can consume on the premises. Or it's a room in any hotel in the world with sofas to sit on before you go into the restaurant. The Germans do have their Bierkellers, but they're dingy basements full of over enthusiastic singers. And it's true the Spanish are so envious of our pubs that they've adopted the word. However, when you see a sign saying *el pub* in Granada, you'll find it's just another plastic-tabled bar.

'Pub' of course is short for public house, and it's the word 'house' that sets the English version apart. Pubs are like second homes. They began life as just that, homes, in Anglo-Saxon times. The woman of the household would brew ale in the scullery and sell it to neighbours or passing travellers. Then some of those alewives recognised a business opportunity, and dedicated a couple of rooms to it. The homeliness of the place meant it became somewhere for friends or travellers to meet and enjoy themselves. It was a – public – house.

The archetypal English pub today still has a welcoming atmosphere, and usually feels old-fashioned, if not downright historic. In fact, Historic England has listed 8,307 of them as being of outstanding or special historic interest. They're like parish churches in one sense – they've survived not as museums but because they still serve the same purpose in life as they've had for many years, sometimes centuries.

But sadly, as you'll be quick to point out, I'm being idealistic here. The smoking ban and cheap supermarket beer means that 'locals' are shutting so fast you'd wonder there are any left at all. In 2009 an average of seven pubs each day got a FOR SALE sign stuck on them and ended up as flats, a Poundland, or something equally humiliating. And though by 2012 the number of closures had fallen to three a day, many of those that have survived still call themselves pubs but are really restaurants, often quite upmarket ones serving delicate international cuisine on tables that leave no room for the casual drinker. A piece of English national identity that goes back many centuries is dying in our time. One of the few remaining archetypal pubs is, I'm glad to say, The Trip to Jerusalem.

As I enter Brew House Yard, there it is. And if proof were needed that pub patrons value an historic feel to their 'local', consider the sign that greets my eyes. In copperplate writing on the white-painted gable end before me are the words 'Ye Oldest Inn In England'. This means the owners are members of the APIOAOIE – the Association of Pubs that Insist Ours is Absolutely the Oldest Inn in England. Most counties have several of them. They usually try to reinforce their claim by putting 'Ye Olde' in front and by calling themselves Inns. Inns are pubs where travellers can stay overnight. Brewers' marketing departments think the word sounds more authentically historical than plain 'pub.'

Ye Olde Trip to Jerusalem may well have the best claim to be Ye oldest in England. It's where, by some accounts, in 1189 a troop of knights and common soldiers called in for a drink before trekking across Europe on the Third Crusade to try to evict the Saracen horde from the Holy City. It's a lovely image, all the locals patting them on the back, wishing them good luck, then – as the flower of Nottingham chivalry disappeared up the road – saying to each other, 'That's the last we'll see of them then.' By 1189 the place had already been going for 100 years.

But no one's quite sure how the name came about, and in fact it's been called several different things, including 'The Pilgrim' in a recent century. What we do know is that it was owned at various times by the Knights Templar and the Knights of St John of Jerusalem, both of whom were that bizarre medieval concoction, warrior monks who travelled to the Holy Land to fight in the Crusades. So it's not hard to see why 'Jerusalem' figures in the pub's name.

The Trip, as it's known in Nottingham, has another distinction. It's a warren of caves with a bit of building tacked on the front. These caves are not natural ones. They were hacked out by hand from the cliff face below Nottingham Castle, and this – as we'll soon learn – is where the Norman connection comes in, very soon after Duke William's triumph at Hastings in 1066.

***

My musings are interrupted when I see Geoff coming out of The Trip's front door with a tray of what looks like coffee and milk. We greet each other, then I get myself a hot chocolate and join him. As you know, Geoff and I were at grammar school together. That was here in Nottingham, where the two of us became fans of history, Nottingham Forest Football Club, and shared a fancy that only Lenny Bruce could match us for cynical humour. Our presence now back in the old city provokes a few too many sentences starting with, 'Do you remember when…?', and our drinks are starting to get cold in the chill morning air when the barmaid comes over to our table.

'Are you two gentlemen booked on the cellar tour?' she asks, and without waiting for a reply adds. 'I've got your tickets here.'

'Tickets?' I exclaim. 'How many of us will there be?'

'Just the two of you,' she replies. 'We ask for a donation of two pound fifty for charity. The Cat's Protection League.'

'Ah ha,' says Geoff and he's away, telling about the seemingly hundreds of such animals he's had as pets during his life, ending with, 'But I'm afraid my friend here hates cats.'

'Well, I wouldn't go that far,' I smile, 'But the two of us balance each other out. The ones I try to strangle, Geoff here rescues and looks after.'

Like most of my jokes, it's ill judged, and the barmaid gives me the sort of look she's probably been saving up for when the Yorkshire Ripper gets let out and walks into The Trip.

Ten minutes later, inside the bar, we meet our guide and landlady. She's tall with long dark hair and has a 'Trip to Jerusalem' badge on her jacket. Her name's Rosie. How reassuring that she's called what pub landladies should be called. She's not a Kylie or a Jocasta. However, Rosie, we're soon to learn, is rather more than your average pub manager. As well as being an efficient businesswoman, she's also a keen amateur historian. She and Geoff immediately begin to compare methods of protecting cats, so I allow words like 'moggy', 'burmese blue' and 'highly intelligent' to drift past my ears, while I peer around. We're in a small cave with leather-backed benches along its sides, and – what puzzles me – a cosy brick fireplace set into the rock face.

'Where does its chimney go?' I ask as soon as the feline exchange starts to die down.

'It's been cut into the rock and comes out just below the castle,' explains Rosie. 'There are several of them. You'll soon see.'

'I remember drinking in here like it was yesterday,' I say. And we explain about our connection with the city.

'That'd be before we sealed the roof,' she says. 'The rock's very crumbly. Bits used to drop in your drink, if you didn't put a beer mat over it.'

'Yes, yes, I can remember that,' I say with schoolboy delight. 'So what did they do in the Middle Ages before beer mats were invented?'

'Real men liked a bit of grit in their pints,' says Geoff in a gruff voice. Chuckles over, Rosie leads us through a door marked 'Cellars'.

Unlike normal cellars that go down, the Trip's version goes sideways, into the cliff face then burrows under the castle above. We're in a brightly-lit rock tunnel and once we've passed the 'Health and Safety' notice and a wall display of those grit-repellent beer mats, there are metal barrels all along the sides. Rosie points out small dents that pepper the face of the rock.

'Those are the marks left by the tools they used to hack out the tunnels,' she explains.

'It must have been a helluva job,' I say.

'It's sandstone,' she replies. 'Very soft, as rocks go. What happened was that William Peverel, a Norman baron who fought alongside William the Conqueror at the Battle of Hastings, was given command of this area, and he built the first castle on the rock above us. We think they started to dig out these caves pretty soon after that. It was a brewery, to serve the castle garrison.'

'Yes, of course,' says Geoff. 'Ale was important. Everybody drank it, even children, because it was the only clean drink available. Untreated water was polluted.'

'Correct,' says Rosie. 'The brewing process sterilised it. And the caves were ideal for brewing because there's a constant temperature here all the year round. And they diverted the River Leen so it came past outside to supply the water.'

'So this wasn't some alehouse cottage industry,' I say. 'It was brewing on an industrial scale.'

'Yes,' says Rosie, 'and we can be pretty sure that as well as supplying the castle, they'd sell it to locals as well. And they were still brewing here till only a few years ago. Now it makes the perfect beer cellar. I think it's great that this has been a home for beer for nearly a thousand years.'

Rosie then takes us down a narrow plank into another cave on a level half a metre lower. 'Be very careful. Mind your step,' she warns, as her 4in-high heels clack on the bouncing wood. 'Now you'll notice that this cave has been hewn out with these side chambers, so the plan of the room is in the shape of a cross.'

'A chapel?' I suggest.

'Could well be, given The Trip used to be owned by the Knights of St John of Jerusalem. Then more recently, this cave wasn't so holy. It's where they used to have cockfighting and gambling.'

As we move on through more caverns, I realise I've got sandy fragments in my hair and over much of my coat. As I thrash about trying to brush it off, Rosie shows us a small cramped alcove in the rock. Unlike the tunnels we've passed through, in here it's damp; the walls and roof are covered in green slime. It's a store for bottles of wine and fizzy drinks. There's a rusty iron-barred gate across its entrance. 'This was where prisoners condemned to be hanged were kept before being taken up to the gibbet above,' she explains. 'It was once part of the gaol attached to the castle.'

'I've got to try this out,' I say, and in I go, pulling the iron bars shut behind me. I sit on a crate of J2O apple and mango juice, trying to imagine what the final moments of life would feel like. Would you fear more the certain tightening of the hangman's knot, or the uncertain eternity to follow, perhaps tormented in the fires of Hell? A drop of ice-cold water falls on my nose, and I'm up and out before the rusty gate gets stuck in the shut position.

As we weave our way back, I ask, 'So how far do the caves and tunnels stretch in here?'

'We don't know,' she replies. 'There have been collapses and some unsafe sections have been sealed off. It could be hundreds of yards in several directions. You've just been in the safe parts.'

Back on the other side of the cellar door, the pub is starting to fill with lunchtime drinkers. Rosie pulls a pint of Olde Trip for Geoff and opens a bottle with a name something like Magic Glitter Juice for me. She insists the drinks are on the house. 'I'll show you the giant chimney next,' she says. This is like an empty inglenook fireplace about 8 to 10ft wide, but when you step into it and look up, you see that its chimney is just as wide all the way up for what looks like 60 or 70ft to where daylight streams in. This vertical passageway, I guess, emerges somewhere close to the castle.

'It was used in later times as a fireplace for heating and cooking, then was sealed off,' explains Rosie. 'When they opened it up again in 1997, they cleared over fifty tons of soot from it. But originally, it was part of the brewery. For the malting, they needed a big fire and a very wide-chimney, and you can walk through the chimney on the floor above. That's where the barley would have been laid out on wooden trays over the heat.'

'So this is the heart of William Peverel's Norman brewery?' I say.

Rosie smiles and nods. 'I'll show you where the roof caved in a few years ago,' she says, as her stilettos tick-tack up a set of steps carved from the rock. 'You can still see where it came away,' she explains, pointing at an upside-down crater in the ceiling. It's directly over a middle-aged couple, seated in front of untouched half-pints and leafing through a map book. 'The whole lot came down,' Rosie adds. 'Luckily no one happened to be underneath.'

The woman who's risking death here today, gives a nervous glance at the huge gouge in the ceiling above her. Geoff and I must look like safety inspectors, because she says, 'We're alright now though, aren't we?' Before I can give a mischievous tut and shake of the head, Rosie reassures them and explains about the rock surface being sealed these days.

Our tour is complete. Geoff and I shake hands with our guide, tell her how much we've enjoyed it, and repeat our thanks several times. The cellar tour is supposed to last twenty minutes. Rosie has been with us well over an hour.

***

The original brewery and alehouse that is today The Trip to Jerusalem were closely associated with the central events of the Norman Conquest. William Peverel, the Norman baron that Rosie told us about, was a favourite of William the Conqueror. At the time of the Battle of Hastings, he was just 26. According to one account, he was the Conqueror's illegitimate son by a Saxon princess, Maud Ingelrica. Maud had visited Normandy with Edward the Confessor shortly before Edward became king.

So who were these new invaders of England? By a slight stretch of history, we could say they were just one more set of Viking raiders. 'Norman' was a variant of 'Norsemen.' While, during the tenth century, one set of Vikings from Denmark and Norway were busy occupying England, others of their fellows were arriving in northern France. But unlike the Vikings in England who didn't mix with the local population, the Norman Vikings did. They adopted elements of the native culture, and their menfolk began to marry women from the neighbourhood. The Normans even started to speak their own version of the local language. Norman French was different from standard French of that time, mainly in its spelling and pronunciation. So, where Parisians, for example, wrote 'challenge' and 'prison', the Normans put 'calenge' and 'prisun.'

Following the victory at Hastings, the Conqueror moved fast. He had himself crowned king at Westminster Abbey, and then he carved up the country into small units which he awarded to his barons. Most Norman noblemen found they had bits of land scattered around England. King William's plan was that none but his most loyal supporters would have a large, single power block, which he recognised might be a future threat to royal authority. It's a mark of the Conqueror's trust in the young Peverel that the lands he received were concentrated in a single region. He became the lord of no fewer than 162 manors in Nottinghamshire and Derbyshire. The castle he built on top of the rock at Nottingham, above the future pub, was the headquarters for the eastern part of his new English domain.

His team must have included an experienced engineer, someone who had the knowledge and expertise to organise the hollowing out of the sandstone beneath the castle to provide a chimney for malting, and who knew how to divert the local river so its waters could be sterilised during the brewing process. Without it, the Norman garrison in the castle would have been vulnerable to dysentery and other intestinal illnesses that were often fatal in the Middle Ages.

It's not likely that the ale produced here would also have been made available straightaway to the local English population – that would have followed later. In the early days of the Conquest, the two sides, English and Norman, were at each others' throats. We can judge the tension between them from a chaotic misunderstanding during King William's coronation at Westminster Abbey. When the Norman bodyguards outside heard a commotion inside the Abbey, they mistook it for a violent attack by the local Anglo-Saxon populace. The royal soldiers panicked, and, for some ill-judged reason, set fire to the surrounding buildings. The noise they'd heard was in fact nothing more than the cheers of the congregation for the new King. Amid the smoke and uproar, the coronation ceremony continued with the presiding bishops trembling in fear. But according to a Norman chronicler: 'The English were greatly enraged when they understood the origin of this unfortunate affair, which led them to be suspicious of the Normans and consider them faithless, so they waited for some future opportunity of revenge.'

The English got no such chance. Over the next five years, a series of rebellions was crushed without mercy. One Benedictine monk wrote that the Norman military operation during the winter of 1069–70, known as the 'Harrying of the North,' left 'no village inhabited between York and Durham.' It was said that 100,000 people died of hunger. No one could know the number, but setting it so high does tell us that this must have been a terrible time for ordinary folk. The Anglo-Saxon upper classes fared no better. The new King ordered the systematic elimination of 4,000 thanes – Anglo-Saxon warrior landholders – right across England. And it was their territory that was handed out to William Peverel and 170 or so of his fellow Norman barons.

Peverel's castle, up above The Trip, would have been an all-wood affair, a tall tower on a mound of earth with a courtyard surrounded by a wooden palisade. These 'motte and bailey' castles were quickly thrown up all over the country by the new Norman rulers. They were like fortified police stations, places from which soldiers could rush out and deal with any sign of armed opposition among the local Saxon population. None of these structures remain for us to see today, though you can sometimes spot the earthworks on which they were built. There's one in Nottinghamshire at Laxton, for instance. And often the original mound of a motte and bailey can be seen incorporated into a later fortification, for instance, at Corfe Castle in Dorset.

The first castles built by the Normans in England comprised a wooden keep on an artificial mound – the motte – above a fenced courtyard – the bailey. Then, during the twelfth century, timber was replaced by stone, but the castle's layout – as this large-scale model of Corfe Castle in Dorset shows – remained the same. (Andrew Hackney)

Wooden defences, however, were obviously vulnerable to fire, rot and even a good push with a battering ram. So once the Normans were satisfied that the English were no longer such an immediate threat, they turned their attention to digging in for the long haul. They asserted their authority in the way that military governments did in the twelfth century: they built fortified stone towers. Many of these keeps have long since been absorbed into the more elaborate castles constructed by later generations. A few still stand, like the one at Rochester in Kent, which has 10ft-thick walls. And the most famous Norman keep is the White Tower, admired today by 2.8 million visitors a year at the Tower of London. Incidentally, Nottingham's twelfth-century castle fell into disrepair and was demolished in the seventeenth century. There's now a museum and art gallery on the site.

The Normans' activities in England went way beyond military operations and governmental systems designed to subdue the Anglo-Saxon population. Bishops and other senior clergy were shipped in to take over the English church. And another construction boom began. Architects, masons and sculptors came over from Normandy, and networks of wooden scaffolding began to rise above cities all over England. New cathedrals were springing up in Lincoln, St Albans, Hereford, Ely, Worcester, Exeter, Carlisle and Durham. In other towns, where the congregation had outgrown the old building or where fires had damaged it, at Canterbury and Peterborough for instance, the Norman builders set about constructing fresh, more spectacular places of worship. Whole communities of monks and nuns – women would soon play a more prominent role in religious life – all followed on the coat-tails of the conquerors too. The Carthusians and the Cistercians arrived during the twelfth century, their abbeys and monasteries often later becoming parish churches. You can usually pick out these English Norman buildings by their rounded archways, often with zigzag dogtooth carvings. Durham Cathedral is the finest example. But there's also many a delightful piece of Norman artwork to be stumbled upon in the little church of some remote English country village.

The north doorway of St John the Baptist Church, Burford, Oxfordshire, built around 1175. The curved arch and zigzag pattern are typical of Norman, or English Romanesque architecture.

Norman influence on English culture far outlasted the Norman kings themselves. In fact, there were only three truly Norman monarchs – the Conqueror and two of his sons, William Rufus and Henry I. Between them, they ruled England for just seventy-nine years. After that, there was a disputed claim to the throne, and from 1135 for the next nineteen years England collapsed into an anarchic civil war. William Peverel's son, William the Younger backed the losing side, and when in 1154 Henry II assumed the crown, one of his first acts was to strip Peverel of all those lordships his father had been granted in Nottinghamshire and Derbyshire, as well as the castle and its brewery in Nottingham itself.

The new King, Henry II, was technically a Norman. He was the great-grandson of the Conqueror. However, his power base was in Anjou in central western France rather than Normandy. So he's considered the first Angevin king, the House of Anjou being the beginning of the Plantagenet dynasty. The Plantagenets were to last the next 250 years. But the Angevins' arrival didn't mean the end of Norman culture. Though Peverel was gone, many other Norman barons, as well as senior Norman churchmen, continued in power under the new regime. One change that did occur, how-ever, was in the language spoken at court, and at the top of English society. Standard medieval French replaced the harsher syllables of Norman French.

This brings us to the greatest contribution of the Plantagenet period to the growth of English national identity. It's true that the parish churches, the stone towered castles, the cathedrals, and of course one or two pubs, all contribute today to the rich legacy of English architecture. But the greatest gift of the Plantagenets to the English today was in what they failed to achieve.

Given the efficient, and at times ruthless, way that the Normans and their Plantagenet successors maintained control of the coun-try – not only of its land, its government and its church, but its legal system and even its commercial operations – you might imagine that their language too would drive out the Old English of the Anglo-Saxons. That's what usually happened in such cir-cumstances. Anglo-Saxon for example, as we've seen, had all but obliterated the Celtic language of the natives.

In the first decades after 1066, the odds looked stacked in favour of French becoming the language of England, because its new rulers stayed resolutely French in their culture and the way they spoke. All kings and most barons for the first 140 years after 1066 saw England as little more than a foreign backyard. They regarded Anjou, Normandy and all their other estates across the Channel, which they maintained, as their true home. The three Norman kings, for instance, spent half their time in France. At one stage William the Conqueror stayed there for five uninterrupted years. Richard the Lionheart at the end of the twelfth century spent only six months out of his ten-year reign in England. So the rulers of England didn't see themselves as English, and French went unchallenged and undiluted as the language of power. So why didn't a version of French become the language of England?

Part of the reason is that Anglo-Saxon, the Old English language had got itself such a firm foothold. It had had 700 years to become the spoken language of a nation. But also Old English had been celebrated in a literature that reflected the history and traditions of the Anglo-Saxons. This was not only in manuscripts such as the *Anglo-Saxon Chronicle* and the English translation of the Lindisfarne Gospels, but also for instance in what's considered one of the most important English poems, *Beowulf* – a heroic epic about the very roots of the Anglo-Saxons.

Old English had numbers on its side too. The Norman kings, the royal court, the Norman barons, their entourages and their soldiers may have added up to no more than 15,000, and by some reckonings, only 5,000. That compared with a general population in late eleventh-century England of around 1.5 million. And these proportions were not much different under the first Plantagenets. So, although – for the moment at least – French was the language of the ruling elite, in the long run French would lose the battle for the tongues and parchments of the wider population of England.

Old English, however, had had a narrow escape. If, as might well have happened, it had been replaced by Old French to become the native language of the English, the implications for a separate English identity would have been catastrophic. We today would almost certainly be speaking French, or a French dialect at best. You'd now be reading something called, *Pour qui se prennent-ils les anglais?* Or more likely, I'd not be writing this book at all, because Englishness might now have become no more significant than, say, Isle of Wight identity or Swindon identity, i.e. not very.

However, Old English itself was changing. French would not replace it. But the language of Charlemagne and William the

Conqueror would have an influence on the development of the English language. As we shall discover at a later stop on our journey, that influence would be very powerful indeed.

***

Meanwhile, the growth of English national identity was about to be given a powerful boost, in fact three boosts. They came during the early thirteenth century, 150 years after Hastings. But the man responsible was no hero. In fact, he has a reputation as the most villainous of all English monarchs. King John. It wasn't John's achievements that promoted the identity of the English as a separate nation. It was his three big failures that reinforced a sense of Englishness among his subjects, and especially among their descendants.

To find out more, we're going to a stretch of the River Thames near Windsor, to see the English celebrate their birthright as only the English can. Oh, and by the way, foreigners from almost every other civilised country in the world will be there too to pay homage to an English institution. Let's go and join them.

5

RUNNYMEDE, SURREY

TYRANNY, TREACHERY AND LIBERTY

KING JOHN WAS A TYRANT NOT A KING, A DESTROYER INSTEAD OF A GOVERNOR, CRUSHING HIS OWN PEOPLE AND FAVOURING FOREIGNERS.

MATTHEW PARIS (1200–59)

We're engaged in a very English occupation today. We're messing about in boats. No Ratties or Moles, however, to be seen on our stretch of the Thames this morning, though the habitat's here, an idyllic selection of north-west Surrey's woods and meadows along both banks. Or it would be idyllic if our eyes weren't drawn upwards every 45 seconds by the growl of an airliner rising from the world's second busiest international airport at Heathrow, 4 miles away. But you get used to that after a while. There're more exciting distractions all around us on the water. Scores of other boats are scattered across the river, and straggling as far as we can see in both directions. Their occupants, like us no doubt, have packed picnic baskets, filled cool boxes, and many (unlike us) have donned fancy dress, all to celebrate one of the proudest days in English history.

Maggie and I have been invited by our friends Clare and Jonathon aboard their motor cruiser *Cygnet* to take part in the River Relay

Pageant marking the 800th Anniversary of Magna Carta. We're heading for Runnymede, the meadow by the Thames, halfway between Windsor and Staines, where in the year 1215 King John was forced by his barons to agree to Magna Carta, the Great Charter, regarded today not only in England but across the world as the most hallowed and ancient beacon of freedom and justice.

'I know *Cygnet's* not quite as shapely as a junior swan,' Jonathan had apologised when he'd first mentioned the event, 'but she is white at least, well, white plastic.' We'd reassured him that it was generous of him and Clare to want us with them on this glorious commemoration of the English origins of the rule of law and the taming of kings. Maggie and I had brought along a couple of strings of bunting to deck out *Cygnet*. We'd been careful to hunt out on the Internet little flags decorated with crosses of St George. We didn't want the Scots or the Welsh thinking they could take any credit for Magna Carta.

Most of the other vessels around us are less plasticky than us, not something we'd of course remark on to our hosts. For a start, there are lots of rowing boats. Not ones like the low, narrow hulls in the annual Oxford and Cambridge race. These are all bigger and slower looking, with their mid-quarters covered by canvas canopies in bright reds, greens and yellows. Their rowers are not beefy young Oxbridge students either. The boat that Jonathan is now attempting to avoid by throwing *Cygnet* into a screeching reverse thrust, has a crew of middle-aged men whose waistlines have seen skimpier days. Their cox, a matron in floppy brimmed hat bursting with what look like violet daffodils, calls out, 'Sorry! Sorry! Awfully sorry,' and bites her lip in an apologetic smile.

Another craft is crewed entirely by town criers, all in identical blue frockcoats and tricorn hats. The cox is a monk who's gripping a tiller and dressed in brown habit and a cowl which starts slipping back off his head as he stands up and leans sideways to see where he's going. 'Steady on there, old son,' yells one of the rowers, 'or you'll have us all in the drink.'

The monk looks cross. 'Who's in charge here?'

Another town crier calls back, 'It'll be nobody unless you sit down, old fruit, and stop rocking the boat.'

They all laugh and row on, as the monk flops back with an 'OK, OK'.

'Look,' shouts Clare. She's pointing to the other side. A perfect straight line of Canada geese is cruising past.

'One, two, three, … six, seven' Maggie counts, just before a Venetian gondola screens them from view. It's manned by four Thomas Cromwell look-alikes, complete with black floppy hats and cloaks, though I soon see that 'manned' is inaccurate. They're all young women.

There are canal boats too, lumbering along like lorries climbing a steep hill. We all get out of their way. The one approaching us now has the shine of a well-cared-for steam locomotive, its night-black sides decorated by thin white lines bordering its name: *Oh Be Joyful*, the next word, 'Cheshire', telling it's come a long way … for a canal boat. The chap at its helm – red tie, straw umpire's hat – turns around a full 180 degrees, and gives a slow, full-armed wave to someone he must have recognised half a mile behind. He's confident that, in a canal boat, taking your eyes off the direction of travel for half a minute, or longer if you like, doesn't matter a jot. The rest of us know that he'll take half a mile to stop or change direction, so it's up to us to get out of the way, which Jonathan nearly manages to do. There's a slight bump as the rubber bit on *Cygnet's* back-end grazes the steel side of the *Oh Be Joyful*.

'I think I'd better take over,' says Clare giving him a playful push aside from the steering wheel. She grins at us. 'He'll never admit he's no good at it.'

'Drink anyone?' asks Jonathan, turning defeat into an opportunity. 'Let's see what's in the Eskie.'

***

I expect you'll be wondering by now what any of this has got to do with Magna Carta and King John. Well, this is just the build-up. The main act is, as I speak, coming around the bend.

Cygnet is now opposite a riverbank that's packed with moored vessels. In fact, there are so many of them that they're tied up to each other, two and three deep. Clare takes us alongside a Mississippi paddleboat, and, after a brief, friendly exchange with its captain, Jonathan puts down his bottle of Heineken and chucks a rope to a crew man on board who secures us to a railing near the iron and wood paddle-wheel at the stern.

Up above us on the deck of our host vessel, a line of folk all wearing the sort of purple or garish green paper crowns you get from cheap Christmas crackers, raise their wine glasses to us, and call out, 'Good one,' 'Welcome' and then, 'Look, look, here she comes.' And as one, they stretch forward a spare arm and squint into their mobile phones, now – if the correct icon's been tapped – in camera mode.

'She' is the *Gloriana*.

Gloriana is what the English called the first Queen Elizabeth. In the twenty-first century she is the second Queen Elizabeth's personal river boat. *Gloriana* is now smoothing her imperious path between the scattering rowers and fibreglass day-boats, her long, white hull topped along its length by red and gold carvings. Her cabin, like a stretched coronation coach, sports a huge royal coat of arms with golden lion and unicorn poking out fierce red tongues. On top, no sails, but half a dozen huge standards that billow and flop in the breeze. Her stern sweeps up high above the Thames, ending in the gilded letters, 'EIIR' and as glittering a crown as you could hope to curtsey before anywhere. But, it's the oars that, more than all that regal colour and pomp, make us gasp. A line of long white poles gently stroking the water in faultless unison. And when suddenly – pair by pair – they peel up till they stand to attention like two ranks of wiry soldiers in a salute, it's too much for us mere commoners in our puny little craft. An 'ooOOOoooh!' is heard all across the river, followed by respectful applause.

'Hmm,' says Maggie, 'I don't get this. I thought today was all about celebrating how a monarch got his comeuppance. Power to the people. Chop off his head. That kind of thing. And here we are all clapping a piece of royal extravagance.'

'That's the English for you,' says Clare. 'We never miss a chance to show off that – unlike those foreigners – we have a real queen.'

'She's not a real queen,' complains Jonathan. 'She's a constitutional monarch.'

'You know what I mean,' says Clare again. 'I'm talking about all the "Gawd bless you Ma'am, God save the queen" stuff. It's our equivalent of American presidents saying, "God Bless America." Royalty equals England equals patriotism.'

One of the women in a paper crown above us on the paddle steamer has overheard this exchange. She calls down, 'I hate to tell you folks, but you're missing the fun.' And she gives a couple of nods over towards *Gloriana*. And there is our monarch.

No, not our much blessed reigning sovereign, Her Majesty Queen Elizabeth II, but that well-known black sheep of the royal flock, King John. He's standing in the stern of the royal barge, silver crown, his famous long hair wafting in the wind, red smock coat with three lions on the front, and he's talking to himself. Or at least there's no on near him to listen. And then he starts wagging a finger at the rest of us, to indicate, I suppose, that he's laying down the law, rather than obeying it.

We all boo. That's more like it.

***

King John has had a bad press over the years. Many historians today though have decided that he did have a few good points. He could be generous, and he took a keen interest in the mechanics of government. And in some ways he was unlucky. He faced a clever and determined foreign enemy in King Philip Augustus of France, and he was blamed for things his brother and his father before him had done when they were kings. The baronial rebellion which brought about Magna Carta had been brewing for decades, and was the climax of dissatisfaction with Henry II and Richard the Lionheart as much as with John. And he wasn't as shrewd as his father, Henry, nor did have his brother Richard's reputation as a brilliant warrior – always a help for a king trying to win the respect of his baronial subjects.

It's true, too, that John could be cruel, for instance in the way he starved to death Lady Matilda de Briouze for refusing to give up her children as hostages. But then kings at that time who did not enforce their authority by occasional acts of brutality could look easy targets for revolt.

John's real problems were that he had poor judgement and he was unpredictable. You didn't know where you were with him. One moment he was heaping a wealth of castles, land and noble

King John's tomb in Worcester Cathedral. The stone effigy was raised on the decorated plinth and moved to a position in front of the high altar in Tudor times. The Tudors regarded him as an English hero, who – like Henry VIII – had battled against the Pope.

titles on you as a reward for your loyalty. The next, he was accusing you of being a traitor, stripping you of the rewards he earlier awarded you, and demanding you hand over your children as guarantees of your good behaviour.

So, in the year 1215, he faced an armed revolt by around forty of his barons. And just as John himself was a mixed bag, so were the country's noble families. For a start, only a minority of them – forty out of a total of around 170 – took to the field in rebellion. Forty more saddled up their steeds, summoned their knights and cross-bowmen, and trooped off to support the king. About ninety baronial families wanted nothing to do with either side. And then there were the leaders of the revolt. They've been described as 'self-serving thugs.' Chief rebel was a man called Robert Fitzwalter, whose pompous self-awarded title was 'Marshal of the Army of God and the Holy Church'. Fitzwalter was a blustering clown. When his son-in-law murdered a servant boy, Fitzwalter led a gang of armed men into the law court to intimidate the judges into dropping the charges. When he succeeded, he fled with his family to France.

So, what brought these two unattractive enemies to this stretch of the Thames in June 1215? And how did we manage to get from their meeting something that makes the English today feel like they invented justice and freedom?

Much of the thanks should go to the Archbishop of Canterbury, Stephen Langton for the brainwork behind the wording of the document. In the early part of the year, neither rebels nor royalists were gaining much advantage, and they agreed to come together to see if they could thrash out a peace deal. Both were stalling for time. The king was at Windsor, and the barons 9 miles downriver at Staines. Langton did some astute shuttle diplomacy and negotiated a treaty between them. They met to finalise the details on the meadow – halfway between the two towns – at Runnymede, where *Cygnet*, *Gloriana*, *Oh Be Joyful* and all the other pageant boats are moored today. The terms of the deal were recorded in a document that later came to be called Magna Carta.

King John's royal seal was pressed into hot wax at the bottom of the document – you'll notice he did not, as is often suggested, sign it – on 15 June 1215. Today's the 14th, so the 800th anniversary is tomorrow. That's when the queen, the Prime Minister and the usual English cast of virtuous VIPs, as well as several hundred lawyers and leaders from across the civilised world, will gather here to commemorate the birth of the rule of law.

But today is the people's day. Or at least the day of those people who can afford to own a boat, have paid for a ticket on one, or have friends (e.g. Clare and Jonathan) who own one. We've chosen the people's day to come here to Runnymede because Magna Carta gave the common people equality beneath the law.

Or did it? Well, no, that's one of the myths.

Magna Carta has sixty-three clauses, and most of them would leave the eyes of ordinary folk today glazed over with boredom. The document is mainly peppered with obsolete feudal technical terms like *halberget*, *trithings* and *amercement*, or it talks about long-forgotten practicalities like fish-traps on the River Medway. And even when we do stumble on a sentence that makes us perk up, historians step in and tell us to calm down. Take clause thirty-nine, the most famous clause in Magna Carta:

> No free man shall be seized or imprisoned, or stripped of his rights or possessions, or outlawed or exiled, or deprived of his standing in any other way, nor will we [i.e. the king] proceed with force against him, or send others to do so, except by the lawful judgement of his equals or by the law of the land.

Stirring stuff. But take a closer look at it. These wonderful rights are available only to 'free men.' So 50 per cent of the population – women – are ruled out to start with. And *free men* made up only a small proportion of the male population. The clause obviously applied to the barons, and also to their knights, but otherwise was restricted to only one in four of the male population. Most of the rest were tied to the land, little better than agricultural slaves. They were not *free*, and could be bullied, beaten up and otherwise punished by corrupt royal officials, without redress, after Magna Carta just as much as before. Clause thirty-nine is upper-class men looking after themselves – hardly a beacon of equality and justice.

But all was not lost. There are a couple of gems hidden in the words of this clause. They state that the king, in the particular circumstances of how free men shall be treated, will abide by the law. That was a first.

Magna Carta didn't set down a general principle. It didn't say, 'The king is no different from anyone else in a court of law.' But it gave examples of that principle. And that was something entirely new: the idea that the king was not above the law.

And the other treasure in clause thirty-nine is this: If we accept for one moment that back in the early thirteenth century, it was as yet unthinkable that women or most men could be included, then we can see these lines in Magna Carta were the thin end of a legal wedge. They were again an example of a principle that arbitrary punishment is wrong. In other words, you can't just be locked up or hanged on the say-so of someone powerful. You must be convicted in a proper court of law first.

But that's not the end of the story. Magna Carta wasn't fixed forever in 1215. Over the next 200 years, it was re-issued at least fifty-five times, often updated. Whenever a king faced opposition, or wanted to raise taxes, and needed to make concessions, those concessions were often incorporated into a revised Magna Carta. The most significant of the updatings came in 1354, under King Edward III. Clause thirty-nine was altered to read: 'No man, of whatever estate or condition he may be ... [shall be punished] ... except by due process of law.' Although it would be many centuries before women achieved equality with men, this was a big step forward. It was an acceptance that justice should be extended to the lowest levels of society.

The most glorious period in Magna Carta's life came in the seventeenth centuries. During the great clash between Parliament and Crown, Parliament relied on Magna Carta to combat the claims of the Stuart kings, James I and Charles I, that they had a divine right to rule – in other words that they were accountable only to God and were not subject to the law or to the will of the people. In 1649, Magna Carta justified the trial and execution of Charles I.

So, this stretch of the River Thames, where so many of us have turned up today, can after all claim to be the birthplace of the rule of law. Such a momentous idea – that we all, including those who govern us, must obey the law – didn't spring into this world fully formed. Like the rest of us, it needed to grow. So there's plenty here today for English commoners to celebrate on this fine English meadow.

***

Cue the arrival of the man who might claim to be the people's most ancient representative: The Speaker of the House of Commons, the Rt. Hon. John Bercow. He's accompanied by government minister Phillip Hammond, who's not only Foreign Secretary but also has the honour of being MP for this birthplace of freedom. By now Clare, Jonathan, Maggie and I have eaten a few salmon sandwiches and are no longer thirsty. We've clambered through the lower deck of the paddle steamer, excusing ourselves and thanking the passengers for their tolerance, before balancing along a plank to reach the meadow, which has been cordoned off for the ceremony about to take place. And – something that would have bewildered Ratty and Mole – we've been searched for weapons and explosives. Now not too far away, a military band is playing something patriotic; it might be 'Land of Hope and Glory', but it's difficult to tell amid the shouts and laughs of the several hundred people milling about.

As well as Messrs Bercow and Hammond, there's at least one mayor in red robes and chain of office, as well as several other unrecognisable but important people looking pleased with themselves. They're standing next to a bright blue sheet draped over something about 12ft tall.

Speaker Bercow then does as his title suggests and makes a speech, all about Magna Carta being the 'bedrock of so much we have come subsequently to honour and to cherish,' before having a wrestling match with the blue sheet. Whatever is underneath, it does not want to come out. The band strikes up 'God Save the Queen', then stops, then starts again once the wind and the red-robed mayor have come to the Speaker's help and the sheet has ballooned off to reveal a statue.

'Who is it?' asks Jonathan. 'Don't tell me it's King John.'

'Maybe it's one of the barons,' suggests Maggie.

'Looks more like George Osborne in drag,' says Clare.

As the crowd starts to thin out, we make our way forward, and find ourselves close to Secretary of State Hammond, by now giving an interview to a BBC reporter.

'It's a statue of the queen,' he says. And then, just in case viewers should have any doubts, adds, 'A very good statue of the queen'.

'What!' I exclaim – in a whisper so as not to broadcast to the nation via the reporter's mic. 'The queen! But Magna Carta's *anti*-queens-and-kings. That's what Magna Carta's about.'

'Shsh!' Maggie hisses. 'Listen.'

But my concerns are not unique, because Mr Hammond is saying, '… might, to some people, appear to be something slightly incongruous in celebrating the 800th anniversary of the curtailing of the power of the monarch by unveiling a statue of the monarch. Not at all. Because while John represented arguably the worst of monarchy, Queen Elizabeth II represents undoubtedly the best of monarchy.'

When he's done and is now being collared by Sky News, we drift off to take a closer look at the newly revealed royal statue. I turn to the others. 'Isn't it typical of a politician?' I say. 'You have two things that anyone with half a brain can see are opposites. One, a weapon against the monarchy. The other, something that glorifies the monarchy. And your politician stands up and says, "Ah, but they both mean the same really." It's classic politician rubbish. They'll argue black's white, and white's black if it suits them'

'Well,' says Jonathan, 'what Hammond says is just about sustainable.'

'You know what I think?' – Maggie this time – 'I think this is a case of the organisers of today's event saying, "Ah, big national anniversary coming up, what do we do on big national occasions in this country? We wheel out the queen! Let's have a statue of her." Without really thinking it through.'

'I'm with Maggie,' says Clare. 'If the English really want to show their appreciation of something that's brilliantly English, the way to do it is with the queen.'

'Yes,' Maggie continues, 'and think about the royal barge and all those paper Christmas cracker crowns we saw. You'd think today was the queen's birthday. For the English, England's glory – whether it's Magna Carta or whatever – equals queen.'

'But she's the queen of Scotland, Wales and Northern Ireland as well, not just of England,' says Jonathan.

'Well, of course that's true,' I chip in, 'but nobody ever says "Elizabeth, Queen of Britain" or "Elizabeth, Queen of the UK". On the other hand, "Elizabeth, Queen of England" trips right off the tongue. We accept that she's head of state for all those places from Scotland to Australia, but the English adopt her as being special to them. What do England football fans sing at Wembley?' And I render the first line of 'God Save the Queen'.

We're now by the statue. 'I still think it looks like George Osborne,' says Clare. The plaque on the plinth says:

HM QUEEN ELIZABETH II
Unveiled by
The Rt Hon John Bercow MP

Member of Parliament for Buckingham and Speaker of the
House of Commons.
Made possible by the generous donations from
SHEIKH MAREI MUBARAK MAHFOUZ BIN
MAHFOUZ
and other donors listed nearby.

'Now, wait a minute,' I say, 'This is getting silly. A statue of the queen paid for not by a grateful English nation but by ... well, who is Sheikh Marei Mubarak Mahfouz Bin Mahfouz?'

'Give me a mo,' says Jonathan, and he starts prodding at his i-phone. After a few seconds, he says, 'Right...he's a 44-year-old businessman from Saudi Arabia.'

'It gets better!' I shriek. 'So, here we have an English charter that curbed the power of monarchs and is seen as the foundation of human rights, celebrated with the statue of a monarch paid for by someone from the country with one of the world's worst records for human rights!'

'To be fair,' adds Jonathan, 'Google says he's an "enthusiastic Anglophile", and there's nothing here about him being involved in any human rights abuses.'

'Yeah, well, nevertheless ...' I protest.

***

The next day, which is the actual anniversary of Magna Carta, the four of us are sitting in front of the television at Clare and Jonathan's. Now it's the turn of the queen herself and Prime Minster Cameron to be where we were yesterday on the river bank at Runnymede. We watch as the queen, in light blue coat and matching top-hat, unveils another plaque, this one making no mention of Middle Eastern potentates and sticking strictly to the celebrating '800 years of Magna Carta' line. The Prime Minister makes a speech saying that what happened on this meadow eight centuries ago is as relevant today as it was then.

This is all standard national celebration stuff. But what sets the event apart, what promotes it to a much higher league of English pride, is the presence of so many foreign admirers. There are leaders from Canada, Australia, India and other Commonwealth countries, and by far the biggest contingent is from the United States.

It's one of the strangest things in Magna Carta's story that, much as we in England revere it, the Americans worship it even more. The eight-columned Magna Carta memorial, for instance, where today's commemoration takes place, was not erected by us, the English. No. Back in 1957, 9,000 American lawyers stumped up the money to get it built here. And so today, as well as the Commonwealth citizens paying homage, there are more than a thousand Americans, mainly lawyers. The most impressive speech of the day is delivered by a woman in sombre black suit. She's Loretta Lynch, the US Attorney General, who tells the crowd: 'While the hands that wrote Magna Carta have long been stilled, the principles they carved out of the struggles of their day and the struggles of the human condition, live on.'

So how did this American adoration of Magna Carta come about? For the answer, we have to go back to the seventeenth century. In England, from that time forwards, Parliament and the law courts more and more became regarded as the ultimate guarantors of English personal freedom, and Magna Carta tended to take a back seat. But during this same period, Magna Carta began to make a new life for itself overseas. It was carried to the American colonies. In the following century, during the War of Independence, it was a weapon turned against its makers. The Americans claimed that their rallying cry of 'No taxation without representation' had its justification in Magna Carta. And when they founded their new nation, the most famous section of the Bill of Rights – the Fifth Amendment – read: 'No person shall be deprived of life, liberty, or property without due process of law.'

It was a direct quote from the 1354 Magna Carta except that the word 'man' had become 'person'. So today whenever Americans cite the need for 'due process', whether complaining that their boss has fired them without reason, or whether to protest at imprisonments in Guantanamo Bay, they are quoting Magna Carta.

The old charter has come a long way, from the grouses of a few upper-class Englishmen about King John to the international watchword today for justice and freedom from oppression for everyone.

The English of course remember with pride that it is their country which, with Magna Carta, laid the foundation of the rule of law, a principle which – despite whatever lapses there have been or perhaps are today – we still see as one of the golden threads running through English national identity. The recognition by other countries of England's role in developing the rule of law enhances that pride. Perhaps, to be generous on such a celebratory day, we should see Sheikh Marei Mubarak Mahfouz Bin Mahfouz's support as a compliment to Englishness too.

***

King John's contribution to the growth of English national identity went beyond bequeathing to us – through his incompetence and ill-judgement – the notion that we are the world's most venerable defenders of the rule of law. John suffered two other catastrophic defeats, both of which boosted the idea that England was an independent nation, ultimately with its own culture, its own way of governing itself, and its own language.

The first of those defeats came in the fifth year of his reign, when he lost Normandy. As we discovered at our last stop, English kings in the late eleventh and throughout the twelfth centuries regarded England as little more than a backyard to their main home which was their Continental possessions. In 1204, following a bitter military campaign, the French King Philip Augustus drove out John's troops and took Normandy for the French crown. It would never again be linked to England, as it had been since William the Conqueror's victory at Hastings in 1066.

The loss of Normandy not only hit the king, his power and his prestige hard, it also had a life-changing impact on the baronial families of England. Those families were the descendants of the barons who had come across with Duke William. He'd rewarded their loyalty by granting them land in England. But they had still retained their castles and their territories in Normandy. Now, with Normandy in the hands of the French king, they had to make up their minds. It would be difficult to owe allegiance for one part of their estates to the king of England, and for another to the French king, two monarchs who were fierce enemies. So, which lands would they give up? The Norman ones, or the English? Many chose to stick with the English side, and the result was that from 1204 onwards, most of the noble families of England were just that, and that alone. They were no longer distracted by spending half their time across the Channel. The baronial families of England would from now on increasingly see themselves as undiluted English folk.

King John – for the moment at least – was in a different position. Although he'd lost Normandy, he was still the lord, or claimed to be, of a vast tract of western France: Anjou, Touraine, Maine, Brittany, Poitou, Aquitaine, the Auvergne and Gascony. But that too was to change.

Ten years later, in the summer of 1214, following the Battle of Bouvines in northern France, King Philip Augustus overran all of these territories with the single exception of Gascony in the far south. Now John, like his barons before him, had to withdraw to England. He was now King of England and lord of little else.

So both the monarch and the barons were thrown back together. It was like a wounded lion facing a pack of wolves, which had been roaming the forest, but were now trapped alongside each other in a narrow compound. The result was an all-out fight, the baronial rebellion that led to Magna Carta.

In the long term, there was a permanent effect on English national identity. For all the centuries to come, those in power – the monarch, the royal court, the great noble families, and hence the machinery of government and the legal system – would be English through and through. That sentiment would in turn filter down to the millions in the lower ranks of society.

The English were beginning to understand who they were.

***

We've heard a lot so far about the top of society, the nobles and the king. And we've made mention of those at the bottom, the unfree common people. But what about those in between? The middle classes have made a powerful contribution to English national identity. They've often been the bastions of stability in English society throughout its history. Below them, there has been an underclass which it has been feared might at any moment erupt into revolt. Above them, there's been an aristocracy which – in the middle ages at least – was prone to drag the rest of the country into its death-or-glory power disputes.

So next we're going to a place where middle-class people lived a century after King John. It sits in the middle of a modern middle-class suburb in Middle England. I like the link. Trouble is, it's not easy to find. You can drive right by and not know it's there.

6

LONGTHORPE, CAMBRIDGESHIRE

....

WE KNOW OUR PLACE

....

WHEN ADAM DELVED AND EVE SPAN, WHO WAS THEN THE GENTLEMAN?

JOHN BALL (1338–81), PRIEST AND SUPPORTER OF THE PEASANTS' REVOLT

What's more miserable than a Middle England town on a wet Sunday afternoon? Maybe a Middle England *suburb* on a wet Sunday afternoon. I'm lost. All I know is I'm somewhere in Peterborough.

The trouble is I forgot to put the address of Longthorpe Tower into the sat-nav before I left home. And of course, I chucked the maps out of the car ages ago because technology had made them obsolete. Then to cap it all, the English Heritage phone number I got via the mobile doesn't answer.

'It can't be that hard,' I say to myself, as I drive out of Peterborough for the third time along the A1260. 'There are bound to be signs.'

I'm going over a bridge, and I catch glimpses of the railway below and an oily looking river. It's starting to rain hard, and when the word 'Longthorpe' next to a right-pointing arrow looms up through the beating windscreen wipers, I turn. Now I'm in the middle of an estate of brick-built bungalows and modern terraced houses with a more than average preponderance of pampas grass on the front lawns. I'm getting desperate. I'm going to have to ask someone.

Ask someone! For an instant, I sense the tenuous nature of our civilisation, dependent as it is on a billion computers meshing together in perfect synchronicity. One small technological slip anywhere in the system and we're doomed. We're reduced to having to 'ask someone.' I give an accusatory glance at the blank little screen suckered onto the side window. Within its silicon brain are the details of everywhere in Europe, from the narrowest alley in Omsk to the breeziest Guest House on the Skegness prom. But right now it's all trapped inside. Like beans in a tin with no can opener.

Anyway, there's no one about to ask. No one who looks sensible, that is. Only a young guy running with his hood up to keep the rain off. He's my only hope, so I cruise in parallel with him on the other side of the road.

'Longthorpe,' I shout. 'Which way to Longthorpe?'

'How...............? This is ...., mate.' What with a bus splashing from the other direction between us, a four-by-four beeping from behind, and the fact that the sat-nav stuck to my window is stopping it opening more than 2in, I can't make out what he's saying.

'Longthorpe?' I shout again.

He doesn't slacken his pace. 'You're in it, mate. This is Longthorpe.'

The thought that the youth of today can't be trusted in the smallest thing flits through my mind, but what choice do I have? So I shout, 'Longthorpe Tower, which way?'

For a moment, the overtaking four-by-four blocks my view, its driver threatening me with his middle finger. Then the youth shouts, 'Never heard of it, mate.' And he trots off down a bungalowed side road.

As the car wanders blindly past a mobile phone cell mast bristling with more long metal rods than a nuclear reactor, I see a sign for 'Thorpe Road.' The windscreen wipers start to squeak as the downpour slackens to a light drizzle, so I turn them off and see on the left – by an electricity sub-station – a flowery umbrella with red wellies beneath it.

I slacken my speed and press the passenger-side 'window down' button. 'Excuse me,' I say, leaning across. 'I'm looking for

Longthorpe Tower.' I hear myself raise the pitch of the word 'tower' in the irritating way some young people do, as though they're apologising.

'Of course,' she replies. 'You haven't got far to go. Only a few hundred yards. You want number 336 on this side. It's a bungalow just before a row of new houses.'

A bungalow! Number 336! She's either misheard, or she's got dementia. So in order not to upset her, I say in a calm, clear, slow voice, 'No, no. I'm looking for Longthorpe Tower. It's got one of the finest collection of medieval wall paintings anywhere in Western Europe. It's an historic house. You know, like Chatsworth or Longleat.'

She smiles, as though indulging her 5-year-old grandson. 'Well, it's not quite as big as that. But if you look for number 336, there's a path on the opposite side of the road, between two houses. And it's just down there. You can't miss it. There's parking by the church a few yards further along the road.'

I thank her, and even though she used the words 'You can't miss it,' (which, along with 'The cheque's in the post,' and 'I'm from head office, I'm here to help you,' is one of The Three Great Lies), I decide to check it out anyway.

Two and a half minutes later, after dumping the car and running back through the downpour, there in front of me is a stocky, square stone structure not much higher than the slate roof of the detached brick house next to it with a Ford Focus on the drive and a trampoline in the garden. It certainly looks old, though hardly the sort of place where you'd find a treasured collection of art. I'm pondering this when the head and torso of a woman wearing a standard-issue English Heritage fleece pops out of a stone door-frame at the top of some wooden steps on the side of the building. She peers up at the black clouds, then waves to me, 'Welcome to Longthorpe Tower. Come in and get dry.'

***

I enter a room not much more than five metres square with a vaulted roof. I'm the only visitor. Janice – that's what my English Heritage guide's badge says – invites me to dump my damp brolly and coat on the floor alongside her desk. Then, chattering all the

Longthorpe Tower
is hidden away at
the bottom of a
suburban garden in
Peterborough.

time about the wet, drab spring we're having, she checks my membership card and takes my £3.99 for a booklet.

I look around. Every square foot of the mellow brown stone walls and the arched ceiling is covered in paintings. There are long-necked birds. There are what look like saints with halos. There are kings in their crowns. There are ordinary people, making baskets, carrying heavy loads, pictured in intense conversation. And there are animals everywhere, a rabbit, an eagle, a monkey – some of them riding what looks like a fairground wheel. Although in places the colours are faded and there are a few blank patches where the plaster has broken away, all of the images have a vivid immediacy about them. The rabbit, for instance looks startled. The king with his hand on the wheel is peering down his nose at me. There are details that draw you in – the bare feet of a beggar, the straining leg of a man digging, the curved fingers of a harpist, the spreading arms of a schoolmaster teaching a difficult lesson to an attentive pupil. And all this in a space I'd guess is no bigger than many of the twenty-first-century dining rooms in the surrounding houses of this Peterborough suburb.

'It's not quite what I was expecting,' I say to Janice. 'A lot smaller... but it's... it's incredible.'

'That's what's so special about it,' she replies. 'It isn't some grand country manor, or huge cathedral. This is a house where, in the early thirteen hundreds, Robert de Thorpe lived with his wife and children. They were middle class. Where you're standing now would have been the room where they entertained their guests.'

'Quite a change from the usual,' I say. 'You see so many aristocratic homes, packed with artistic treasures, it's a delight to come to a place we can more easily relate to.' Janice gives me a blank expression, as though I'm speaking an obscure dialect. Or could it be the polite reaction to someone talking rot. So I expand the thought. 'We can put ourselves in their shoes and see how we would have coped, with no central heating or smartphones, or Ready-to-Eat M&S chicken curries.'

I've clearly overstepped Janice's line now, and with measured courtesy, she puts me on a different track, the right one. 'Well...' she replies, 'it's not quite like that here. I always like to quote to visitors what the historian Richard Jones said about the de Thorpe family.' She picks up her notebook and fits her specs on her nose. 'He said: "I suspect that because we can visit where these people lived, we think that they were like us, but they weren't."' She lets her specs fall back on their little chain, and looks up at me repeating, 'They weren't like us.' And with that, she turns to attend to a couple in plastic macs who have just rushed in.

'Fwoof!' says the man, 'It's coming down hard again.' I say hello to them. It's as though we're all fellow guests invited for drinks, or supper in the little room.

The painting that grabs my attention first is on the wall over the fireplace. It's the large wheel with various creatures around it, and the king standing behind. The booklet describes it as the wheel of the five senses, each one represented by an animal. Seems obvious really. The hawk – eagle-eyed – must be sight. The pig with its big snout – smell. The monkey has its fingers in its mouth, so I guess it's taste. The cockerel and the spider are a puzzle though. I consult the booklet again. It turns out my score is one out of five. The bird is actually a vulture, which represents smell. The pig isn't a pig, it's a wild boar, which is hearing. Then the spider in its web is touch. The cockerel on the bottom right is sight. I got the monkey right.

Janice sees me frowning. 'The main point of the picture,' she says, 'is to show us that even the animals have got sharper senses than us. So the lesson that the painting is putting across is that we humans can't rely on our ears, eyes or sense of touch.'

'That's pretty fundamental,' I say. 'If you couldn't trust your eyes and ears to tell you about your surroundings, where would you be?'

The chap in the mac now chips in. 'You can see how magic would take a hold,' he says. 'If you reckon everything you see and hear is no more than smoke and mirrors.'

'Exactly. Come and look at this,' says our guide, and she goes over to the small window nook. She shows us a faintly scratched symbol of intersecting circles on the wall. 'Archaeologists have only just discovered its meaning. It's to ward off witches' spells.'

'I can't imagine what it would feel like to be vulnerable to diabolic forces in your own home.' I say.

'You're right,' says Janice 'And it all goes to show of course just how hard it is for us to understand how people back in Robert de Thorpe's day thought. In some ways, we share with them emotions, loves and fears and ambitions. But in other ways, they lived in an alien world.'

The other two visitors are looking at what seems to be a fierce a dog, growling at one end, and firing something foul from the other, like an explosion from a cannon. 'It's shooting the contents of its bowels at its pursuer,' explains Janice. 'It's called a Bonnacon. It's a mythical beast.'

'Not a very nice image to have in front of you at suppertime,' observes the woman in the mac.

'Well, there you are again,' replies Janice. 'Robert de Thorpe, solid middle-class, but with different ideas about what was and wasn't acceptable. You notice it's over the door, so one theory is that it had the power to keep away unwelcome visitors. Then there's another idea – that it's a sort of political satire, and was intended to make fun of some well-known person. We don't know who.'

'I guess, middle-class as he was,' I say, 'he must have been quite rich to afford an artist of such talent to decorate his room.'

'That's true,' replies Janice, 'But, you know, wealth could have its dangers back in the fourteenth century. And this very room where we are now was where a terrifying criminal attack happened one night in the year 1329.' And she goes on to explain that marauding gangs of robbers roamed most country districts at that time, and that one such band broke into the de Thorpes' family home. The Tower served as a kind of fourteenth-century panic room, where the family could flee and barricade themselves in if there was a burglary. Robert, now aged 55, and his family didn't manage to secure themselves in time, and the gang held them prisoners in their own home until the de Thorpes revealed where they kept their cash and treasure, before the robbers escaped into the night with their trophies.

I sit for a while to try to absorb all that I've learnt. And questions drift into my head. What was he like, the man who lived here? Why did he decide to fill this room with such artistic, philosophical and entertaining images? Who was Robert de Thorpe? And given what we now know about the problems of understanding someone from 700 years ago, can we answer these questions at all? We'd better stick to the facts. So once I've climbed the stone stairs in the corner and found myself in another small room – this one without magnificent attractions on its walls – I sit and study the booklet I bought.

***

The de Thorpe family, it turns out, were not some noble Norman barons who had come to England with William the Conqueror. The de Thorpes had sprung from the lowest of the low in society. The great-grandfather of the Robert de Thorpe who commissioned the paintings here in the early fourteenth century, had been a peasant farmer, a villein, called Thurstan. He was one of those unfree men who – as we discovered at the last stop on our journey – were considered too inferior to be granted the right to a fair trial in clause thirty-nine of Magna Carta. As a villein, Thurstan rented land from the local lord. In lieu of payment, he had to work three days a week for his master, and even more at spring sowing and autumn harvest. That same master could demand he pay taxes, either in kind – eggs, chickens, lambs – or in money if he had it, at any time without warning. Thurstan's land could be sold with him and his family on it without a by your leave. And he, his wife and children could be used and abused by the lord or his officials in any way they liked, with the generous proviso that villein Thurstan and his family couldn't be murdered or beaten up so badly they were maimed for life. It amounted to agricultural slavery. That was the lowly stock the owners of Longthorpe Tower came from.

But, at some point during King John's reign, Thurstan and his family won their freedom. Whether he bought it from his lord and master or whether it was given him as a favour, we don't know. But it was the start of the family's climb up the social ladder. By around 1250, Thurstan's son William had acquired enough land, and with it relative wealth, to be able to build not only a fine house in Longthorpe including the tower we're visiting today but also a new chapel for the local village.

Robert de Thorpe was William's grandson. He trained as a lawyer, probably at one of the legal institutions which were then being established in London and which survive today as colleges for barristers: the inns of court. In 1309, he was appointed to the important position of steward of the Abbey of Peterborough. That meant he was the abbot's chief legal officer, with a staff of clerks working for him.

The amount of land he held is described in the records as 'one quarter of a knight's fee', an area difficult to estimate. A knight's fee wasn't a standard measure. It meant enough land to support a knight, his family, servants, retainers and the peasants to farm the fields. A quarter of such an estate would have been somewhere between 250 and 1,250 acres.

Robert de Thorpe was in an unusual and ambiguous position. On the one hand, he was a professional man with a prestigious, well-paid job that made him richer than many knights. But at the same time, he did not have the social rank that his well-respected career might in another age carry with it. In the strict pecking order that applied in fourteenth-century England, he was the lowest grade of freeman and no more.

Some time around 1319, Robert got his reward. He was knighted. But it may be that even afterwards he was still regarded as what later generations would call 'nouveau riche' with all the sneers that the landed classes of England have always attached to such words. We could see his decision to commission the extraordinary wall paintings in his home as a statement. It said: 'I am a man of taste, wealth, and intellect. Be impressed.' But that would be guesswork about what went on inside his head, so we had best be careful.

***

Nothing better illustrates England's rigid class system than the so-called 'sumptuary laws' passed during the lifetime of Robert de Thorpe and during later decades of the fourteenth century. These laws attempted to specify – by threatening to fine transgressors – what food and particularly what dress were permitted for members of each social class. The sumptuary laws defined four ranks in society. Agricultural labourers and others on a low income were at the bottom. Then above them came merchants and skilled craftsmen – Robert de Thorpe in 1315 would have been put here. Next higher were knights. And near the top of the tree, just below the king, were earls and other barons. In 1336, Edward II issued a proclamation prohibiting merchants and the servants of gentlemen from eating more than one meal of meat or fish per day. The following year, an Act of Parliament decreed that furs could be worn only by persons 'of gentle birth' or those who earned more than £100 a year.

But the powers that be became particularly obsessed with one bit of apparel: what folk wore on their feet. One law at this time decreed: 'No knight under the estate of a lord, esquire or gentleman, nor any other person, shall wear any shoes or boots having spikes or points which exceed the length of two inches, under the forfeiture of forty pence.' We don't know whether anyone was actually prosecuted for such a heinous crime. But by later in the century, pointy-toed footwear must have been running out of control, with the lower orders trampling on the feet of their social superiors. According to some reports, shoe ends had become so outrageous that they had to be fastened by chains to the waist or knees, in order to allow the wearer to move about. So Parliament made a desperate attempt to reinforce traditional class distinctions with a decree that only the nobility could wear 24in pointed shoes. Gentlemen would be restricted to 12in extensions, and merchants had to make do with a pair of humiliating 6½in. Robert de Thorpe himself was a victim – or perhaps a beneficiary? – of the sumptuary laws. His appointment as Steward of the Abbey entitled him to wear 'half a width of the better kind of clerical cloth, with a fur lining suitable for a clerk'. That fixed his position in society: superior to labourers but inferior to knights.

Underlying what can seem to us a laughable obsession with footwear and fur collars were some serious social issues. Fundamental changes were taking place in society. England was coming to be a prosperous nation. That was mainly down to the growth of the wool trade; English sheep were providing a product that was exported all over Europe. And that meant many more opportunities were opening up for ambitious men. Take, for instance, William Grevel, merchant, of Chipping Campden in Gloucestershire. He made so much money from wool that by the end of the century he was building in his home town a church to rival many cathedrals. And, as ever according to economic theory, the wool trade created other jobs suitable for folk right down the social ladder. Towns prospered with skilled tradesmen working not only as weavers and dyers of wool, but masons, farriers, potters, candle-makers, goldsmiths, and more than forty different crafts. Great estates – like the abbey at Peterborough – now needed a permanent legal department to uphold their rights in a changing world, providing careers for Robert de Thorpe and his small army of clerks.

While the governing, landowning classes benefited from growing prosperity, it also made them nervous. The old hierarchical structure of society was under threat. The remnants of the Norman, feudal, military aristocracy were having to come to terms with the fact that some of those beneath them were getting rich and therefore powerful. By specifying what clothes each class could wear and even what they could serve at their dining tables, those who had traditionally been at the top of society sought to remind the rest not to get above themselves.

But it wasn't just the rising wealth of the middle classes that was seen as threatening by the old elite. Deep beneath the prosperous world of fourteenth-century England, the foundations of society were beginning to shake. A restless discontent among the lower orders would soon rattle the rigidity of the class structure.

In 1348 bubonic plague, the Black Death, hit England and rapidly spread through the country. More than one person in five died from it, a sudden and painful death. In some areas it killed as much as half the population. But despite these shocking figures, the improvement in England's economic health continued almost without pause. Demand for wool didn't slacken, and trade thrived. Nevertheless, one result of the Black Death's ravages was a labour shortage. Those who had been spared by the disease and who worked for pay in the fields and towns found that there were more jobs vacant than there were people to fill them, so they demanded higher wages. In 1351, the landowners decided to look after their own interests, and a labour law was passed to try to fix pay rates at their pre-plague levels.

This crude attempt by those in power to prevent the lower ranks in society from sharing in England's prosperity provoked a violent kickback.

In 1381, Wat Tyler – a man about whom we know nothing other than that he came from Kent – marched into London at the head of a mob armed with cudgels. And as discontented city folk joined them, Tyler proclaimed the objectives of their uprising: 'There should be equality among all people save only the king. There should be no serfdom and all men should be free and of one condition.' Tyler and his followers attacked the jails, and chased and killed anyone to do with the royal government. The next day, the king, Richard II, tried to calm the dangerous situation by meeting Tyler face-to-face. However, at the same time that these peace talks were taking place, another mob was breaking into the Tower of London. There they beat to death the Lord Chancellor and the Lord High Treasurer. It was another two days before the king began to regain control. In a clash between royal troops and the rebels at Smithfield, Tyler was killed. Over the next few weeks, other uprisings as far apart as East Anglia, Scarborough in Yorkshire and Bridgenorth in Somerset were quelled. Most of the leaders were hunted down and executed. At least 1,500 rebels were killed.

Those in power at the top of society may have won, but the so-called Peasants' Revolt had been a warning to them. And they heeded it. During the decades to come there was a reluctance to impose heavy taxes on the general populace for fear of the turmoil and bloodshed such a levy might provoke among the lower classes. A new class system was being built to replace the old feudal hierarchy. And it was to become a very English institution over the following centuries. The rise of a strong middle class in England would help make English society more stable than any other European nation. The English middle class would often be derided, by the landed gentry above them with such sniffy put-downs as, 'Oh, so you people are *in trade*', and by the working class below them as narrow-minded, self-satisfied conservatives. But Robert de Thorpe had everything to gain from a society that was undisturbed by revolt or discontent. And the English middle classes that followed him have always been a bulwark against riot and revolution. The Robert de Thorpes would often be a steadying influence on English society during the storms that lay ahead.

***

In the first decades after the Norman Conquest, 200 years before the walls of Longthorpe Tower were decorated, one of the most notable divisions in social class was according to which language you spoke: the upper-class Norman conquerors used French, the vanquished Anglo-Saxons English. But, as we saw on the last stop of our journey, that linguistic barrier started breaking down once King John and his barons had lost most of their territories across the Channel. The ruling classes began to see themselves as English rather than as foreign occupiers. That trend was boosted in the fourteenth century with the outbreak of a war between the English and the French that was to last, on and off, for 116 years. The so-called Hundred Years War would mean that French became, irrevocably, the language of the enemy.

But the declining popularity of the French language in English society was not something that happened overnight. Robert de Thorpe in the early fourteenth century – like most of his equals and betters – would have been trilingual. He spoke English with his wife and children, probably to the artist who painted the pictures on his walls and in the everyday encounters outside work. And as a lawyer, and particularly as a lawyer working for an ecclesiastical institution, he would need to know Latin. Most ecclesiastical and some legal documents were still written in that ancient tongue. But in Robert's time it was also still fashionable to speak French, and as an up-and-coming gentleman he would converse in that language with his social superiors. And French was still often used in governmental letters and decrees as well as in Parliament and the courts, so fluency in French as well as Latin would be essential workaday skills for Robert. It wasn't until 1362 that Parliament recognised the need to start using English if the law was to be understood by at least some in the wider country who were literate. But even that didn't stop all use of French in government documents. The following year, in 1363, one of the sumptuary laws defined the four classes as *garçons* (labourers), *gens de mestere* (merchants and craftsmen), *chivalers* (knights) and *seigneurs* (barons).

So how did English become the single common language of the nation? Well, it wasn't some sort of we-win-you-lose process. The English language made gradual inroads into those areas of life where French and Latin had ruled, government, the church, the law. But in doing so, English vocabulary didn't replace the Latin and French words commonly in use. Instead it welcomed them with open arms, and adopted them into the English linguistic family. We can see how French entered the language in the work of one of the most colourful and prolific of English poets, who was writing at this time. Geoffrey Chaucer's *Canterbury Tales* begins thus (words of French influence in bold):

When that **April** with his shoures soote
The droghte of **March** hath **perced** to the roote
And bathed every **veyne** in swich **licour**
Of which **vertu engendered** is the **flour**

When **April** with its sweet showers
Has **pierced** the drought of **March** to the root,
And bathed every **vein** in a liquid
From whose **virtue** the **flower** is **engendered**.

At the same time as taking in foreign vocabulary, English hung on to the old Germanic words that had the same meanings. The result is that today English speakers end up with lots of choices when they write or speak. We can decide whether to *wish* for something (if we're feeling Anglo-Saxon) or to *desire* it (if a French mood takes us). Our *clothes* (Anglo-Saxon) can become *attire* (French) if we're being formal. And as we *climb, mount* or *ascend* (Anglo-Saxon, French and Latin) the social scale, we might swap our *house* (Anglo-Saxon) for a *mansion* (French). If such a building gets destroyed, we could *ask, question* or *interrogate* someone as to whether it happened by *fire, flame* or *conflagration* (Anglo-Saxon, French and Latin).

Sometimes, even today half a millennium or longer after this process of absorption took place, we show off the richness of our language by using two words of different origins alongside each other. We can say that it's *fit* and *proper* (Anglo-Saxon and French) to have a bit of *peace* and *quiet* (French and Latin) while we draft our last *will* and *testament* (Anglo-Saxon and Latin), otherwise the whole thing will go to *wrack* and *ruin* (Anglo-Saxon and French).

Chaucer's stories – some polite, some ribald, some heroic, some funny – became popular, especially in the century after his death when printing arrived in England. That popularity, driven by growing numbers of schools and therefore of people who could read and write, helped to reinforce in the minds and mouths of those who delighted in Chaucer's verses the new, rich English language. By the year 1500, English had incorporated tens of thousands of Latin and French words to sit alongside those that had come from the Anglo-Saxons and the Vikings. The language of Chaucer is not the language of today. But with a little guidance it's understandable. Modern English was being born. The fact that English can almost always offer a word suitable to the context, not only in meaning but in sound and style, is one of the main reasons why the English language has become perhaps the most varied, most colourful way of communicating on earth.

***

There was only so long that the growing number of middle-class men like Robert de Thorpe could be denied any say in how the country was governed. The lords and earls and other barons had for centuries had the right to advise the king, and if they spoke with one voice on some important matter such as war or taxation, only a foolish king would ignore them. But lawyers like de Thorpe, or wool merchants like William Grevel, couldn't threaten armed rebellion if they didn't get their way. They weren't soldiers. So how did power leak down to them? To find out we're going to somewhere you'll know well, if only from TV news bulletins. It's a place which has enabled the English to claim that they were the founders of modern democracy. It's a strange institution though. Quirky, inefficient and hidebound by traditions whose meanings today are often lost in the fog of time. The funny thing is, though, it works.

7

CHAMBER OF THE HOUSE OF COMMONS, WESTMINSTER

....

A FUNNY FORM OF DEMOCRACY

....

THE KING OF ENGLAND CANNOT RULE
HIS PEOPLE BY LAWS OTHER THAN
THOSE THE PEOPLE HAVE ASSENTED TO.

SIR JOHN FORTESCUE (1394–1479), JUDGE AND MP

A London-based management consultancy is appointed by the government of a newly emerging East African state to advise on the establishment of its key democratic institutions. In formulating the essential elements of the Parliament, the consultants draw up a list of best-practice requirements, as follows:

The dimensions of the chamber of the Lower House should not exceed 21m by 16m (for guidance, no larger than a primary school assembly hall).

Benches, rather than individual chairs, should be provided for MPs to sit on.

There should be an inadequate number of these benches, so that at busy times, even when the MPs are sitting squashed together, approximately 10 per cent of members will be obliged either to stand or to sit on the floor.

No fixed seats should be allocated to named MPs, except for the Prime Minister and the Leader of the Opposition (and these may be occupied by other members when the Prime Minister or Opposition leader are absent).

No desks should be provided for MPs, (for guidance, any surface which could be used by MPs to support papers while they write or take notes, should not be allowed).

In order to avoid sword fights between opposing front benches, they must be separated by a distance of 3.9m.

Procedures for the conduct of business as follows:

No applause, such as hand–clapping, shall be permitted

All members shall be encouraged to shout or jeer at all times during speeches so that it is difficult to hear.

MPs shall elect from their number a 'Speaker', who on appointment shall pretend s/he does not want the job so that other members have to drag her/him forward.

MPs who wish to speak must rise to their feet without saying anything, along with at least thirty other MPs doing the same thing at the same moment. This is called 'catching the Speaker's eye' and should happen whenever the current speaker pauses for breath.

It should be forbidden for any member to call any other member a 'liar', a 'hypocrite' a 'pipsqueak', a 'swine', a 'rat', a 'blackguard' or a 'tart.'

At the end of debates, a bell shall be rung just before 10 p.m., not only in the Parliament but all around the surrounding neighbourhood, so that any MPs in bars or in someone else's bed, can rush over to vote.

Votes should be counted according to how many MPs walk through a certain doorway compared with the number who walk through a different doorway.

If the motion under debate is passed, the Speaker should then announce this by the use of an antiquated word in use only among very old people in the East Midlands of England and parts of Scotland.

Any electronic system of voting must be absolutely prohibited.

… at which point, the management consultants are fired.

If this story doesn't make much sense to you, the odds are you're not English. But read on.

***

'Order! Order!' shouts Mr Speaker Bercow, pronouncing the second word in a tone that suggests he's fed up with asking MPs to behave. 'Statement, the Prime Minister,' he calls when the hubbub of chattering has dipped a few decibels.

Half a dozen members are still wandering in to see if they can find somewhere to sit as David Cameron stands and takes a sip of water. Conservative MPs – around 100, at a rough estimate – shout 'Hear, hear', or it could be 'Yeah, yeah', the words slow and slurred as though large volumes of claret have been consumed and the port is now doing the rounds. There's no suggestion that MPs here this morning are drunk. They always sound like this – Labour members as well as Tory – when they wish to demonstrate their loyalty or that they agree, even when they don't yet know what the speaker is going to say.

'Thank you Mr Speaker,' says the Prime Minister in a business-like way, ignoring his supporters. Two dozen MPs have risen from their seats at the same time as Mr Cameron. Do they each think they've suddenly been promoted to lead the government? But as soon as the real Prime Minister starts to speak, they all sit down again – or in fact squeeze their bottoms back onto the bench, because in leaving their seats they've allowed their neighbours to steal a bit of their territory. Around twenty MPs can't find anywhere to sit at all and are having either to stand by the door, legs akimbo, arms folded, or else they're sitting on the steps between the benches, knees almost touching chins.

By now the Prime Minister is saying, 'Yesterday, I published all the information in my tax returns for the past six years. This is unprecedented, but I think it is the right thing to do.' Amid scattered calls of 'Quite right' and 'Not enough' and other less distinguishable comments, he goes on, 'Mr Speaker, there have been some deeply hurtful and profoundly untrue allegations made against my father.' By now, his words are competing with a rising background of Hear-hears and Yeah-yeahs from the Conservative benches behind him as he defends his father's investment fund, which was run from the Bahamas. Then he makes a joke. 'The BBC, the Murdoch newspapers, and – to pick one council entirely at random – Islington ...' (He pauses, while the Conservatives all throw back their heads and go 'Ha ha ha!' because the Leader of the Opposition, Jeremy Corbyn represents Islington in North London) '... all have these sorts of overseas investments.' The Labour Opposition MPs do not find this funny. They either stare expressionless across the aisle, like John McDonnell the Shadow Chancellor, or tut-tut and give little shakes of their heads like the Shadow International Development Secretary, Diane Abbot. Mr Corbyn himself doesn't look up from the papers he's riffling through on his lap. 'This is not to criticise,' adds the Prime Minister. 'It is entirely standard practice and is not to avoid paying tax.'

A jumble of heckling and counter-heckling now breaks out all around the chamber, and the Leader of the House (not really a 'leader' at all, more an admin job deciding what's discussed when), Chris Grayling, just behind the Prime Minister, keeps doing a passable impression of one of those little model dogs in the back windows of cars that used to nod unrealistically whenever there was a bump in the road. 'We should defend the right of every

British citizen to make money lawfully,' adds Mr Cameron, and the Chancellor of the Exchequer, George Osborne, behind the Prime Minister on the other side, joins his colleague in synchronised head rocking.

The Prime Minister sits down to the sort of crowd noise that must have accompanied cockfighting in the eighteenth century, and the Speaker calls Mr Corbyn.

'The Prime Minister's statement,' he opens, 'is absolutely a masterclass in the art of distraction.' Now it's the turn of Labour MPs to roar their approval, and the Deputy Leader of the Opposition, Tom Watson, creases his face into a smile till his rounded red cheeks push his spectacles up his nose. Mr McDonnell's features remain stern. 'There is now one rule for the super-rich, and another for the rest,' declares Mr Corbyn, and he details how the country has gone through what he calls 'six years of crushing austerity'.

'Much of this,' he notes, 'could have been avoided if our country hadn't been ripped off by the super-rich refusing to pay their taxes.' There's now such a hullaballoo across all sides of the chamber that it's hard to hear his closing words.

Fifty or more MPs get to their feet, not to shout, not to raise their hands, but in a competition to see who can look most calm. It's like that children's game called 'Statues'. In the midst of a chaotic rumpus of cheers, waving papers, uninterpretable hand gestures and MPs who have decided it's time for a cup of coffee so are heading for the door, these frozen beings are judged by Mr Speaker Bercow. The winners get to have their say.

First up is Liz Kendall, defeated candidate for the Labour leadership. From the backmost of the back benches, she asks, 'Why does the Prime Minister think so many companies are registered in Panama in the first place? Why not in London or New York?' ('Yeah, yeah.')

Mr Cameron says it's because they want to market their services not simply to UK residents but to other people. Ms Kendall rolls her eyes to the heavens in a gesture that says, 'Huh. Typical.'

The next winner in the game of Statues is the neat-suited knight with primped white-hair, Sir Alan Duncan, Conservative MP for Rutland and Melton. Once the Speaker has chosen him to perform, he unfreezes to become the very model of a steadfast Tory. 'May I support the Prime Minister?' he croons, 'particularly in thinking of this place. We risk seeing a House of Commons that is stuffed full of low achievers, who hate enterprise, and who know absolutely nothing about the outside world.' Here he points with distaste at the Opposition benches, amid squeals of approval from those around him.

But then a pin-dropping silence falls around the wood-panelled walls of the chamber. An 84-year-old ex-coal miner from Derbyshire, a man who in forty-six years as an MP has never been seen skulking off (not voluntarily anyway) to the bar while ever there was a jaw-aching speech or an earbashing heckle to be heard, gets to his feet. Dennis Skinner, Labour MP for Bolsover, one couldn't-careless hand in a pocket, the other pointing at the Prime Minister, addresses the nation's leader in measured tones: 'I asked him a very important question about the windfall 'e received when 'e wrote off the mortgage on the premises in Notting 'Ill, and I said to 'im 'e didn't write off the mortgage on the 'ouse the taxpayers were 'elping to pay for in Oxford. I didn't receive a proper answer then. Maybe Dodgy Dave will answer it now.'

Outrage. The conservative benches are howling and baying, if not for blood, at the very least for the aged Skinner to say sorry for using such a nasty word.

This is Mr Speaker Bercow's big moment. He's got to sort this out before bedlam befalls the Chamber. 'I invite the … Order! … I invite the honourable gentleman to withdraw that adjective he used a moment ago … Order!' (This time he screws up his face and squeaks the word) '… He's capable of asking the question without using that word. It is up to him, but if he doesn't wish to withdraw it, I can't reasonably ask the Prime Minister to answer the question. All he has to do is to withdraw that word and think of another.' Now there's laughter from the Labour benches. 'Sorry, sorry?' says the Speaker, unable to hear what's being said to him.

'Which word? Which word?' they're calling to him.

'The word beginning with D and ending with Y that he inappropriately used,' replies Mr Bercow with a Victorian spinster's patronising distaste for the children of ill-bred parents.

The honourable member for Bolsover springs to his feet with an energy that must have surprised his 84-year-old limbs. Now red in the face, and waving an arm, he has to shout to be heard through the cries of 'Chuck him out' and 'Disgraceful!'

'This man,' he cries, pointing at the Prime Minister again, ''as done more to divide this nation than anybody else.'e's looked after his own pocket! I still refer to 'im as Dodgy Dave!'With that he sits, though only on the edge of his bench, poised to rise again, then dismisses the Speaker with a shrug of the hand and shouts above the clamour, 'Do what you like!'

Mr Speaker Bercow bends forward and is given a piece of paper by one of the bewigged clerks who sit in front of him, and he pronounces sentence. 'Under the power given me by Standing Order Number 43, I order the honourable member to withdraw immediately from the House for the remainder of this day's sitting.'

Mr Skinner tosses a final remark at the Speaker, but it's lost in the hubbub, and he turns and trudges off like a tired miner at the end of his shift.

'Bye bye … Bye bye,' the Tories shriek with pleasure, and the House of Commons – mother of parliaments, respected around the globe as the founder of representational democracy – resumes its business.

***

So what has parliamentary democracy got to do with national identity?

The word 'democracy' of course comes from the two ancient Greek words for people and government. Parliament as we know it now, or any other democratically elected national assembly, brings together in one place the representatives of the whole nation. And though those representatives will never all agree, they do all recognise that their authority comes from the people and that their job is to decide what is best for the nation. So Parliament needs a sense of national identity in order to function. And at the same time, Parliament – through its decisions – defines the political identity of the nation, because of course politics isn't just some rarefied philosophical study. The decisions of Parliament define every aspect of daily life across the nation: war, peace, taxes, education, health, safety at work, what is a crime, what isn't, down to which side of the road we drive on and whom we can and can't marry.

Full-blown, one-adult-one-vote parliamentary democracy in this country didn't come about overnight. In fact, it took many, many centuries. 'Parliament', in the sense we understand the word today, was the outcome of a very slow process. Nevertheless, the most startling feature of the early English parliaments is the way in which they recognised the theory of democracy, even though they didn't yet implement it in practice. Very few people had a vote in the early days. And yet, although there was no community in the sense of equal voting rights, time after time we see references in early official records to the 'community of England', to the 'people of the land'. Parliament, more and more in its early centuries, was associated with a definition of England and the English as one nation with common interests. Parliament promoted an English national identity.

The first gathering to call itself a parliament met in 1257. Henry III was planning expensive adventures on the continent, even though he was already short of cash. Seven barons, led by the Earl of Leicester, Simon de Montfort, swore an oath together that they would bring the king under control. De Montfort was a terrifying figure. He was a fearless and merciless warrior, he was greedy and he had a self-belief driven by religious faith that came close to mania. He and his six colleagues confronted the king in Westminster Hall, and demanded that he summon a 'parlemenz' at Oxford. Henry is said to have replied to de Montfort, 'I fear thunder and lightning terribly, but, by God's head, I fear you more than all the thunder and lightning in the world,' – not exactly the words to assert kingly power over a rebel, and Henry indeed gave in.

The parliament that then met at Oxford bore little relation to what we would understand by the word. On the face of it, it was no more than the sort of gathering of nobles and bishops that kings had traditionally summoned from time to time in order to seek advice on important matters of state. But the Oxford parliament broke new ground in several directions. First, the leading lay and church leaders who attended were asked to take an oath in the name of 'le commun de Engleterre'. And the king himself swore an oath to agree a new system of government. A series of committees would be set up, jointly selected by the barons and the king. One of these committees, to be known by a title that survives to this day, the Privy Council, would oversee the work of the royal government. The king also agreed under oath to summon 'parlemenz' three times a year. All this was promised in writing by Henry as 'king on Engleneloande' to his 'loandes folk', the people of the land. It was the first royal document issued in the English language since Anglo-Saxon times.

Henry soon backtracked on his word, and renounced the agreement. Armed rebellion followed, and in 1264 de Montfort took the king prisoner and required him to summon another parliament. And this meeting, too, was revolutionary. For the first time, elected representatives attended. Not many, and their influence in discussions was limited. Burgesses were chosen by the larger towns to speak on behalf of the boroughs in the presence of the usual convocation of barons and bishops. The seeds of something bigger had been sown. Democracy was taking root.

This latest parliament, however, turned out to be no more than a brief interval in a conflict which was to be settled by the sword and crossbow rather than in reasoned argument. The country was split. Many barons and the more senior knights stayed loyal to the crown, and continued fighting, led now by Henry's son, Edward. The war came to a head at Evesham in Worcestershire on 4 August 1265. Ten thousand royalists, outnumbering the rebels two to one, occupied the high ground that commanded the area to the north of the town. De Montfort's men were massacred. And through the chaos of battle, the rebel leader saw a troop of a dozen royal knights bearing down on him. He knew it was the end, and his final words were spoken as though he were already in heaven observing his fate from on high. As his killers got close, he said to his bodyguard, 'How beautifully they advance. Our bodies are theirs, our souls are God's.' His body was indeed theirs. They castrated it, and dismembered it, and carried off de Montfort's head high in the air, speared on a lance.

***

So how important was de Montfort in developing parliamentary democracy? Well, we shouldn't run away with the idea that

Simon de Montfort, moments before his death at the battle of Evesham. The image is from a popular history published in 1864. The Victorians saw de Montfort as one of the heroes of English history.

this noble earl and his cohorts wanted the lowest orders of the population to be directly represented in government. The rebels were experimenting with ways to try and control unacceptable behaviour in a king, short of threatening to kill him. The only way they knew to rein in the monarch was through the traditional Great Councils of the most powerful in the land. Admitting representatives of the towns was more a mark of the growing wealth and influence of the boroughs than it was a nod towards democracy. And there was probably an element of spin-doctoring in the words, 'le commun de Engleterre' and the 'loandes folk', with the rebel barons trying to sex up their cause with a claim that the whole nation was behind them.

Nevertheless, it does seem that these phrases now had some basis in fact. Peasants and less well-off knights had fought against the king. For instance, a bunch of farmers in one small Leicestershire village who had attacked a troop of royal soldiers, later told a royal court that they'd done it in the name of 'the community of the realm.' A common English political identity was, at the very least, beginning to take shape. And the 'martyrdom' of de Montfort, whose grave was for some time visited by pilgrims, was seen as lending that infant political identity a degree of God-given respectability. What's more, the new ideas about government seen in de Montfort's parliaments were not killed off along with their chief proponent. By 1295, parliaments were being summoned by the king whenever he needed support for his plans, and a settled system had developed. As well as the barons and the bishops who attended by virtue of their titles, each county now sent two knights and each town two burgesses. These commoners, however, were still in a precarious position. It was the king who summoned them to Parliament, and opposition to his plans or any other behaviour that he regarded as mischievous, could result in a burgess or even a knight being excluded.

Despite such threats, the influence of Parliament – especially when it was united so it was harder for the king to pick off individuals – was growing. And in 1327, a parliament met and put into effect what, by fourteenth-century standards, was the ultimate expression of power. It was the reign of Edward II, a king described by one present-day historian as, 'irresponsible, lazy, vicious, politically reckless, somewhat eccentric and indifferent to the interests of any but his personal entourage.' Following mob violence in London during which one of the king's supporters, the Bishop of Exeter, was beheaded with a bread knife, opposition to the king found its focus in Parliament. During an unprecedented seventy-one-day session, clergy, nobles and knights, plus the elected representatives of the towns – what one chronicler called 'the whole community of the realm' – declared Edward deposed.

But that wasn't all. Parliament's debates were held in the vast Norman building that still survives today as Westminster Hall, and a 'great multitude of people,' came to listen. And they shouted too, demanding the king be replaced by his son. And that's what happened. Edward II was murdered, probably with a red-hot iron inserted into his body, in an act of brutality symbolic of his alleged homosexuality. Parliament – or 'the whole community of the realm' – had legitimised the overthrow and execution of a monarch.

Up to now, Parliament had been a single body, with commoners and nobles meeting together. That changed in 1341, when Parliament split into two separate sessions with the Commons acting apart from the Lords. And so the House of Commons was born. And thirty-five years later we see this lower house asserting itself as an independent force.

By now Edward II's successor, Edward III was in his 60s. He was in poor health and was finding affairs of state too much. Instead of ruling the country, he was often to be found in the bedchamber of his mistress, Alice Ferrers. Many key decisions were being left to his ministers, and there was more than a suspicion that Ferrers was twisting the king around her little finger. It was the Commons rather than the Lords who this time led the attack on the king. In order to press their case and to try to spur the Lords into action, they elected one of their number to act as spokesman, Sir Peter de la Mare. De la Mare was the first Speaker of the House of Commons. He declared that the king had surrounded himself with 'certain councillors and servants who are not loyal or profitable to him or his kingdom'. The king had de la Mare thrown into prison. But within a year, Edward was dead, de la Mare was released and the office of Speaker was established.

And so to this day, when MPs have elected one of their number to be Speaker, tradition has it that he or she must be dragged, reluctant, to their presiding seat, a reminder of the days of de la Mare, when a Speaker whose job it was to bring unwelcome news to the sovereign might find himself rotting in a dungeon beneath the Tower of London – or worse.

∗∗∗

Over the following centuries, power would ebb and flow between Crown and Parliament, often driven by force of arms and threats of violence, backed up by constitutional arguments. The king would quote the traditional supremacy of the monarchy, Parliament the ancient principle – going back to Roman law – that 'what touches all shall be approved by all'. And by the early fifteenth century, Parliament's claim to represent the 'community of the realm,' was edging closer to reality. In 1429, many more ordinary citizens were given the right to vote for their member of the House of Commons. Now any male who owned land worth at least 40 shillings a year outright joined barons, bishops, knights, merchants and craftsmen from the towns in being represented directly by a Member of Parliament. That amounted to tens of thousands of English citizens who were now enfranchised.

Although this number was a big increase in those who had a vote, it still made up no more than 2 or 3 per cent of the total population, then of around 3 million. The franchise would not be extended beyond this limited group for another 400 years, and it would be 500 years before women would be included. We shall return to that struggle later. But for now, English democracy was stuck. Power was firmly lodged with a very small group of the most privileged and wealthy in society.

Nevertheless, during the early centuries of Parliament's history, a principle had been established that the 'community of the realm' – however inadequately defined – must have some say in decisions that affected it. Parliament had played a vital role in creating an image of an English nation, a sense throughout the country that England was one people, with some authority to decide how it would be governed.

There was another way, too, that Parliament pushed forward English identity. The English were ahead of the field; they were the first European nation to produce an assembly of government that contained an increasingly important number of elected representatives. Although the monarch and an unelected nobility still wielded much of the power, Parliament by the year 1500 was the thin end of a democratic wedge. And in later centuries, it would become a model for the representative assemblies of other nations. It would be the 'mother of parliaments'. And that phrase has been used by the English as one of the ways to define themselves.

***

So, what about those bizarre traditions that we saw operating in the House of Commons today? What do they tell us most about the political and social values that are peculiar to the English? To get to the bottom of these idiosyncrasies, we have to ask how they came about in the first place, and why they have persisted.

The mythical management consultants who were sacked by the newly emerging nation might have got away with their best-practice advice if they had included one more requirement for the perfect parliament:'The methods of operating listed above should be introduced one by one over a period of at least 750 years.' But even management consultants can be credited with enough common sense to recognise that this injunction might be easier to say than do, given the need for haste in newly emerging nations.

The origins of the strange traditions of the House of Commons are often obscure. Why, for instance, do MPs behave like boisterous students on a Friday night out? It's probably to make up for the ban on clapping at the end of a speech. Instead of that, supporters of a speaker show their approval, the moment they hear him or her say something they like, with those growled shouts of 'Hear, hear!' – a corruption of 'Hear him! Hear him!' called out by MPs in the seventeenth century. Of course, the opposing party then has to strike back with their own brand of ridicule to drown them out. The ban on clapping is said to be because otherwise speeches would start to be judged by the length and vehemence of the applause instead of by their content. The danger then would be that this kind of ovation could be orchestrated to see which side could outdo the other. One glance at the TV images of North Korean Workers' Party Congress members crashing their hands together in synchronised applause as though their lives depended on it (which of course they do) to salute their dear leader Kim Jong un should be enough to convince us that the clapping ban might be a sensible rule after all.

The layout of the House of Commons, its inadequate size, shortage of seats and lack of modern facilities simply reflect the way it was 200 or more years ago. They set it apart from any other elective assembly in the world. Just take one example, the devolved Scottish Parliament at Holyrood in Edinburgh. Its spacious and airy chamber contains rising tiers of desks arranged in a congenial semi-circle that does at least suggest that collaboration, not conflict, might be possible. Each member has an allotted place, where they can write notes and work at their lap-op computer, provided to each member. Voting takes place at the civilised hours of 5 p.m. Monday to Thursday and 12 p.m. on Fridays. Votes are counted electronically, each desk with a handy couple of buttons. Members clap without overdoing it, and – usually – behave themselves. How very different from our own Parliament.

There's something very English about the eccentric way the House of Commons is run. Eccentricity is a trait that we shall see recur time after time on our journey. The English House of Commons is as it is because that's the way it has been not quite always but certainly for a very long time. A modernisation committee, set up under Prime Minister Tony Blair, brought some efficiencies in the process of enacting legislation, but the commission backed off from proposing any changes to the daily oddities and inconveniences of a chamber 400 years behind the times. Which prompts the question: why do MPs reject a bit more comfort, a bit more twenty-first-century technology? And why don't they agree to behave in the sort of civilised fashion that the smallest parish council in England takes for granted?

The reason, I believe, goes to the very heart of Englishness. In the chamber of the House of Commons, you cannot help – every moment of every day – being aware of history. As an MP you are reliving it every time you utter a low, slow Hear-hear, every time you jeer, every time you stand up to try to catch the Speaker's eye, every time you file through the division lobbies at 10 p.m., every time you can't find a seat and have to squat on the steps, every time Dennis Skinner is thrown out for saying 'dodgy'. It's bizarre, it's different, it's ancient, it's a constant reminder of our past and it tells us something of fundamental importance. Our parliamentary democracy – for all its shortcomings – has been going for hundreds of years. It may seem daft to foreigners, but it works. It's solid and unchangeable. What it says is: The English don't do violent revolutions. England is a land of social and political stability. These values are symbolised in the unchanging rituals of the House of Commons.

Although Parliament's democratic base got stuck in the fifteenth century, its authority would steadily grow. Under Henry VIII in the sixteenth century, Parliament was to play a key role in the break with the Church of Rome. The great constitutional shifts that happened during his reign would all be put into effect through Acts of Parliament.

***

During the era of Henry VIII and the two Tudor monarchs who followed him, the English became a nation divided, not in some new struggle for power but in an argument about how to pray. To find out more, we're going to Oxford, city of dreaming spires and civilised academic debate – except that what we're going to find there is anything but dreamy and civilised. Instead, Oxford's tale is one of terrifying brutality and state-sponsored killing. A warning: it's not for the faint-hearted.

8

Oxford

BAD DAYS

THE PRIESTS TOLD THE PEOPLE THAT
WHOEVER BROUGHT FAGOTS TO BURN
HERETICS WOULD HAVE AN INDULGENCE
TO COMMIT SINS FOR FORTY DAYS.

JOHN FOXE (1516/17–87)

'Of course,' says Mike, 'they used to think that by torturing you, they were doing you a favour.'

I look at him and pause, expecting his face to crack into a grin. But I wait for the joke in vain. 'OK, how's that?' I give in.

'Well, if you were a devout Catholic, you believed that Catholicism was the only way to heaven, so if you could torture a Protestant till he recanted and adopted your faith, you were sure you'd saved him from the eternal flames of Hell.'

'Hmm,' I say, and before I can add anything incisive, I'm dodging sideways, as a young woman on a sit-up-and-beg bike ting-a-lings her bell and swerves to my left, her long brown hair and short black gown flapping behind her.

Mike and I are standing outside Balliol College in the middle of Broad Street in Oxford. It's not quite as dangerous as it sounds. Broad Street is a traffic-free zone, except for the hundred or so students peddling past for all they're worth from library to lecture, tutorial to seminar, or just from bed to late breakfast with some mates.

That would have been Mike and I many decades ago. My college was Christ Church just down Cornmarket and straight on.

Mike was at Balliol, so this is his old home. We're standing here examining a jagged-edged square patch of cobbles in the tarmac, no more than a couple of feet wide. The stones are in the shape of a black cross, picked out by a white surround. They mark the spot where, during the reign of the Roman Catholic Queen Mary, nicknamed 'Bloody Mary', three of England's leading Protestant churchmen were executed. In 1556, Hugh Latimer, Bishop of Worcester, and Nicholas Ridley, Bishop of London, were burned at the stake here, to be followed five months later by Thomas Cranmer, Archbishop of Canterbury.

It has sometimes been assumed that this form of execution was relatively humane because the prisoner would become unconscious from the smoke fumes before feeling the pain of the fire. But this was often not so. Wind and rain could slow the process down and blow away the smoke, so prolonging an agonising death. And the executioner and his assistants would sometimes deliberately control the fire so that the victim burned slowly as the flames gradually destroyed his body from the feet up. He might be screaming and writhing for anything up to two hours, while his skin was destroyed and his blood boiled and seeped away, before a merciful death at last ended his suffering. I say 'his' suffering, but being burned alive was a favourite way of executing heretical women, too.

Mike and I have come to Oxford to walk in the final footsteps of Cranmer, Latimer and Ridley, and to find out how the bloodiest days of religious persecution in England's history helped mould the country's identity. At various times during the sixteenth century, both Protestants and Catholics were hunted down and executed. Cranmer, Latimer and Ridley were the most famous of all these victims.

***

Mike and I head off to find the prison where the three churchmen were held while they awaited trial and execution. It is no more than 100 paces from the place where they died. It was called the Bocardo. It's a strange, Italianate name, but it turns out to be a particularly Oxford joke, the sort of convoluted witticism that University dons are fond of but which makes others roll their eyes. A *bocardo* was a term used in philosophical logic to denote a statement that students found it hard to argue their way out of. Hence the Bocardo was a prison that convicts found it hard to escape from. But I'm not sure what we're going to find. I know the sixteenth-century gaol cells haven't survived, though I've read that the prison was part of the Church of St Michael of the North Gate, which is still here.

Just around the corner, in Cornmarket, the grey stones of the square church tower rise above us. It's almost 1,000 years old. Clutching the base of its wall today is a purple-canopied stall with the words AMT COFFEE on the front. Nearby, a thin, bearded guy in tight leather trousers is strumming a guitar, an upturned cap with a few coins in it on the ground before him. Next to him, a figure with his head covered by a red hood, cigarette in one hand, leaning with the other against a lamp post as though he's stopping it falling over, is complaining, 'Yeah, but these people today don't know anything.' The guitarist nods, gazing into the distance.

Now, what we need to find inside the church is someone with a keen knowledge of sixteenth-century history, who might just happen to know exactly where the prison was and how it tied in with the church, and if there's anything left to link it to Cranmer, Latimer and Ridley. In we go, and – hallelujah! – straight in front of us, where a sunbeam streaks through a window like a heavenly spotlight, is sitting a chap in a pure white roll-neck sweater with the warmest smile the angels themselves could devise.

'Hello,' I say, still walking towards him. 'Do you know anything about the old Bocardo prison?'

'I certainly do,' he replies. 'Sit down, and I'll tell you.' We introduce ourselves, and then Joshua – Well, what else would he be called? – explains that back in the sixteenth century, the north gate to the city was immediately alongside the church tower. And straddling the gate like an archway, linking the tower and the building on the other side, were the prison cells. The only way you could reached them was through a door from halfway up inside the old Saxon church tower. And Joshua produces a print of gate, church and prison from the eighteenth century. 'It hadn't changed much,' explains Joshua, 'from two hundred years before when Cranmer, Latimer and Ridley were held here.'

The three men had been arrested soon after Queen Mary came to the throne, and at first they were cast into the Tower of London.

Oxford's North Gate from inside the city. The Bocardo prison was above the archway and would have looked much like this in the sixteenth century. The only way in or out was via the church tower. The archway and the prison were demolished in 1771. (By kind permission of ©St Michael at the North Gate Church)

Mary and her advisers knew that these were no ordinary heretics. They were highly intelligent men, and their trial for heresy couldn't be left to some lowly ill-educated priest who might get tied in knots by their Protestant rhetoric. So they were packed into the back of a cart, bound and under armed escort were trundled through the streets of London and on up the road here to Oxford. The University was dominated by Catholic churchmen who supported Mary's campaign to exterminate the Protestant heresy and its proponents, and would be well able to cross verbal swords with the prisoners.

Following Joshua's directions, Mike and I climb up the steps inside the tower. On the first level there's a small display of treasures. As well as a silver chalice and some ancient stone carvings, there's also a leather cup with a slot in its cover. This was given to prisoners to lower down through their cell windows on a piece of string, so that relatives or kindly passers-by could deposit a coin in it for them. On the next floor up there's a large window that back in the sixteenth century would have been the doorway across into the prison, and on the floor above that, propped against the wall, is a dark oak door with three huge iron hinges and a bulky lock. A sign nearby tells us that this was the very door to the cell where Archbishop Cranmer was imprisoned. You can never be quite sure about these claims. But it's good enough for the romantic in me, and I stroke its rough rusted ironwork and its oaken panels worn glossy smooth by time. We keep going to the top and out onto the roof. We're on a level here with the all the towers and steeples of Oxford's many college halls and chapels. Joshua has told us that back in the 1550s you would have had a clear view from here of the land outside Balliol College where the heretics were burned. Today, modern buildings block that view. While Latimer and Ridley were being be burnt, Cranmer was brought up here and was forced to watch the terrible death of his friends.

***

So, what were the events that led to the arrest and eventual executions of Latimer, Ridley and Cranmer?

It began with one man's failed marriage. The teenage King Henry VIII had been on the throne for one month when he married Catherine of Aragon in 1509. Royal marriages usually had nothing to do with love or companionship. They were political. They were often designed to forge useful overseas alliances, and were always the means to ensure the continuation of the ruling dynasty by providing a son who would live into adulthood. Catherine was the daughter of the king of Spain, so that was useful. But as an heir-making machine, she turned out to be a failure. After two stillbirths, two miscarriages, and two deaths in infancy, she finally in 1516 produced a baby that survived. But it was a girl, christened Mary. And daughters were risky; the continuing tradition of the warrior king meant queens were more likely to be overthrown. Henry, who had fathered an illegitimate son, concluded that the marriage was the problem. It had been cursed by God.

At this moment, Henry, conveniently, fell in love. Not with a foreign princess, but with an English commoner's daughter, Anne Boleyn. He decided he would marry her and she would bear him the longed-for son and heir. And given that his union with Anne would be a divine gift, and that he didn't want a son born out of wedlock, he also decided they would not have sex before the wedding. That was to take five years, and we can only guess how much one man's sexual frustration during that time was responsible for the violent and revolutionary events that followed. Whether or not we blame Henry's libido, getting divorced from Catherine certainly became an obsession with him.

Divorce, in the sense we understand it, was impossible in the sixteenth century. Legal separation could be achieved only by the Pope's ruling. After lengthy diplomatic negotiations, the Pope refused. And so, Henry decided to take the first step himself. In January 1533, he married Anne Boleyn. It turned out to be not quite the first step. He had already given in to his sexual desires. Anne, on her wedding day, was pregnant. On 7 September, she gave birth. It was a disappointment for Henry. Another girl, who was christened Elizabeth. Now it was necessary to pass laws which would justify Henry's marriage. In rapid succession, Acts of Parliament removed the English church from the Pope's jurisdiction and made Henry its head instead. Other Acts declared his marriage to Catherine void, and his offspring by Anne to be his legitimate successors.

Henry placed the strategy and tactics of his religious policy in the hands of his two most trusted appointees: his secretary Thomas Cromwell and the Archbishop of Canterbury, Thomas Cranmer. The break with Rome provided an opportunity to fill the royal coffers, and Cromwell organised the dismantling of monastic life in England. Monks were turned out of their ancient abbeys and monasteries, their treasures were carted away, and the buildings themselves were either torn down or sold off to become the ancestral homes of later generations of noble English families.

It was not a total revolution, however. Not yet anyway. The way the nation worshipped, along with traditional Catholic beliefs, were largely unchanged. This included the Catholic doctrine of transubstantiation – the king and English people continued to hold that the wine and bread in Holy Communion were, literally, transformed into the body and blood of Christ. And Henry continued, after the break with Rome as before, to have Protestant Lutherans burned to death as heretics, even though they – like him – opposed the papacy. At the same time, those who stayed steadfast for the Pope as the head of the Church in England, suffered similar fates. Most prominent of these was the Lord High Chancellor, Sir Thomas More, whom Henry – in an act of mercy – allowed to be beheaded, a quicker, less painful death than the stake. Not so fortunate – if that's the right word – were a group of Carthusian monks, who had resisted the destruction of their monastery. They were hanged carefully so that, with their necks not broken, they remained conscious while they were castrated and disembowelled, before their bodies were chopped up into four pieces.

Meanwhile, Anne still failed to bear Henry a son. He took at face value gossip that she'd committed adultery with a young court musician as well as with one of his personal attendants, and he had her beheaded in May 1536. The story of Henry's matrimonial entanglements has been told many times, in novels, TV and films. For our purposes, it's enough to note that four more wives followed, and that one of them, Jane Seymour did give birth to a son, Edward, who became king on Henry's death in 1547.

Henry's Catholicism without the Pope vanished during the two short reigns of Edward VI and Mary, the first an evangelical Protestant, the second an uncompromising supporter of the papacy. As a result, England was subjected to violent swings in official religious policy.

Edward was only 9 years old when he came to the throne, so inevitably he was a puppet of others. Cranmer, who was becoming more and more a reformist, more and more an evangelical Protestant, was in charge. He grew a beard, brought his wife out of hiding and demanded harsh punishments for immorality, including life imprisonment for adulterers. Under Cranmer's guidance, too, communion was now no longer a miracle, as Catholics taught, but was more a group commemoration. But King Edward was a sickly boy, and both he and Cranmer realised that he might not live long. That raised the spectre of his half-sister Mary becoming queen. Mary's mother had ensured that she was brought up a strict Catholic, recognising the supremacy of the Pope. It was clear that Mary's succession would be a catastrophe for Protestants and their beliefs. Edward therefore planned to have his 17-year-old Protestant cousin, Jane Grey, named as his heir. In 1553, Edward's lung disease suddenly got the better of him, and he died after a reign of only five years.

Mary moved fast. She rallied support and put down an uprising led by Jane's family. One by one the plotters were caught and beheaded. Possession of heretical or treasonable literature became punishable by death. It was not long before England's leading Protestant churchmen, Bishop Latimer of Worcester, Bishop Ridley of London and Archbishop Cranmer were rounded up, and made ready to face trial here in Oxford.

***

On Thursday 12 September 1555, Cranmer, dressed in the black gown of a doctor of divinity and clutching a long white staff, was brought from his cell, across into the church tower and down the steps out into the street. There he was helped into the back of a horse-drawn cart in which was taken through the narrow streets of Oxford to the University Church of St Mary the Virgin.

That's where Mike and I go now. We weave between the walls of colleges – Jesus, Exeter, Lincoln, Hertford, Brasenose – and, as we reach the round, domed neoclassical library that is the Radcliffe Camera, there before us is the University Church of St Mary the Virgin, its mighty tower and steeple in the midst of a long, spreading nave unchanged since Cranmer saw it that Thursday morning in 1555.

We make our way through the crowds of tourists: Japanese with their selfie sticks, American retirees with natty rucksacks by the coachload, French, German, Spanish speakers, and accents which I can't recognise but which could be Russian or some other Slavic language. Inside, the nave is much grander and brighter than the more cosy interior of the North Gate church. Its pointed arches and massive windows with their perpendicular lines, dating from a period before Queen Mary's reign, look now much as they did when Cranmer arrived here.

We know a lot about the conduct of the trials that took place here and about the subsequent executions themselves. It was all recounted in one of the classic – though now infrequently read – books of the English language: John Foxe's *Book of Martyrs*, which was published eight years after the executions of the three church-men in Oxford. Foxe was a diligent journalist. He visited Oxford, and there tracked down and interviewed eyewitnesses. At the same time, however, he was not free from bias. His book was designed to reinforce the Protestant cause. We can neither prove nor disprove his account. Much of it, though, has a ring of truth about it.

When Cranmer entered the church, the sight that met his eyes was different in two ways from what Mike and I see this morning. First, the pews were packed with people, probably all men, a mix of Protestants and Catholics. Second, a 10ft-high platform had been erected on a wooden scaffold in front of the high altar. It was decorated with cloths in red and white to signify the majesty of the state. On top, with due pomp, sat the Pope's representative, James Brooks, Bishop of Gloucester. Below and in front of him were the queen's own commissioners, Dr Thomas Martin and Dr John Story. It was all designed to intimidate Cranmer, who was not to be given the benefit of normal judicial procedure. There was no independent judge.

Cranmer refused to be bullied. He declined to doff his cap before the Pope's man and the queen's commissioners. And once Martin and Story had made opening speeches, accusing him of blasphemy and heresy, Cranmer announced that he didn't recognise the court. 'Neither would I have appeared this day before you,' he added, 'but that I was brought hither as a prisoner.' He was asked whether he still supported the king rather than the Pope as head of the Church in England. Cranmer replied that he had 'taken a solemn oath, never to consent to the admitting of the bishop of Rome's authority into this realm of England again,' and he wouldn't change his mind now. Brooks seemed to back off. He perhaps decided that it might be beyond his authority to condemn a man of Cranmer's exalted archi-episcopal rank, so he decided that Cranmer should be sent to Rome to answer before the Pope himself. With that, the archbishop was led out, and taken back to his cell in the Bocardo.

Then it was Latimer and Ridley's turn. Ridley had been moved from the Bocardo soon after their arrival, and instead had been given accommodation in the home of the jailer, a man called Mr Irish, whose wife cooked meals for him. It's not clear why

Ridley got this special treatment – at 55 he was ten years younger than Cranmer, and thirteen years younger than Latimer, who at 68 was in frail health. Latimer and Ridley were subjected to the same ritual kangaroo court as Cranmer. Latimer felt he wasn't up to the pressure of a debate so submitted a written testimony denying the fundamental Catholic doctrine of transubstantiation. Ridley, addressing Brooks, made a similar assertion.

In all three trials, there was a political element. The queen and her advisers believed the three prisoners could be, if not the organisers of rebellion, the inspirations for it. And in Ridley's case, there was a particular need for judicial vengeance. He'd backed Lady Jane Grey's claim to the throne, and had pronounced Queen Mary to be a bastard and so not qualified to be monarch. Brooks felt on safer ground with Ridley and Latimer, and without wasting time he found them guilty of heresy and condemned them to be burned at the stake.

On his last night on earth, Nicholas Ridley was as usual served his evening meal by Mrs Irish, the jailor's wife. She had grown quite fond of him over the previous weeks and was now in tears. To cheer her up, according to Foxe, Ridley made light of his fate. 'Though my breakfast will be somewhat sharp,' he joked, 'my supper will be more pleasant and sweet.' The next morning, he was taken out to join Hugh Latimer in the street. Together they were marched along the city wall perimeter, through the shouts and taunts of the pushing crowd. Hundreds, if not thousands had come to witness the terrible event – every household in the city had been ordered to send a representative.

Mike and I are now back standing close to the cross in the tarmac outside the gates of Balliol College. It would have looked more like a field back then. The place would have been chosen because it was close to the prison but also far enough away from buildings that there was a reduced risk of sparks flying off and starting a house fire, a common event in any town in England at the time.

The stake had been hammered into the ground, ready, with logs piled up around. Ridley was dressed in a black gown bordered with fur. Latimer was clothed in a long white shroud that reached his feet. The two of them looked back towards the church tower. Cranmer didn't acknowledge them – he was arguing with a friar.

According to the account in Foxe's book, the two men tried to give each other courage in the final moments. Ridley hugged Latimer, and said to him, 'Be of good heart, brother, for God will either assuage the fury of the flame, or else strengthen us to abide it.' They knelt by the stake, and prayed together, 'earnestly', says Foxe. Then they had a short private conversation, before being made to listen to a sermon from a Catholic prelate, who harangued the crowds on the sins of those about to be consigned now not only to flames on earth but also to the everlasting fires of Hell. Ridley was then stripped of his fur gown.

A blacksmith stepped forward and fixed the two men upright to the stake with an iron chain passed around their waists. Ridley told him to make sure it was secure. His brother had come to be close to him in his final moments, and he was allowed to hang a small bag of gunpowder around each man's neck. The idea was that this would explode as soon as the first flames caught hold and so spare the two victims any further suffering. It did not work as planned.

A burning torch was placed first at Ridley's feet. Latimer called over to him, 'Be of good comfort, Master Ridley, and play the man. We shall this day light such a candle by God's grace in England, as I trust shall never be put out.' That, again, is according to Foxe; whether Latimer did indeed say this, we can't know. It is of course exactly the sort of quote that any good Protestant journalist would like to be able to write, and the words became an inspiring legend to later English generations.

Ridley cried out, 'Lord, Lord, receive my spirit.'

As the fire was now reaching Latimer, he too shouted, 'O Father of heaven, receive my soul!' and, Foxe claims, Latimer stroked his face with his hands, as if he were bathing in the fire. Then he died. Whether the gunpowder hastened his end, we don't know.

Ridley was less fortunate. The wood on his side of the pyre was, it seems, too green, and it burned slowly. His gunpowder packet must have been damp because it failed to explode. His brother, who was watching from the front of the crowd, realised the problem and, risking getting burned himself, stepped forward and tried to pile up the logs and branches so Ridley would expire more quickly. But he somehow managed to make matters worse,

An illustration from Foxe's *Book of Martyrs*, showing Latimer and Ridley moments before the flames are lit. Latimer, on the left of the stake, is saying, 'Father of Heaven receive my soul.' Cranmer, watching from the church tower, top right, says, 'O Lord, strengthen them.'

and Ridley's agony went on for some time before his final scream was silenced.

***

Archbishop Cranmer, who had been watching from the top of the tower of St Micheal's church, never did go to Rome to appear before the Pope. Over the next few months he was subjected to a variety of psychological pressures, threats and promises. He was summoned before a new papal commission in Oxford. He was ordered to appear stripped of his archiepiscopal robes and dressed in old rags, as though he were a beggar rather than the most senior churchman in the country. But this dire humiliation didn't work. Cranmer still refused to renounce what the commissioners saw as his heretical views. So, they switched to a bad-cop-good-cop routine. Cranmer was sent to the lodgings of the Dean of Christ Church, who treated him with kindness and respect. A deal was put on the table. Cranmer could go back to being Archbishop of Canterbury, if he'd just recant. And what's more he'd even regain

Queen Mary's favour. It was all a lie. What the commissioners knew, and Cranmer didn't, was that the queen had already made up her mind: whatever Cranmer said, he was destined for the flames outside the north gate of Oxford. But Cranmer was taken in by the blandishments. He signed a document that began, 'I, Thomas Cranmer, late archbishop of Canterbury ... acknowledge the Bishop of Rome to be supreme head on earth, and Christ's vicar, unto whom all Christian people ought to be subject.' Over the following weeks, he put his name to no fewer than four more such recantations. It ought to have been enough to save him from the executioner's torch. But the queen was determined that he should go. Cranmer was too influential a figure, and back in power he might become the focus for further opposition.

On 21 March 1556, as he knelt praying in his cell in the Bocardo prison, Cranmer could hear the stake once more being hammered into the earth a few yards away outside. The wood was being piled up ready. And the blacksmith was testing the strength of his iron chain. But before that horror was enacted, there was a sensational shock to come. And it was Cranmer who delivered it. At 9 o'clock on the morning of his execution, the former archbishop – dressed again in torn and dirty clothes – was taken from the prison back to the University Church of St Mary the Virgin, where he had first faced his accusers. Cranmer had agreed to preach there one last time. The plan was that he would praise the righteous nature of Catholic doctrine and the supremacy of the Pope over all Christians in England. The most senior supporter of the Reformation, in public, confessing that he'd been wrong, and that Roman Catholicism and all it stood for, were right. It was a coup that the queen and the papal party relished. But it was to be the biggest PR disaster of Mary's reign.

The church was packed with folk who had come to see and hear the drama. Some were supporters of the queen and the Pope, but others were Protestants who were sympathetic to the break with Rome that Mary's father had made. Some tutted and whispered in commiseration at the ragged clothes that the once powerful Cranmer had been forced to put on. Cranmer begged the congregation to pray for him. He fell to his knees and a wept.

Then he struggled to his feet, and turning to the congregation, he announced that now, before he died, he had something to say which would glorify God and edify his listeners. He had only signed all those documents in support of the Pope, he said, 'for fear of death, and to save my life.' The congregation was aghast. The Pope, announced Cranmer, 'is Christ's enemy, and Antichrist, with all his false doctrine.' There was uproar all around the church – shock among the Catholics, amazement among the Protestants. Cranmer tried to continue with his denunciation of the papacy, but the presiding priest intervened. 'Lead the heretic away!' he screamed, and the guards jumped onto the stage and grabbed him. They hustled him out, while the monks and friars on the front row insulted him and called him vile names. Many people ran from the church to keep up with him and to see what would happen next.

When he was brought to the place outside Balliol, Cranmer was allowed to kneel for a few moments in prayer. Then he was bound with the chains to the stake. The kindling at his feet was lit, and as the flames rose higher, he punished the hand that had signed those documents that he now denied. Here's how Foxe recounts Cranmer's final minutes:

> Stretching out his right hand, he held it unshrinkingly in the fire until it was burnt to a cinder, even before his body was injured, frequently exclaiming, 'This unworthy right hand! This unworthy right hand!' His body did abide the burning with such steadfastness that he seemed to have no more than the stake to which he was bound; his eyes were lifted up to heaven, and he repeated 'This unworthy right hand!' as long as his voice would suffer him; and, using often the words of Stephen, 'Lord Jesus, receive my spirit,' in the greatness of the flame, he gave up the ghost.

***

Almost 1,000 people were executed, Catholics and Protestants, for their religious beliefs during the reigns of Henry VIII and Mary Tudor. The faith and bravery of Cranmer, Latimer and Ridley – and of many other Protestant victims – were immortalised by John Foxe in his *Book of Martyrs*, which rapidly became a best-seller. Foxe's role as a propagandist often gets the better of his journalism. So he sometimes leaves out what doesn't suit his Protestant cause. In his account of the lives of the three Oxford martyrs, he ignores the fact that all three were themselves persecutors, with some responsibility for others being burned alive. Latimer even preached the sermon at the burning of a Catholic martyr during the reign of Henry VIII. Nevertheless, what Foxe wrote did much to mould English attitudes to religion and freedom during the decades and centuries that followed. His vivid accounts of gruesome torture and agonising executions, often accompanied by graphic illustrations, helped create a national tradition of English resistance to religious persecution.

And his book also helped foster an English tradition of resistance of another kind too. Opposition to Bloody Mary, a nickname coined by Foxe, also had a strong political – we might say, patriotic – element to it. Mary had married King Philip of Spain. Philip drew Mary, and England, into a disastrous war against France, which ended in 1588 with the loss of the very last English possession in French territory, the city of Calais. Mary knew what a catastrophe she had caused, and she is said to have remarked, 'When I am dead, you will find "Calais" engraved on my heart.' That day came sooner than she'd expected. Within weeks, she was coughing and sneezing and confined to her bed. She died of influenza. Mary had not just been a brutal monarch. She'd been a failure, and she was perceived to be the tool of foreign powers, of the Pope and of Spanish royal ambition. Her opponents, revered in Foxe's popular book, became English heroes, symbols of English resistance to foreign oppression.

The Victorians, in particular, glorified these martyrs. Two hundred yards from the site of the burnings, around the corner in St Giles, stands the Martyrs' Memorial – it's actually in the wrong place because the Victorians misunderstood where the three men died. But no matter. The sheer size of this huge neo-Gothic column, its tower encrusted with statues of the martyrs themselves and its giant steeple, topped by a cross 60ft above the traffic of St Giles, tell us much about the importance in English history of the events in Oxford of 1555 and 1556. For the Victorians,

Cranmer, Latimer and Ridley were heroes, fighting for religious and political freedom against unjust persecution.

We today may feel that's a bit simplistic. But we can agree that the events behind the martyrs' deaths did play an important role in defining the English nation. The break with the Pope in Rome nationalised England's religion. The bible used in every church in the land, for instance, would from now on be in the English language, not in Latin. And with the finish of the Roman church in England, the foundation was laid for a national institution, the Church of England, which would spread English influence across the world. Over many centuries, the Anglican church has come to embody what are often regarded as typically English values: an avoidance of extremes in doctrine, preaching and methods of conversion; the idea of the church as a sort of social club, where kindness and politeness are the unwritten rules ('a vicar's tea party' being synonymous in the English language with peaceful respectability); and even the church as a focus of patriotism – remember the hymn, 'And did those feet in ancient time walk upon England's mountains green.' Today, the Anglican church, as it has become known, whose foundations were laid by the Reformation, has 62 million practising worshippers worldwide, from the United States to Africa, the Asian subcontinent and Australasia. Its head, the Archbishop of Canterbury, presents himself more as a spiritual guide than as the absolute ruler of a global congregation, unlike the Pope in Tudor times – that lesson has been learned. And the spread worldwide of an English institution with English values has added to a sense that the English can still wield an influence for moderation, stability and peace beyond our shores.

The Reformation also strengthened the English sense of their independence from foreign authority. Henry VIII's break with the Pope in Rome ended a 1,000-year-long claim by a foreign power to control the Church in England, and, because of the fundamental importance of religious matters in society back then, that meant ending foreign interference in the daily lives of English folk. Under Mary's successor, her sister Elizabeth, this contributed – as we shall see on the next stop of our journey – to an English feeling of pride in being different from their neighbours, a pride in being peculiarly English.

Finally, there was the impact on Parliament. There was an irony in Henry's claim that he now had the God-given right to be the head of the Church in England. Behind his grand scheme were reams of detail, from defining the meaning of Holy Communion, to laying down how church services should be conducted, to setting out who could marry whom, when a marriage could be declared null and void, and even the rules of royal succession. The king could no longer just issue an edict putting these points into effect. They required legislation. And so, the Reformation further emphasised the role and power of England's Parliament. The king, despite his claims to be the supreme head of the Church, could not act without the support of the Lords and the Commons, institutions which, as we've seen earlier, claimed to represent the wishes of the English people nationwide, however imperfect that representation was in the sixteenth century.

***

However, although the Reformation and Counter-Reformation did undoubtedly strengthen the national identity of the English, we should not think that England was now one nation, undivided. Religious and political turmoil were far from finished in England. The accession to the throne of Mary's half-sister, the Protestant Elizabeth, in 1558 turned the searchlight back on Roman Catholics. Some 130 priests were executed for religious treason during Elizabeth's forty-four-year reign. And another sixty lay Catholics were also put to death. Torture was used more than in any other English reign.

Yet, at the same time, there was an atmosphere of celebration and fun during the first Elizabethan age. That was perhaps because Catholics made up only an estimated 1 per cent of the population, so persecution was not felt to be a threat to the vast majority of the people. The English found time to relax. They took themselves off to alehouses and theatres. They learned to laugh at themselves as slightly mad, hard-drinking merrymakers who weren't very good at learning other people's languages. Sound about right? Let's go and find out more in Stratford-upon-Avon, where a certain Master Shakespeare grew up and learned to make the English laugh, cry and feel proud of themselves.

9

Stratford-upon-Avon, Warwickshire

....

BARDOLATRY

....

This blessed plot, this earth, this realm, this England.

William Shakespeare (1564-1616)

Is William Shakespeare – apart from his many other claims to immortality – England's greatest patriot? For a start, he wrote the most stirring and most oft-quoted call for English bravery and sacrifice. Only the hearts of the most cynical of internationalists wouldn't flutter at the words he put into Henry V's mouth in the days before the English victory over the French at Agincourt.

> I see you stand like greyhounds in the slips,
> Straining upon the start. The game's afoot:
> Follow your spirit, and upon this charge
> Cry 'God for Harry, England, and Saint George!'

And Shakespeare clinched his role as England's No.1 patriot by arranging with the Almighty to be born and to die on the same day, the day we celebrate England's patron saint, St George, 23 April. It's that date today, but it's not just any 23 April. Today is the 400th anniversary of the Bard's death. Across the globe, people are celebrating his life and his work. So where else would we be on this special day but in Stratford-upon-Avon, where Shakespeare was born and is buried.

***

Stratford, at half past nine this morning, has got its bunting out, its coffee shops percolating, its traffic re-routed from the town centre, and its temporary railings erected at its roadsides. It's ready for the crowds now streaming over the river bridge from the sports ground car-park to be greeted by a flashing sign on the Memorial Theatre saying 'Happy Birthday, Shakespeare'. A middle-aged man dressed like a seventeenth-century lawyer – black flat-cap and gown – is trying not to notice the microphone being pushed under his nose by a bouncing young guy with 'BBC Radio Coventry and Warwickshire' on his jacket, who is attached by a cable to a thin young woman with a clipboard.

'So tell me about your costume,' he asks, grinning and nodding.

'It's the formal attire of Stratford town councillors,' comes the response.

'And what does this day mean to you?'

'Well,' replies the councillor, 'Pride in the town, pride in being English.'

A 6ft-tall brown bear with a large head and an old school tie round its neck, is giving a double thumbs-up behind the councillor's back in the mistaken belief that it's on live TV.

There's going to be a parade, and the tables outside the Encore – just recognisable as a pub from the swinging sign with the caricature of Shakespeare above the date 1685 – are all taken by customers refreshing themselves before the action begins. They're sacrificing the chance of an uninterrupted view of the procession for coffee and croissants. The throng is already three-deep around the corner in Bridge Street and is pressing against the barricades at the kerb edge.

A cross between a vampire and a bridesmaid – bat-winged cloak, black lipstick and eye mask, shiny orange-coloured hair and a bunch of flowers in one hand – pushes a large piece of card at me with two holes in it and a dangling elastic string.

'Oh, thanks,' I say.

'No problem. Enjoy,' she replies. 'We're giving out 10,000 of them.' And before I can say, 'Wow', she's dodged off to get rid of some more.

I turn the card over, and there's Shakespeare's eyeless face between a bald pate and an Elizabethan ruff. It's a mask. On the other side, there's a list of the day's events, from which I see that the parade will soon be mustering up in the town centre. That's where I decide to go. It's a slow passage, what with all the buggies, and the kids in their masks – too big for them so they can't see where they're going – banging into adult legs, and there are as many people trying to come down the street as there are going up it. Then there are the twenty-odd people blocking the route by HUFFKINS TEASHOP, while they salivate at the mountain of lardy cakes in its window.

Accents around me are global. There's Brummie, Southern States American drawl, Australian, and more Brummie. I hear French and Spanish, German and a Scandinavian lilt which linguistic ignorance stops me pinpointing. Once, when I'm jammed by a static queue outside Greggs, I peer over the ranks of spectators who have already chosen their spots, at a row of shields fixed on poles in the middle of the street. I make out the words Pakistan, Poland, India, China, Thailand – which I assume means folk from these countries will be in the parade.

At last I make it to a point opposite the corner where, on top of a black-curtained podium, a man in blazer and tie is telling us that to commemorate Stratford's most famous citizen, children from the town's primary schools have been taking part in a competition. They had to answer the question, 'What does Shakespeare mean to you?' The winner is an 8-year-old who produced a 'motion representation of the graveyard scene from *Hamlet* in Lego.' I take advantage of the distraction caused by the announcement of this epic achievement, to edge forwards, and by the time the laughter and cheering have stopped, the crowd hereabouts discover they've got a new neighbour with a decent view – me.

Above the crowds on the opposite side of the little square, every window is crammed with faces. Children are waving Union Jacks over a Costa Coffee sign on a Tudor half-timbered building. Families and friends of the employees of Barclay's Bank, who have been let into the building to watch, are trying to take selfies, leaning backwards over first-floor windowsills in a way that could soon give the St John Ambulance first-aid crew below something to test their training. Eight different TV crews have their own barricaded pen nearby. 'We've got media here from all over the world,' explains the commentator, 'from Brazil, the United States, France, Germany and Sweden, and of course you'll be able to see yourselves on the BBC, ITN and Sky tonight.'

Suddenly, the four loudspeakers above us begin to vibrate with ponderous, deafening bell tolls. 'This is – [boom!] – the death – [boom!] – knell for - [boom!] – the Bard - [boom!],' we're informed from the podium.

As well as a white bust of Shakespeare in the middle of the square, there are other strange Shakespeares all over the place. No one, apart from kids, wants to wear their masks. They get in the way of picture-taking. And their size means you can't put them in a pocket. So, people are wearing them on the backs of their heads. This has the disconcerting effect of making you think people are either walking backwards, or have managed to swivel their necks round 180 degrees. I hang mine by its elastic from the front of my belt, like a Shakespearean fig leaf.

But there's no time to worry whether this will look equally weird, because an ancient coffin bier has been wheeled before us. There's no corpse in a box on it, but instead a large spray of white flowers with a label saying '1564 to 1616' in gold letters. And the paraders are arriving. I've never seen so many red robes, gold chains and tricorn hats in one place. Mayors from towns all over the country have been invited, and are now strolling around the Square, chatting to each other about important municipal matters. Then they file away into a side street to await their turn to move off.

This brief appearance before a retreat to the wings sets the pattern of behaviour for those to come. There are men in dark suits and women in hats like the queen wears, so you can tell they're the Great, whose Goodness is beyond question, or at least yet to be tested. Then there are morris dancers who give a skip and a jingle every few yards, while a man in a top hat, who becomes a cardboard horse from the waist down, careers about in front of them. And the entire pupil population of King Edward VI's School Stratford then chatters its way four abreast past us, each teenager holding a small bunch of flowers as if it were delicate porcelain that might fall and smash any moment.

There's one more ceremony before the parade gets underway. 'In a moment, ladies and gentlemen,' says the commentator (the death knell has now stopped), 'I'm going to ask you all to put on your Shakespeare masks ...' and here his voice rises to a climax, '... for a Shakespeare Mask Moment! It will be a world record for the number of people in one place all wearing Shakespeare masks... if only because people have never gathered together before all wearing Shakespeare masks.' He pauses. 'OK. Now!' And we all do it, though it's a bit of a fumble because we need to get our mobile phones into camera mode at the same time as lining up our eyes with the two holes in our masks.

Then there's a bang, and confetti and sparkly coloured ribbon shoots up in the air and rains down on the scene. The front door of Barclays Bank bursts open and out comes a band to lead the procession. Not, as you might imagine, the Royal Shakespeare Company players, or a local school orchestra, but a New Orleans Jazz band, playing a syncopated version of 'Happy Birthday to You', Two young women behind me – who're both too short to have seen much of the build-up and have been talking non-stop up to now, mostly about a boring colleague where they work – have been jolted into the present by the exploding confetti, and are now bobbing up and down in time to the New Orleans' beat.

By the time the trumpets and tubas have dissolved in the general clamour of the crowds, the Stratford school kids have filed past us – still holding on to their bouquets and calling to each other with embarrassed excitement – followed by the South Asian delegation, and the mayors and the morris dancers are now coming into view. They're all heading towards the Shakespeare Memorial Theatre and then on for a quarter of a mile to Holy Trinity church, where the bones of the Bard are interred. So I decide to do the same. This proves even more difficult than my slow passage up here a couple of hours earlier: thousands more folk have joined us, with those at the bottom of the street determined to see what's going on at the top, those at the top anxious to follow the procession to the bottom, others not knowing where they're going but looking for a cup of coffee, all with different ideas about the speed those ahead of them should be doing, while countless multitudes are still not moving at all, thus creating a 500-yard-long bottleneck for the rest of us to seep though.

Once I've put the theatre behind me, I think I'll be clever and – not even pausing at the queue by the Mr Whippy van ('Often licked but never beaten!') – take the path through the trees alongside the river. I've gone about eight steps when I'm confronted by a human tide surging towards me. It's the kids from the King Edward VI school who have done their bit by the Bard and laid their bouquets on his tomb. Now they want to get on with the rest of the fun. I pin myself to a tree trunk for stability while they wash through. Tantalising snippets of chatter reach me: '... Yeah, yeah, I know, but the disco goes on till ten ...' and '... not me. I'm going to get a free doughnut then go home ...' and '... my heels are digging in the grass ...' which leave a lot of questions to wonder about.

At last I get to the churchyard. There's no question of going inside. Those on parade have that exclusive privilege. But I soon discover there's even more to this procession than I'd seen back in the town centre. The banners tell all. The Worshipful Company of Fruiterers (fur-trimmed green gowns and black flat caps) next to the World Lyrical Dance Federation (which is neither lyrical, dancing nor federated, but is represented by a single walking and possibly unhappy girl). Then there's Maria's Children Russia (adults and children in what could be Slavic capes and headgear, holding up multi-coloured banner saying 'An Arts Rehabilitation Center for Russian Orphans'). And there are representatives of other Stratfords from across the globe. First up, a dozen folk in red fleece tops holding small Australian flags. A thin middle-aged chap with glasses on a chain around his neck leaps out from the watching crowd and grabs the hand of a burly Ozzie in the procession. 'I've been there! I've been to Stratford, Australia! I know your town! I've been there!' he blurts, his face bursting with enthusiasm.

'Magic. Thanks, mate,' says the Australian, 'Great little place, isn't it?'

'It is! It is! I've been there.'

Then when a group in black broad-brimmed hats arrives, he does the same again. 'Hello! Hello! I've been to Stratford, New Zealand! I've been to your town! I've been there!' And he grabs a passing kiwi hand.

'Wonderful. Did you like it?' asks the startled woman he's gripping.

'I did! I did! I've been there! I've been to Stratford, New Zealand.'

'Coincidence, huh?' And she eases herself free.

Then it's the turn of representatives from Stratford, Connecticut, USA. Once the 'been-there' routine has been repeated a third time, I try to get through the procession so I can ask him if he collects Stratfords, like some people collect antique cigarette cards or miniature green bottles, but he's already disappeared into the throng milling around the gravestones.

As I'm meandering back, letting the current of people lead me where it will, I find myself outside the Black Swan pub, known by all as the Dirty Duck, the name given it by American servicemen during the Second World War. It's got a couple of strings of bunting flickering in the breeze on its railings. One lot has 'Pimm's No.1' on each little triangle. The others have little crosses of St George on them. I suddenly remember that today is St George's Day – but these tiny flags are the only mark of that event I've seen anywhere in the town. Maybe there was a cross of St George on a pole at the start of the parade, but it wasn't noticeable even if there was. But none of this surprises me. While the Scots celebrate St Andrew's Day as a national holiday, and the Welsh so love St David that more Welsh boys are christened Dafydd – shortened to Dai – than any other name, the English don't bother much about their saint's day. Why, I wonder. Is it because it's hard for us to feel we've much in common with him? George was, after all, a Greek soldier in the Roman Empire who had probably never even heard of this island. Or is it because many English people don't like the way his red cross has been hijacked by extreme right-wing nationalist groups and noisy England football fans? There's now an attempt to win back the flag for more mainstream moderate English nationalism, by those who want to see some form of devolved power in England, just as the Scots, Welsh and Northern Irish have. But until that happens, St George is relegated on his day in Stratford to a few bits of plastic cloth on a pub.

A few steps further on, I hear the bouncing rhythm of Joe Loss's 'In the Mood', and there in front of me are five women of various ages and sizes in long black and white skirts and skimpy tops, swaying their hips and rippling their arms in time to the beat. I read on a small sign that they are the 'gorgeous belly dancing goddesses from Stratford-upon-Avon.' They're having fun, and the crowd gives them a smattering of applause as the music fades and they take their bows.

The thought strikes me, '*C'est magnifique, mais ce n'est pas* ... Shakespeare.' But perhaps the fact that I'm reduced to quoting, or misquoting, from French, means that there's no equivalent expression in English. So maybe that means we don't think there's anything bizarre about celebrating Shakespeare with belly dancing. It's normal. The words 'irrelevant' or 'eccentric' don't come into it. But surely an alien from Mars, sneaking through the crowds in Stratford this morning, would resort to these two words when reporting on today's events to friends back home. A New Orleans Jazz Band, morris dancers, a worshipful bunch of fruiterers, Russian orphans. Of course, we could say, 'Well, if you're having a party, anything goes.' Fair enough. And of course, Shakespeare is not being forgotten, with those 10,000 cardboard Bard faces, all the flowers on his tomb and ... well, that's it.

***

So what about the hundreds of thousands of other reasons why we're celebrating the man today? I mean all the words in his plays and his poetry that have made millions of us laugh, weep and stop to think, over the past 400 years? Unless I've missed it somewhere, no one has heard, during the hour and a half build-up nor the procession itself, a single line that Shakespeare penned. I know that tonight there's going to be a gala, a star-studded show at the Memorial Theatre with extracts from his work. But that's then. What about this morning, for the thousands of us who have got up early and driven here? I hope it's not because the organisers were worried about boring us with language we might not understand.

A recent survey in fifteen selected countries overseas found that more people there claim to enjoy Shakespeare's plays – 65 per cent – than those who said they did in this country – 59 per cent. One theory is that part of the reason why foreigners so love the Bard is that they often see his plays in translation, which may make them easier to comprehend. Many of those polled abroad said their knowledge of Shakespeare made them view England favourably, and made them want to visit here. This of course is just the sort of thing to make the English feel proud, and to give them a sense of who they think they are. The idea that an English person – one of us – should be so admired around the world reinforces our sense of ourselves as special.

Another reason for the spread worldwide of what the *Guardian* newspaper calls 'Bardolatry' is that Shakespeare's dramas have been transformed into other art forms. In Italy, Verdi composed four operas based on Shakespeare plays, *Macbeth*, *Otello*, *Falstaff* and *Lear*. There are also lesser-known German and Finnish operatic versions of *Lear*. The French composer Delius did *A Village Romeo and Juliet*. Berlioz wrote *Béatrice et Bénédict* based on *Much Ado about Nothing*. *Hamlet* also turns up in French opera. The Americans have done their bit with Leonard Bernstein's *West Side Story* (*Romeo and Juliet*)

From the title page of the First Folio edition of Shakespeare's plays, published in 1623.

and Cole Porter's *Kiss me Kate* (*The Taming of the Shrew*). Then there's ballet. Prokofiev's *Romeo and Juliet*, Mendelssohn's *A Midsummer Night's Dream*, and Sibelius set *The Tempest* to music. And there are too many films and TV adaptations in foreign languages to list.

Shakespeare has often turned up in both the most unexpected and the most inspiring places beyond our shores. For eighteen years, during the hopeless days of his life in the prison cell on Robben Island, Nelson Mandela kept one book with him. It had to be smuggled in past guards. He made notes in its margins and read extracts to his fellow captives. It wasn't even written in his native language. It was the complete works of Shakespeare. 'He always seems to have something to say to us,' Mandela wrote later. One of his favourite passage was this from *Julius Caesar*:

> Cowards die many times before their deaths.
> The valiant never taste of death but once.
> Of all the wonders that I yet have heard,
> It seems to me most strange that men should fear,
> Seeing that death, a necessary end,
> Will come when it will come.

The French historian, Alexis de Tocqueville on a tour of America in 1831 observed that 'there is scarcely a pioneer's hut where one does not encounter some odd volumes of Shakespeare.' In 1848, the crew of a whaling ship whiled away their days sailing through the South Pacific Ocean by performing *Othello*. And I can report that a few years ago in a village supermarket in eastern Spain, on a display cabinet between the chorizo and the Rioja, I came across several slim volumes, including *Hamlet de Guillermo Shakespeare, una traduccion* and *El Mercader De Venecia*.

***

Shakespeare has a habit of infiltrating our lives, whether or not we're fans. English speakers both here and the world over quote from him almost every hour of the day. For instance, let's say we tell someone, *more in sorrow than anger* (this phrase, like those in italics over the next two paragraphs, was devised by Shakespeare), 'You have me *in stitches*, you do, you're living in *a fool's paradise*, and it's *a foregone conclusion* that *all of a sudden* there'll be *a sea change*, and then *at one fell swoop, come what may*, you'll find yourself *in a pickle*, so you may think you're *as pure as the driven snow* and *fancy free*, but the rest of us are waiting *with bated breath* to see whether you've got *a charmed life*, or more likely will *vanish into thin air* and be *as dead as a doornail*, because you've always *worn your heart on your sleeve*, and the way you *lay it on with a trowel* – you're not *the be all and end all*, you know – huh, well, it makes my *hair stand on end*, there's *neither rhyme not reason* to it. So, *more fool you*, and *good riddance*, I say.'

The list is long, rich and surprising. There are so many household words in the queen's English that are quotes from Shakespeare – or I should say, *household words* in *the queen's English*. But it's high time I stopped, you can have too much of a good thing (*high time, too much of a good thing* – OK I'll stop).

Shakespeare gave the English language not just 130-odd vivid idiosyncratic everyday phrases, but also, where he couldn't find suitable words, he invented them. Around 1,700 in total that we today utter with never a second thought. *Amazement, bedroom, drugged, eyeball, fashionable, gossip, hobnob, impartial, jaded, luggage, marketable, negotiate, outbreak, puking, remorseless, scuffle, torture, undress, varied, worthless, zany*, are all new words that he gave us. Some were simply old words with a new grammatical form: Shakespeare made *drugged* from drug, for instance. Others may seem inconsequential to us today, but without the Bard's invention we might still be calling the place where we sleep a bedchamber rather than a *bedroom*. Others of his neologisms are earthier, more expressive than what was available before. It's more delightful to *hobnob* with neighbours rather than fraternise or socialise with them. And those of us who have had to lug our *luggage* through an airport, rather than just carrying our bags, should be grateful to Shakespeare for pinpointing the laborious effort involved.

***

But Shakespeare gives us even more than the most sublime literature in the English language, and an enrichment to the daily way we've all spoken ever since. He also provides a guide to the progress of English identity in the late sixteenth and early seventeenth centuries. His plays are full of references to what it's like to be English in Elizabethan England. Englishness now is a well-defined concept, in a way that it had not been in previous centuries. In Shakespeare's plays, we hear the country – the land and its people – glorified almost to the heights of heaven. Take John of Gaunt's words in *Richard II*. Though Shakespeare's play is about events two centuries before he was writing, the sentiments are very much those of 1595:

> This royal throne of kings, this sceptred isle,
> This earth of Majesty, this seat of Mars,
> This other Eden, demi-paradise;
> This fortress built by Nature for herself,
> Against infection and the hand of war,
> This happy breed of men, this little world,
> This precious stone set in the silver sea,
> Which serves it in the office of a wall,
> Or as a moat defensive to a house,
> Against the envy of less happier lands;
> This blessed plot, this earth, this realm, this England.

But Shakespeare sees his role as much more than that of national cheerleader. He tells us too about what people saw as the oddities of the English back in the late sixteenth and early seventeenth centuries. These oddities are not necessarily ones we see in ourselves today. But what's significant is the very existence of such widely-recognised traits in the character of the English at that time. Shakespeare, as you'd expect, paints colourful pictures.

The English are argumentative. In *The Merry Wives of Windsor*, Master Slender explains how he loves bear-baiting, and would 'as soon quarrel at it as any man in England'.

Their nature is to be curious but uncharitable. 'Every holiday fool in England,' we learn from Trinculo in *The Tempest*, 'would give a piece of silver to see a strange fish, though no one will give a doit [a small coin] to relieve a lame beggar.'

They drink too much. Iago in *Othello* says the English are 'most potent in potting [swigging pots of ale]; your Dane, your German, and your swag-bellied Hollander are nothing to your English.'

They're gluttonous and aggressive.'They will eat like wolves and fight like devils,' according to the Constable of France in *Henry V*.

They're eccentric. Hamlet, according to the gravedigger, is mad, and will go to England to 'recover his wits; or, if he do not, 'tis no great matter there.' In other words, the English are all as crazy as he is, so no one will notice.

English soldiers are young tearaways, and all the better for being so. In *King John*, they're 'Rash, inconsiderate, fiery ... with ladies' faces and fierce dragons spleens ...' but are still '... dauntless spirits'

The English are modest, or pretend to be. Henry V again:

I thought upon one pair of English legs
Did march three Frenchmen.Yet, forgive me, God,
That I do brag thus! This your air of France
Hath blown that vice in me.

And – does this sound familiar? – the English can't be bothered to learn anyone else's language. 'An English nobleman,' according to the Lady of Belmont in *The Merchant of Venice*, 'can speak no language but his own.' And when Shakespeare finds one who can, in *Henry VI, Part 2*, he's condemned because he 'can speak French and therefore ... is a traitor'.

It's not these characteristics themselves that matter for our history of English identity. It's the very fact that he says these things at all, and – we may assume – gets the groundlings, the ordinary English folk standing before the stage at the Globe Theatre, laughing and cheering at them. Englishness is now real in Elizabethan England. English people now recognise themselves as different, proud, odd sometimes, and often superior to other nations.

***

So, where does this new self-consciousness and this new self-confidence of the English in the age of Shakespeare come from?

Three great conflicts, against powerful foreign powers, the French, the Pope and the Spanish, over the previous 250 years, had forced the English to define themselves as different from their enemies. And success in these conflicts had furthermore left the English feeling they possessed some special God-given qualities.

The Hundred Years War between England and France, which had started back at a time when Robert de Thorpe was still showing off his paintings at Longthorpe Tower, had year by year, battle by battle, driven out any remains of Frenchness harboured at court or by the baronial classes who traced their ancestry back to the Normans. And although, inevitably in such a long conflict, fortunes flowed back and forth between the two sides, great English victories over the French like those at Agincourt and Crécy were turned into heroic stories, oft-repeated to inspire a new generation of English soldiers, until military prowess and modest bravery became part of what the English thought they were.

The second great conflict that reinforced Englishness was Henry VIII's declaration of independence from the Roman church, which we investigated at our stop in Oxford. As we saw, that had further strengthened England's sense of independence from foreign interference.

Then under Elizabeth I, another foreign enemy was seen off. In 1588, a fleet of 130 Spanish galleons set sail from La Coruña in Spain. The plan was that it would escort an army from Flanders to invade England. The aim: to overthrow Queen Elizabeth, stamp out Protestantism and restore England to the Catholic Church in Rome. Elizabeth herself addressed her troops at Tilbury Docks. Her words tell us much about the woman herself, and too, how the spirit of Agincourt lived on: 'I know I have the body of a weak and feeble woman,' she told the men, 'but I have the heart and stomach of a king – and of a King of England too, and think foul scorn that Parma or Spain, or any prince of Europe, should dare to invade the borders of my realm.'

The Spanish ships sailed up the Channel until they were anchored off Calais. At that point, Sir Francis Drake, commander of the English fleet, launched his attack. He ordered his men to set fire to a number of wooden vessels and send them drifting in among the enemy. The Spanish ships scattered, and many were damaged in the battle that followed. It was a catastrophe for the Spanish. The remains of their fleet fled, forced by Drake to take a long route around the north of the British Isles. The English commander launched hit-and-run attacks on them along the east coast.

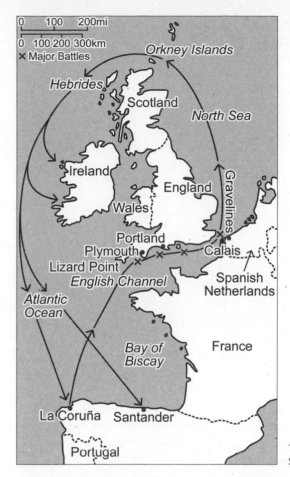

The route of the Spanish Armada.

By the time they reached the seas off the west coast of Ireland, on-board supplies were running out, and many of the ships, battered and holed in the fighting, were barely seaworthy. But worse was to come. A series of violent storms blew up and smashed many of the Spanish vessels on the rocks, taking their crews and fighters with them to oblivion. The survivors struggled on, and as they limped into their home ports, the true extent of the losses became clear. Only sixty-seven out of the original 130 ships made it back to Spain. More than 5,000 Spanish seamen and soldiers had died, drowned, starved to death or been slaughtered in battle.

For Elizabeth's England, the defeat of the Spanish Armada meant the survival of English Protestantism. It meant freedom from the threat of foreign oppression. And it meant that England, now ruling the waves, could expand and colonise new worlds. The Spanish had been trounced by an English navy led by an English hero with the job finished off by God himself blowing the Spaniards to a watery grave. For Elizabethans, the Almighty was clearly on the side of the English. Elizabeth herself became Gloriana, a glorious woman. And she promoted this image by commissioning portraits of herself as pure and powerful. Her reign was a time of optimism. Art, music and literature flourished; much of it, like the plays of Shakespeare, extolled the virtues of the English. And, as ever in the history of human nature, it takes self-confidence to be able to laugh at yourself. So one minute Shakespeare is raising our nationalist spirits with talk of *'This royal throne of kings, this sceptred isle'*, and the next he's winking at us as he makes the English out to be binge drinkers and slightly nuts.

Shakespeare, more than any other individual, helped shape English identity. His genius, now admired the world over, has generated English pride. He contributed to the richness of the language in a way that no one else had done before or would do after, and he not only reflected the new-found national self-consciousness and self-confidence of the Elizabethan age but he strengthened those feelings through the popularity of his work. His patriotism may today sound over-the-top and jingoistic, and we may not always now see ourselves as quite so ungenerous and quarrelsome as he sometimes did. Nevertheless, Shakespeare's words, in the mouths of kings or of bear-baiting fans, still have the power to stir English hearts or make us chuckle at ourselves 400 years later.

***

Though Shakespeare was still writing until his death, thirteen years after the end of Elizabeth's reign in 1603, the glory of England associated with her rule and given voice in his work would not last much longer. The Elizabethan Age would turn out to be no more than a relatively peaceful interlude in a prolonged violent drama.

The theme of the new century was announced in 1605 when one Guido Fawkes was arrested in a cellar beneath the Houses of Parliament. With him were thirty-six barrels of gunpowder. His plan had been to explode them during the state opening of Parliament, so assassinating Elizabeth's successor, James I. Fawkes and his fellow conspirators were Catholics who had soon discovered that there would be no tolerance of their religion under the new king. The plotters were captured, tried and convicted. Fawkes was tortured. Each man was tied to a wooden frame, and dragged through the crowded streets of London. They were then led up the scaffold, and each wearing only a shirt, was hanged, but then quickly cut down. Still conscious, they were castrated and disembowelled, and their bodies were cut into four pieces. Fawkes managed to struggle forward and jump from the platform with a violent drop that broke his neck, so avoiding the agonising death he'd witnessed his friends suffer.

The Gunpowder Plot and its suppression was a taste of what would follow over the next sixty years. The old divisions between Catholics and Protestants would soon blaze up again and play a key part in a ferocious civil war and an unchecked dictatorship. In the end, these fearful times would – in a strange way – produce some of the most attractive characteristics in the English. But before that, England was going to have to suffer the worst of times.

That's what we're going to look at now. So the next stage of our journey will be a rough ride. We're going to witness mass slaughter, divided families and the suppression of the rule of law. But at least we can get a good cup of tea. So it's on to Stow-on-the-Wold.

10

Stow-on-the-Wold, Gloucestershire

....

Massacre in Middle England

....

Truly England and the Church of God hath had a great favour from the Lord, in this great victory given us.

Oliver Cromwell (1599–1688)

There's a strange thing about English place names. They often fit the character of their towns. Not all of them, but enough to suggest a pattern. I'm not thinking of the obviously descriptive ones, like Ironbridge in Shropshire or Southend-on-Sea in Essex. I had in mind, for instance, Stoke-on-Trent. If you'd never been to Stoke, you'd guess it might have smoking furnaces, or at least used to. Or take Wigan, the abrupt, no-nonsense name you'd choose for a mill town, probably with some tough working-class lads who play rugby league or an uncompromising style of football. And then there's the sound of 'Surbiton': it has to be a very suburban Surrey suburb. So it's not surprising that Stow-on-the-Wold, like its neighbour, Chipping Campden, turns out to merit the adjectives 'quaint', 'historic', 'genteel.' And there's something else about Stow-on-the-Wold, and other multi-worded little towns in the Cotswolds: they're so … so … there's no other word for it … English.

I'm standing in Stow-on-the-Wold's huge market square. A jumble of ancient stone buildings surrounds me, their walls all shades of gritty mustard, sometimes weathered to white, sometimes grooved and pitted with age. No two roofs are the same height, none slant the same way. Window frames here defy right angles. I'm looking at one opposite that's got a 20-degree list. Sixteenth-century cottage architecture, topped by sagging tiles, nestles next to a neighbour whose eighteenth-century facade of carved pillars rise up four storeys to twirling capitals and a flat roof. The shops that now inhabit these ancient structures sell everything from porcelain ducks, to postcards of old Stow, to home-made ice cream and jars of sweets like the ones you knew as a child.

To my left, presiding over the town like a pompous Victorian parson, stands the glowering edifice of St Edwards Hall in all its neo-Gothic glory. It houses the town's library and a collection of seventeenth-century paintings, and is where Stow's venerable Civic Society holds its meetings. To my right, there's a set of stocks in the middle of a grassy triangle. All the scene seems to lack is children skipping around a maypole, or a troop of morris dancers, waving white hankies, with bells on their toes. Behind the green there's an antique shop, an art gallery and the Old Stocks Inn. Near it is the White Hart. Further along, the King's Arms, then the Talbot, and opposite me, the Queen's Head.

And there are lots of examples of another very English institution here: teashops. Whole books have been written on the history of tea, how it ousted coffee as the favourite drink of the English in the seventeenth century across all classes, while at the same time dividing English society according to the vessel it was drunk from, china cups held with a raised little finger, or mugs fixed in a builder's firm grip. In Lucy's Tearoom, close to the churchyard, a porcelain pot of it is served with cucumber sandwiches, a scone or two or a slice of lemon-drizzle cake. Lucy's is one of a dozen such emporia in Stow where you can get – in a phrase whose subtle inferences about the nature of Englishness are untranslatable to any other language – a 'nice cuppa'.

A minibus pulls up next to me, and a family – parents and three children – get out. I hear American accents. The teenage daughter takes in the whole town with a sweeping glance, and exclaims, 'Oh my gosh, look, it's so cute!'

Stow attracts around 140,000 tourists a year, from all around the country and from overseas – Japan, Australia, France, Germany and Canada as well as the USA. The town's population is a little under 3,000. Forty per cent of its residents are folk from outside the area who have chosen to move to this haven of contentment in their retirement.

So what is it about Stow-on-the-Wold that makes us see it as being so quintessentially English? Its buildings, no two the same, mostly historic, but in a modest, cottage-sized way, suggest that Stow is a survivor from some Golden Age. A non-existent era when life was simpler, when we weren't driven into conformity, when we were moderate in our opinions and habits, a time when tradition not change ruled the day. We see places like Stow-on-the-Wold as the much-loved remnants of a merry old England, a country, in the words of the former Prime Minister, John Major, of '... county grounds, warm beer ... dog lovers ... and old maids bicycling to Holy Communion through the morning mist.' The square in this ancient Cotswold town tells of a middle ground, a quiet satisfaction with things as they are, somewhere where violent extremism has no place. If you're a foreign visitor to England you'll want to experience the essence of Englishness, so Stow becomes a must on the tourist trail between Windsor and Stratford-upon-Avon.

The delightful irony about Stow is that there have been times in its past when the very opposite of these moderate values dominated life here, when violence and fanaticism were rife in this now peaceful little town. And here's a further irony. Those violent events go a long way to explaining how the values of stability, moderation and compromise became such central threads in the fabric of English identity. There are a couple of clues to that more brutal side of Stow's story to be seen here in the square today.

A small crowd is gathering outside St Edward's Hall. At their centre are two chaps armed and ready to do battle. They're dressed as infantrymen from the time of the English Civil War. I edge forward to listen.

One of them steps forward and introduces himself as Roger. Then standing to attention, he explains he's dressed as a seventeenth-century pikeman – metal helmet, breastplate, and he taps two short steel aprons flapping over his thighs and the vulnerable bit in between. 'They're called tassets,' he tells us. 'They were very uncomfortable, so the pikemen often threw them away before the fighting started.' His companion-in-arms, Brian, peers at the crowd from beneath the wide brim of a brown hat flopping over his shoulder-length hair and thick grey beard. He's holding a musket, its wooden stock resting on the ground.

Roger drops his pike from upright. 'This one's shorter than they would have been in the seventeenth century,' he explains. 'Originally, they would have been eighteen feet long …' – and he points the weapon up towards a high window on the side of the Hall – '… up to about there.' This meets with the approval of the spectators, who give a collective 'Hmm.' He shows us how he would have crouched with his pike pointing forwards, and explains that, with hundreds of other pikemen doing the same, the effect would have been like the side of a gigantic, fearsome porcupine. The enemy would line up the same way, so the two sets of opposing pikes would slowly approach each other till their sharpened steel blades stopped an inch or so from the enemy noses. 'Then it was like a game of chicken,' he says, 'waiting to see who'd crack first. And if you did manage to skewer your opponent,' he continues, 'there was no room to pull your pike free and you'd be hemmed in by all the others around you, so you'd be trapped. And the battle just turned into a barroom brawl!'

Now it's Brian's turn. He's going to show us how you loaded and fired a musket. He pours gunpowder down the muzzle, and forces it home with a metal ramrod. A lead ball goes in on top of that, then a piece of wadding follows to save the embarrassment of the ball rolling back out before you'd had chance to fire it. 'Next,' he says, 'you'd light a taper on the top of the weapon ready for when you pulled the trigger. I'm not going to fire it today.'

'Oh, go on!' shouts a voice from the back.

'Sorry,' says Brian with a shrug, 'health and safety. Anyway, the musket wasn't a very effective weapon. For a start, you couldn't get an accurate sighting, so it was a matter of luck if you hit your target. And there was another problem. Sometimes, it didn't work properly and the gunpowder would flare up without firing the ball. That's where we get the phrase "a flash in the pan", when there's a lot of commotion but no result. If you were really unlucky, the whole shebang could explode in your face.'

Brian raises the musket to his shoulder and aims it over the heads of the crowd somewhere towards the old police station. Then he lowers it again and goes on, 'It took about thirty seconds to load it and get it ready to fire one shot, maybe twenty seconds if you were very good at it. But the musketeer often found himself overrun by the enemy before he could finish loading.' The musketeer then had a choice. He could either turn the musket around and use it as a club. Or he could try to balance it in one hand, while he drew his sword. Brian pulls his own sword out of its metre-long scabbard and points its tip up towards the rooftop of St Edwards Hall. 'But as Roger told you, there was no room to swing it, so, you see the metal strips round the handle that protect my fist? You had to use that as a knuckle-duster, and try to hit your man in the face.' And he gives a playful punch in the direction of Brian's chin. We all laugh, nod our approval, and, as Roger and Brian take a bow, we break into restrained clapping.

Down at the other end of the Square, there's a stone cross on top of a pillar in the middle of the road. At its base, a small brass plaque reads:

THE ENGLISH CIVIL WAR
BATTLE OF STOW 21ST MARCH 1646.
NEAR THIS CROSS SIR JACOB ASTLEY
SURRENDERED TO PARLIAMENTARY FORCES
FOLLOWING DEFEAT AT THE BATTLE OF STOW.
SOME 200 ROYALISTS WERE SLAUGHTERED IN
THE SQUARE
AND 1500 IMPRISONED IN THE CHURCH
OVERNIGHT.

THIS WAS THE FINAL BATTLE
OF THE FIRST CIVIL WAR LEADING TO THE END
OF THE ROYALIST OCCUPATION OF OXFORD.
- STOW AND DISTRICT CIVIC SOCIETY

***

The Battle of Stow was decisive. Three years later King Charles I was beheaded, and soon England was a military dictatorship under Oliver Cromwell. So how did these cataclysmic events produce an English nation renowned for its peaceful moderation?

These days, we often think of the Civil War as a conflict between Cavaliers and Roundheads, with Puritans and Parliamentarians on one side, papists and monarchists on the other. But, as often in history, popular notions of what happened in our past are wide of the mark.

'Cavalier' and 'Roundhead' were terms of abuse that each side slung at the other. 'Cavalier', a supporter of the king, came from *caballero*, the Spanish word for an upper-class horseman – in other words, a hated domineering foreigner. Royalists hit back, slandering the Parliamentarians as 'Roundheads', best translated as 'skinheads' in our day, after the shaven-headed apprentices of London, who were renowned street troublemakers. The words tell us a lot about the colourful language of the two sides, but not much about who was a typical Roundhead and who a typical Cavalier. In fact, there was no 'typical'. Civil War loyalties didn't slice the country neatly down the middle into the two opposing camps. Most ordinary folk across England had little interest in what was at stake. Every town and village was divided, often because of nothing more principled than a dislike of the local lord, or because some quarrel with a neighbour had bubbled to the surface.

When it came to the political and religious issues underlying the conflict, the overwhelming majority of the population were in the middle. That made them monarchists, for no other reason than that England was a monarchy, and it did not necessarily mean supporting the current king, Charles I. The idea that there wouldn't be a king or a queen at their head was unthinkable to most people at this time.

As for religion, almost all, again, were middle-of-the-road Church of England rather than supporters of the fundamentalists on either side. Those extremists were the offspring of the religious divisions of a century earlier that we saw on our visit to Oxford. On one side, the most zealous of Protestants were Calvinists, who believed in predestination and that God chooses an 'elect' few for salvation. Everyone else, according to the Calvinists, was doomed to the fires of hell for eternity. These 'godly' Puritans dressed in black or grey, their churches were dull and gloomy, they prayed with sighs and groans, and wanted to eradicate what they regarded as superstition in those who held different beliefs. At the other end of the spectrum was a kind of neo-Catholic 'High Church', whose followers believed in free will, colourful ceremony and highly decorated churches, just the sort of 'superstition' the Calvinists wanted to wipe out. The majority of the population steered clear of both extremes, whether Puritan 'ranting', or High Church 'popery'.

Many of the men who armed themselves with the sort of weaponry Brian and Roger were showing off and joined one side or the other did so because they were forced to by their local lord – sometimes at gunpoint. Some were convicted criminals pushed into one of the armies by a parish constable who wanted to see the back of them. The motives of others are summed up in the words of one soldier who made it clear he didn't care about either side's cause. 'I fight for your half-crowns,' he said, 'and your handsome women.'

So how did this muddle of beliefs and indifference provoke a civil war?

The heart of the conflict had much to do with the way the king behaved. Charles I was clumsy and inept. He claimed that he – and all monarchs – had a divine right to rule, that he was responsible to God for his actions not man. He was therefore determined to rule without the interference of Parliament, and that's what he did for eleven years. He permitted no parliament to assemble for the whole of this time.

But, whatever the opinions – or lack of them – among the population of England at large, the chief factor that drove the leaders of the opposing camps to choose one side or the other was religion. When Charles appointed as Archbishop of Canterbury William

Laud, an exponent of the High Church wing, the Puritans' opposition to the king hardened. They feared that Laud and Charles, urged on by Charles's wife, the Catholic Queen Henrietta-Maria, were conspiring to turn the country back into a Catholic nation.

In 1637, the king needed to raise taxes, and he was forced to summon a parliament to Westminster. And when the MPs met, it was the Puritans who made the running. The angry ranting of these godly men, in turn, struck fear into some of the moderates who had previously opposed the king. They now moved to support him. And so England's governing elite was split down the middle.

The spark that lit the fires of war was struck when Queen Henrietta-Maria pointed to the king's opponents in Parliament, and said to her husband, 'Go you coward, and pull those rogues out by the ears.' And go he did. On 4 January 1642, he marched into the Palace of Westminster with around 200 armed courtiers to arrest one peer and five members of the House of Commons. But it was a botched job. The six men escaped, and Parliament pronounced the king a 'public enemy to the Commonwealth.' It was, in effect, a declaration of war.

***

During the early stages of the Civil War, the Royalists dominated the fighting. But we shouldn't imagine huge armies battling for win-or-lose strategic objectives. By 1644, no fewer than eight small armies were fighting in different regions of the country. And although some famous encounters have stuck in the popular memory, Edgehill, Marston Moor, Naseby, in fact most of the engagements were either sieges of country houses or skirmishes involving a few hundred or even a score or so men. Soon neither side could claim real mastery of the other.

The man who changed that was Oliver Cromwell. Cromwell, born the younger son of a prosperous Cambridgeshire landowning family, had secured his own wealth by acquiring cathedral properties at knock-down prices. In his 30s he had suffered bouts of depression. Then he found God. 'He it is,' wrote Cromwell, 'who enlighteneth our blackness, our darkness.' And he became a radicalised, 'born-again' Puritan. So, in 1640, when he arrived at

Westminster as the newly elected MP for Cambridge, he aligned himself with the Parliamentarians opposing the king's attempt to raise taxes. On the outbreak of war, he went back to his home county and recruited a cavalry troop from among his fellow land-owners. Cromwell soon became a respected commander.

Three years later, his chance came. Parliament appointed him to a role that would allow him to bring together his two new-found passions: religion and war. He moulded a Parliamentarian fighting force, which he knocked into shape with brutal discipline based on Puritan ethics. He stamped out such evils as drunkenness and fornication with terrifying punishments. Blasphemers, for instance, had their tongues pierced with a hot poker. The result was the New Model Army, described as 'a rod of iron in Christ's hands to dash his enemies to pieces'.

The war on the Parliamentarian side by this stage had a whiff of English patriotism about it. Charles, with a French, Catholic-practising wife, was believed to be moving the country's religion back to Rome, away from its English roots. And as the king came to rely more and more on Welsh and Cornish troops – Cornwall had never fully accepted it was part of England and saw itself as Celtic – Parliament sought to rally English yeoman stock by claiming that the king was 'un-English.' At the same time, Cromwell ejected from his New Model Army any 'strangers' – that is, foreigners.

At the Battle of Naseby in Northamptonshire, 13,500 troops of the New Model Army, commanded by Sir Thomas Fairfax and Cromwell, routed 9,000 Royalists, led by the king himself. So in early 1646, Charles retreated to Oxford. His subsequent attempt to re-form his forces, in order to regain the upper hand, failed. That happened right here at Stow-on-the-Wold.

Charles needed to hold his army together. No reinforcements were coming from France, Scotland or Ireland, and Royalist morale was low. But the king held one trump card. His commander here in the West Country was the most experienced serving soldier in the land, Sir Jacob Astley. Astley was still going strong at 66 – a remarkable age at a time when the average citizen was dead before 40. As well as being a gnarled old fighter, he was also something of a wit, and if TV and radio reporters had been around in the mid-seventeenth century, he would have been in demand for interviews. Once, during battle, an enemy arrow suddenly hit the ground between his legs, an uncomfortable occurrence for any gentleman. He gave it a scornful look and declared, 'Hah, rogue, you missed your aim!' He also composed the famous Soldiers' Prayer, which he recited to his troops before the Battle of Edgehill in 1642: 'Lord thou knowest I'll be busy this day, so if I forget thee, forgettest thou not me.'

The king ordered Astley to gather his forces and march to Chipping Norton – 10 miles east of Stow – where he would join up with the king. But the enemy knew of the plan. Parliament's general, Sir William Brereton, had managed to smuggle a spy into Astley's Royalist ranks. Astley's route would take him close to Stow. He had between 2,000 and 3,000 men under his command, and they were harassed for much of the way by the Parliamentary troops. There was a bit of skirmishing here, the odd outbreak of shooting there. But it didn't come to an all-out winner-takes-all fight till the early hours of 21 March. Then, the two armies formed up, facing each other in the cold before dawn, a thin light from the moon and a few blazing torches on each side the only illumination.

Sir Jacob Astley, the defeated commander of the royalist troops at the Battle of Stow, 1646. (By kind permission of the trustees of St Edward's Hall, Stow-on-the-Wold)

The exact site of the battle that followed is a mystery. For years it was believed to have been on a ridge-top next to the hamlet of Donnington, 2 miles north of Stow. But military historians then suggested the main fighting took place closer to the town, an idea that was itself knocked down when the Battlefields Trust organised a survey of that area in 2015, and no musket balls or other leftovers of war were found there. What we can be sure of is that the battle happened close enough to Stow that many hundreds of men, weighed down by armour, encumbered with weapons, and running uphill, could reach there before being caught.

At around 4.45 a.m., as the first glimmers of light came over the hills to the east, Brereton gave the order. Word spread down the line and the Parliamentary troops attacked the Royalist ranks. The charge by his cavalry on the left met fierce resistance from the Royalists. The Parliamentarian commander there and thirty-one of his comrades were brought down as their horses were shot from under them or they themselves were hit. The rest of the Parliamentary horsemen pulled back to regroup. Meanwhile, the Parliamentary infantry had mounted its own assault against the centre of Astley's Royalist ranks. At first they made little headway. But then in a second charge, the superior numbers of cavalry on Parliament's side forced the Royalist horsemen to turn tail and flee. And it was at this point that Astley's infantrymen realised the tide had turned, and they made their dash in the early morning gloom towards the town of Stow. The men, some wounded, all knowing they could now face death, stumbled uphill, pausing at times to defend themselves against the slashing swords of Parliamentary cavalrymen harassing them, as they fled towards Stow's market square.

To get some impression of the sight that met them, we have to erase from our view the Victorian St Edward's Hall which stands in the centre of the square, as well as the buildings behind it, which were not here in 1646. The Square is in fact a long, almost triangular shape, 170 yards long by 40 wide at its centre. Its narrower north end is where the routed fighters were now arriving. Whether the Royalist foot soldiers had enough discipline to form up for an organised defence here, we don't know. But it mattered little. Within minutes, the Parliamentary horses were pounding up

Saxons and Normans clash at the annual Battle of Hastings re-enactment. (Antonio Borrillo)

St Mary's, Deerhurst, Gloucestershire. Today a B&B is tacked onto the church. It was part of the original Saxon priory. The garden, where the tent and other children's playthings are now, formed the cloister.

A highly decorated page from the Lindisfarne Gospels, created in the eighth century. The tiny scribbles above the Latin words are the Old English translations added 200 years later.

The Trip to Jerusalem pub in Nottingham. It was carved out of the sandstone cliff soon after the Norman Conquest to serve as a brewery for the castle garrison on the rock above.

Wat Tyler, leader of the Peasants' Revolt in 1381, about to be killed by Sir William Walworth, Lord Mayor of London, with the young Richard II looking on. The image is from the following century.

The University Church of St Mary the Virgin, Oxford, where the three Protestant martyrs Cranmer, Latimer and Ridley were put on trial in 1556. The papal judge sat on top of a tall intimidating platform erected in front of the altar.

Elizabeth I, from the school of Nicholas Hilliard. Following the defeat of the Spanish Armada in 1588, she became 'Gloriana', a cult figure. The artist has reflected this in her fantastical dress and the emblem of an English lion.

In 2016, on the 400th anniversary of Shakespeare's death, Ten thousand Bard masks were handed out during the processions. Most spectators didn't know what to do with them.

Stow-on-the-Wold, Gloucestershire. The cross near where the 66-year-old Royalist commander Sir Jacob Astley sat on a drum to surrender, following the Civil War battle here in 1646. Beyond is the King's Arms, where Charles I had stayed the year before.

The neoclassical facade of Newby Hall as remodelled by William Weddell in the mid-eighteenth century. (By kind permission of ©the owners of Newby Hall)

The stern of HMS *Victory*, where Nelson had his quarters, looks like a fairytale mansion compared with the rest of the fighting ship.

Inside Nelson's quarters, the atmosphere of a gentleman's home is created with polished oak furniture and imitation marble flooring. The cannon may look out of place. But it was not. When the enemy was sighted, the gun barrel was pointed through a window, and the Admiral's cabin became just another battle station.

The gundeck of HMS *Victory*. Here the crew of over 800 ordinary seamen ate, slept, shared eight 'heads' and, in the heat of battle, were deafened as they loaded, fired and reloaded the cannon.

Barrow Hill Roundhouse engine shed in Derbyshire. The age of the steam railway – driving force of the Industrial Revolution and of massive social change in England – still lives on here. (By kind permission of ©Fred Kerr)

The yard once shared by eleven families in the back-to-back slums of nineteenth-century Birmingham. (By kind permission of ©Kitten Von Mew)

Bamburgh Castle, rebuilt from a ruin by the industrialist and engineer William Armstrong in the 1890s. (©xlibber/Flickr)

St Pancras Station, London: one of the finest examples of Victorian neo-Gothic architecture. (Colin/Wikimedia Commons/CC BY-SA 3.0)

Liverpool's Albert Dock became the trading heart of the Empire when it opened in 1846. But it was built for sailing ships and became derelict in the twentieth century. It was restored and reopened in 1988, mixing past glory with gift shops and fast food.

On Second World War Day at Duxford Air Show, Battle of Britain pilots waiting to be 'scrambled' into action. The real pilots, back in 1940, were much younger than these re-enactors. Many were only 19 or 20.

The White Cliffs of Dover, timeless symbols of England's impregnability. In times of turmoil they have offered a promise that peace and normality will return.

the muddy road in large numbers. They soon overcame whatever opposition the Royalists could manage, and the thunder of hooves was mixed with cries of agony.

The peaceful square we see today was the scene of a gladiatorial slaughter. By around seven in the morning, some 200 Royalist soldiers had been massacred. A legend grew – still repeated in Stow today – that there was so much blood on the ground that it flowed like a stream down Digbeth Street at the far end of the square till it made a ruby red pond at the bottom deep enough for ducks to swim on. Another 1,500 or so common soldiers were captured, as well as sixty officers. They were herded away like the sheep of olden times. They were locked up in St Edward's Church, a place of sanctuary, now a wartime prison.

Among those taken was the Royalist commander Sir Jacob Astley himself. Later in the day, Astley made a formal surrender to Brereton. The ceremony took place by the market cross, where we saw the local Civic Society's plaque. At the age of 66, without sleep the previous night and following a battle which he would know spelt the end of the Royalist cause, he must have been exhausted to the point of near collapse. A drum was provided for him to sit on. The ground around him would not have been solid road, as it is today, but compacted earth, and it's not hard to imagine that the blood of his fallen comrades still stained it. To his left, he could see the church where those of his comrades who had survived, many wounded, were held in less comfortable conditions than he. And just five steps to his right stood an inn, the King's Arms, where his leader Charles I had stayed during another campaign a year earlier.

His surrender complete, Astley turned to the victorious Parliamentary commander and his adjutants, and made one of his famous sound-bite observations, 'Well, boys, you've done your work,' he said. 'Now you can play … unless you fall out among yourselves.' He could see that already his captors were arguing about how they'd share the spoils of victory. But Astley had not foreseen the ambition of one man, who would rise above the squabbles: Cromwell. He would soon accrue to himself enough power to change the face of England.

After a brief upsurge of further resistance among Charles's supporters, Cromwell and the army commanders decided enough was enough. The king was taken prisoner, and Cromwell marched on London. He stripped out of Parliament those MPs who had backed the monarch. The Civil War was at end. It had led to proportionately more people being killed or injured than any other conflict England would ever suffer. It's estimated that 86,000 soldiers were shot, stabbed or beaten to death in battle. Another 129,000, mainly civilians, died from starvation, gangrene, dysentery or other diseases directly attributable to the war's upheavals. More babies and infants died, as a percentage of the population, than at any other time in our history. And again, relative to the 4 to 5 million people in England at the time, total English casualties were higher even than during the First World War.

***

The trial and execution of King Charles I followed in 1649. And so England became a republic. The monarchy and the House of Lords were abolished. What was left of Parliament – a thinned down House of Commons called 'the Rump' – was smashed further by Cromwell. With a military escort at his side, he stood up in his role as an MP and condemned his fellow members: 'whoremasters and drunkards, corrupt and unjust men and scandalous to the profession of the gospel. I will put an end to your prating.' He ordered his men to break up the assembly. Then, pointing to the man regarded as the untouchable leading representative of the Commons, the Speaker, Cromwell said, 'Fetch him down,' and added, indicating the mace, symbol of democratic authority, 'take away these baubles.'

In December 1653, senior army officers drafted a new constitution and made Cromwell, now aged 54, Lord Protector. 'Government,' said Cromwell, 'is for the people's good, not what pleases them.' The new republic, as many around the world would after it, had turned itself into a dictatorship. Opponents were imprisoned without trial, judges were purged, rebels were sent into slavery. Cromwell declared he was obeying God's will. Intolerance of the 'ungodly' was accompanied by legalised brutality. A man named John Naylor, whose crime was to ride into Bristol on a donkey, re-enacting Christ's journey into Jerusalem, was branded,

Statue of Oliver
Cromwell, erected
outside the Palace of
Westminster in 1899.
The Victorians saw him
as a hero of English
democracy fighting
against an autocratic
monarch. Historians
today point out that he
suppressed Parliament
so he himself could
be an autocratic ruler.
(Beata May)

pilloried, bored through the tongue, flogged twice and then sent
to prison for the rest of his foreshortened life.

The Protectorate was Cromwell, and Cromwell, with his
uncompromising ethics, was the Protectorate. When he died suddenly in 1658, his son became a feeble replacement. Within two
years, the monarchy was restored.

On the 25 May 1660, an English ship, formerly the *Naseby*,
renamed the *Royal Charles*, brought a new king, Charles II, from
exile. On board was the diarist Samuel Pepys, who observed, as
they approached Dover, that the king had with him his pet dog,
which 'shit in the boat and made us laugh and me think that a
king and all that belong to him are but just as others are'. And as
Charles II set foot on English soil, 'the shouting and joy expressed
by all', Pepys added, was 'past imagination.'

***

The suffering that English people had endured changed their outlook forever. War had split the nation, killed hundreds of thousands

and left many more bereaved and without a breadwinner. Eleven years of a republican dictatorship had imposed the most uncompromising religious zealotry and had snuffed out any semblance of democratically agreed law or appropriate punishment. In welcoming the demise of both evils, Pepys spoke for the majority in the country.

The reaction to these oppressive events reached a peaceful, constitutional climax in 1689. It was a very English coup. The Dutch prince William of Orange had landed on the shore of Devon with his wife Mary. Parliament offered them the throne, to replace the Catholic James II. The old king fled, and William was crowned. It had all been achieved without a shot being fired. It became known as the Glorious – or sometimes the Bloodless – Revolution.

Two parties had by now emerged in Parliament: the Whigs, moderate descendants of the Civil War Parliamentarians, and the Tories, with a distant line back to the old Royalists. The two sides did something that would have been unthinkable in Cromwell's day: they agreed. They declared England a Protestant country and so brought to an end 130 years of religious conflict. But they also did something even more powerful, something that was the foundation of the way we are governed today. They defined for the first time two great, interlocking principles: Monarchs would no longer have absolute power. And Parliament was now supreme.

From the Whigs we get the principle, founded in Magna Carta, that those who rule us must obey the law like the rest of us. From the Tories comes the principle that disagreeing with the government does not give us the right to take up arms in rebellion. We could argue that these two ideas are incompatible. But the English have made them work together for the past 325 years.

The result of the Glorious Revolution was a very English way of thinking and acting, not only in politics, but in much of everyday life in England, even today. In the words of the twenty-first-century historian Robert Tombs, the English have become a people who show 'suspicion of Utopias and zealots; trust in common sense and experience; respect for tradition; preference for gradual change; and the view that compromise is victory not betrayal'. These values have grown out of the bad days of the sixteenth and seventeenth century: brutal religious persecution, a ferocious civil war and a cruel dictatorship. The English said, 'Never again.' Instead they come to take tea in moderate, traditional, middle-of-the-road Stow-on-the-Wold.

***

In the century that followed the Glorious, Bloodless Revolution, the seeds of tolerance that had been sown in English society took root, grew and blossomed. Tolerance meant that arguments could be settled by rational debate rather than with pike, sword and musket. The Age of Reason was born. Grand, finely balanced buildings were constructed in the civilised style of the ancient Greeks. But tolerance of what others thought and did could also mean 'Anything goes'. Tolerance could sometimes drift into permissiveness, which showed itself in eighteenth-century England as drunkenness and sexual freedom. To investigate this new phase in the development of English identity, we're going to Yorkshire, to a magnificent house where – as soon as I arrive – I get into trouble.

11

Newby Hall, North Yorkshire

Rational, Rich and Rowdy

Reason is the great distinction of human nature.

Samuel Johnson (1709–84)

'May I ask why you're taking notes?' asks our guide Angela in a stern voice but running the question on without pause from her description of a brown and rose-coloured Georgian coffee pot.

'Oh, you know, it's just something I do,' I mumble, realising as I say it that I sound as convincing as a naughty child caught red-handed. The other half-dozen visitors in our group edge away, for fear of guilt by association.

She squares up to me and fixes me with a fiery glare. 'We get suspicious when people take notes,' she says. 'And you may imagine my concern, having already had to point out to you that photography is not permitted inside the house.' It's true, she has, and I look down at my shifty shoes. 'We've had several thefts here at Newby Hall,' she adds, 'and they knew exactly what they were looking for.'

'Oh no, no!' I blurt out, 'I can explain …'

But Angela is not to be interrupted. 'That fine Thomas Chippendale satinwood and marquetry coffee table cross-banded with amaranth and lemonwood, just there …' She opens her hand as though about to pat the vulnerable little wooden creature. 'We only got it back last year after it was stolen five years ago. They threw a brick through the window, grabbed the table and left without touching anything else. They steal to order, you know. Some of these collectors come in, looking perfectly respectable, and *make a note…*' she stresses the words, shooting her eyes at the paper pad in my left hand, '… of what they fancy, then they commission a thief to steal it for them.'

'Oh my goodness gracious, no!' I exclaim, rushing to frame the most innocent and unworldly denial I can. 'My gosh, that's awful, quite frightful. No, I'm just taking notes because I'm doing research. For a project. I'm going round the country, studying who the English think they are.' At this she raises one eyebrow in restrained disapproval. 'The English …' I persist, 'their identity … and history …' The words trail away.

She gives me a silent, noncommittal look which seems to last for several minutes, then says, with a formalised smile, 'Of course. But I'm sure you understand why we have to be so careful.'

'Absolutely,' I say stuffing the notebook and biro into my anorak pocket. 'There are some terrible people about these days.'

***

Newby Hall with its four-square Georgian windows, its fountain-dotted garden with half-mile-long walk between flower-dense borders, sits amid many verdant acres of parkland within a short horse ride of the North York Moors and the elegant towns of Ripon and Harrogate. Newby is one of England's finest – if undeservedly less-known – stately homes.

Stately homes. There's something very English about the phrase, with its suggestion of slow moving, cosy elegance. And stately homes themselves are peculiarly English, or at least our addiction to visiting them is. England has over 1,500 of them. I had raced from Newby Hall's car park to the ticket counter through a downpour, hoping to catch the three o'clock guided tour. Angela's small group had already gathered in the entrance hall and was collectively looking up at a gigantic painting, 10ft by 6ft, of goats, sheep and cows arranged like members of an Edwardian family posing for a photo. My fellow visitors, like the cattle, looked nonplussed by having to wait for me. Angela, in straight skirt, sensible shoes and faintly grey hair tied back, was explaining that she's worked here for seven years, part-time, Tuesdays and Fridays. Then she gives us a potted history of Newby.

The core of the house was the brainchild of its owner Sir Edward Blackett, who was the local MP in the great 1689 Glorious Revolution parliament. Blackett employed Sir Christopher Wren, who designed the place in his spare time from overseeing the construction of St Paul's Cathedral. Shortly afterwards, it was visited by one of the most extraordinary women of the period, Celia Fiennes. Miss Fiennes, who never married, spent twenty years on horseback riding the length and breadth of England. In the days when long-distance travel with all its risks and discomforts was undertaken only if necessary, the idea of travelling purely for pleasure was considered an unfathomable novelty, and for a woman to do it accompanied only by a single servant, was unthinkable. Not for Miss Fiennes, who recorded all her adventures in a diary. In 1697, she wrote that Newby 'is the finest house I saw in Yorkshire'. It was soon to become even finer.

By the mid-eighteenth century, the house and its estate passed to William Weddell who inherited them from his uncle. Weddell was the very model of a young English gentleman. He prided

Portrait of William Weddell (1775/76) by the Italian artist Pompeo Batoni, . Note how he poses with an open hand, as if inviting us to admire his fine taste in art.

himself on his exquisite taste, and he made dramatic changes to Newby. He employed Robert Adam and other of the great designers and architects of the day to enlarge the house in the fashionable neo-classical style, inspired by the arts of ancient Greece and Rome. Newby would become the magnificent showcase for his prized collection of ancient classical treasures. And it's Weddell's Newby that we're looking at today.

But as we soon discover, under Angela's protective guidance, Newby is home to even more than the glories of the ancient world. There are elaborately carved tables, chairs, commodes, desks, in mahogany and teak, gilt-framed mirrors, gleaming marble busts, Venetian glass vases, cherubs and urns in pale pitted limestone, china plates some scalloped, some lozenge-shaped, and there are giant gold-cased clocks topped by gold statuettes of winged victory, weighty chandeliers hanging from golden threads, minute gilded chains looping around tiny moulded shelves each just big enough to hold a miniature porcelain bowl adorned with intricate blue patterning. And there are paintings, not only of cows with courteous expressions but of castles, countesses as well as Greek gods and goddesses too, enough to fill a medium-sized warehouse with a dozen left over. And all of this within walls decorated with Robert Adam's pastel-shaded neoclassical designs.

If, from this description, you have in your mind's eye an image of treasures spilling, piled and cluttered like the contents of some heavenly junk-shop, you need to think again. Instead, picture all these glorious objects in neat, balanced and sometimes symmetrical arrangements. On occasions, they surround giant sofas begging you to sprawl on them, provided you were prepared to not to move an inch for fear of breaking, or even touching the delicate artefacts around you.

Newby is perfect. Every object looks to have been restored and maintained so it glows as it did on the day the craftsmen put the last loving touch to it. Nowhere is visible the tiniest smear, the thinnest hairline crack (my fingers don't even want to type the word), nor even the merest micro-grain of dust. It's almost hypnotic. I could imagine my brain is so enchanted by the beauteous sights being sent to it by my eyes that it's forgetting to control my body. I expect this is why I started to take notes when Angela drew our attention to the Georgian coffee pot. Well, it's a good excuse anyway. And I do notice, after the fourth or fifth room, a subtle shift in my appreciation of Newby and its many peerless objects. It's as though I've been served a meal consisting of dishes of sugar and honey and nothing else. After a while, you yearn for a knob of ripe stilton or a forkful of lamb jalafrezi, something spicy. So when Angela says, 'In there is the small Chamber Room, but we'll move on,' I get suspicious and dodge inside, followed to my surprise by the rest of our small group.

For 'Chamber Room', read 'Chamber Pot Room.' Cabinet after cabinet of them. But of course, Newby being Newby, they're not cheap, white 1940s models such as might have been found under your great-grandmother's bed. A neat engraved sign informs us: 'Many of the pots are extremely rare and they form a unique collection ranging from rough peasant ware of the sixteenth century to some of the finest examples of eighteenth- and nineteenth-century china.' Apart from the odd Japanese one, which by its delicate decoration and the fineness of its porcelain could be mistaken for the oversized accoutrement of a geisha's tea ceremony, most of them have one thing in common. Be they rough peasant ware or fine china, they have jokes inscribed on them. On some, it's a face painted inside, often of a man leering up at the most embarrassing parts of the user's anatomy, and some with the face of a maiden, distressed, as she's every right to be. One has a picture of Prime Minister Gladstone on the bottom. 'What's that one about?' I say to Angela, who's now taken up a reluctant position in the doorway.

'It was made for a high Tory,' she replies, 'so he could show his displeasure at the Liberal government.'

Several of the pots have got inscriptions round the rim. One says, 'Hand it over to me my dear. For a kiss I'll hand you this.' Visions of a lecherous butler and a blushing chambermaid flit through my mind. Another pot has a large, anatomically correct eye looking up at you, and nothing else. It's surreal and disturbing.

A second information sign tells us that they were collected 'from all over Europe and the Far East,' by Robert de Grey Vyner. This raises questions. Why did he go for potties instead of, say, stamps, or thimbles, or Titians or Tintorettos? Did he have a personality disorder? Maybe he was a copromaniac (the sort of obsession that respectable maniacs turn their noses up at). You could imagine him announcing to his wife one evening after dinner, 'Eleanor, my dear, you know you have been urging me for a while now to take up a pastime which would occupy my leisure hours?' She nods her encouragement. 'Well, you will be delighted to learn, my dear, that I have taken a decision. I shall devote my life to the study, collection and display of personal receptacles for human urine and excrement.' It is several minutes before the poor lady can be revived by the administration of *sal volatile* and the slight loosening of a corset.

'So does anyone live in Newby Hall today?' I ask Angela as we all climb a sweeping oak-panelled staircase.

'Mr and Mrs Richard Compton,' she smiles, pronouncing their name with reverence.

'Ah, they sound like down-to-earth folk,' I comment. 'Not like the old days, huh?'

Angela feels the need to offer supportive evidence for my suggestion of a plebeian perspective among Newby's present-day proprietors. 'Mr Richard often enjoys a game of billiards,' she replies, 'with his two grown-up sons, Mr Orlando and Mr Ludovic.'

'Orlando and Ludovic!' I exclaim.

'If you'd like to follow me, please into the Print Bathroom,' she continues, and we do.

The Print Bathroom resembles a small but luxurious sitting room with a comfortable sofa, a Persian rug, a walnut marquetry cabinet and heavy drapes framing the long window. Then you notice the bath and a lavatory, and remember that this is the eighteenth-century aristocratic equivalent of an en suite. It adjoins the Print Bedroom. These two rooms are so called because their walls are adorned with eighteenth-century sepia prints by Gillray and Hogarth. The bed – four-poster and canopied, obviously – is enormous, close to 10ft wide.

'Good for when you have an argument last thing at night,' says a fellow visitor, an elderly chap in tweed jacket and knitted tie. We all chuckle.

'And the chairs are mid-eighteenth century, by Thomas Chippendale,' says Angela. 'They're very fine indeed. There were often complaints about the prices Chippendale charged for his furniture.'

'But his rich clients never paid him,' comments a middle-aged woman with bright-red hair who's been bending over one of the chairs to inspect its quality. 'That's why the old chap went bankrupt.'

'Well I'd like to think that *we* paid him,' she smiles. And it dawns on me that Angela has not simply adopted Newby's treasures as her own, she also sees herself as a member of the family, with a certain responsibility for the actions of family ancestors as well. It's quite touching. I'm starting to warm to her.

'If you look out of the windows,' she says, bringing us back to the fixed itinerary, 'there are beautiful views across the park over Newby land as far as the eye can see. This is where the best guests stay. Mr Richard and Mrs Lucinda Compton accommodate the Prince of Wales here on his visits,' she says, a note of understated pride in her voice.

'With Camilla?' I ask.

'The Prince is accompanied, of course, by the Duchess of Cornwall,' clarifies Angela.

'Have you seen the prints?' cries a bulky man in trainers, track-suit bottoms and green polo shirt. 'Look at this one, the young chap's fully dressed, with a naked woman – his bride, I guess – and the maid's just stripping off as well! And look at this one. What do you suppose *she's* letting him do?'

***

Our tour is nearing its end. But the best is being saved till last. We all troop into The Grand Salon. There is not one of us that doesn't mouth, 'Wow,' or 'Oh my gosh' or an exclamation to that effect. Each of its walls is covered by a single golden tapestry fitted to the exact dimensions of the room, down to the last fraction of an inch, around every mantelpiece, every corner, every polished dado. The carpet and the gilded furniture all echo the same exploding golds and reds like a distant fire. The tapestries came from the Gobelin factory in Paris during the 1760s and took six years to make. They were commissioned by William Weddell during his Grand Tour of Europe.

The Statue Gallery at Newby Hall, Yorkshire. (By kind permission of ©the owners of Newby Hall)

'When important visitors came to Newby, the family would receive them here in the Grand Salon,' explains Angela. 'It had no other purpose than to impress. It's never been used for anything other than to be looked at and be admired.'

Thus rattled with jealousy, Weddell's guests would be taken through to dinner, and afterwards, he knew that he had an even bigger bombshell waiting, which would stun visitors with his exquisite taste and limitless wealth. Angela leads the way, into the Statue Gallery. Gods, emperors and generals stand on their plinths with sightless marble eyes, testimony to the brilliance of the civilisation of ancient Rome that once stretched from the Mediterranean to Hadrian's Wall.

Weddell had spent much of the years 1765 and 1766 on that de rigeur completion of a young gentleman's education in the eighteenth century, the Grand Tour. He'd roamed through France and Italy in the company of a tutor who taught him about the glories of the ancient world through the ruins and sculptures that they observed there, and Weddell did what most tourists do: he brought back a few souvenirs. More than a few, in fact. The ancient Roman and Renaissance sculptures that he acquired on his travels, and that grace the salon before us now, filled nineteen large chests, and he had to charter a ship in Rome to transport them all back to England. Weddell had been exposed to, and was now an enthusiastic *aficionado* of, the great cultural wave that was sweeping Europe in the eighteenth century. The educated classes across the Continent adored all things ancient Greek and Roman, which they believed best represented their own values of rational thought, politeness, and forbearance. Weddell now was a neoclassicist. And this was the Age of the Enlightenment, the Age of Reason. His collection is probably the finest today in England still in private hands.

'Is it all genuine?' I ask Angela.

'A few of them are Renaissance imitations,' she replies, 'immensely valuable in their own right. Oh, and this one here, this statue of Venus is a modern copy. The family sold the original at auction in 2002 to fund the restoration of this beautiful house as you've seen it today. It was valued at £3million.' I shake my head in wonder. 'It fetched eight million,' she adds. I can only shake my head faster.

For a few minutes, everyone in our group tiptoes around paying homage to Roman art and Empire, to William Weddell and to Newby Hall. Then it's time to go and we give Angela a round of applause. She smiles with modest pride.

'I'm sorry about our little misunderstanding,' she says to me.

'Oh, that's OK,' I reply. 'I'm flattered. It's quite exciting to be mistaken for a thief. It's been a great afternoon. Thank you.'

***

It's a near certainty that if Napoleon, or the Kaiser, or the Nazis had ever managed to invade England and occupy rural Yorkshire, the marvels of Newby would have been plundered and carted off years ago to some Teutonic bunker or Gallic *palais*. The fact that Newby's treasures are still here for us to admire is a tribute to that uniquely English element of our history: the Hastings factor, 950 years without successful foreign invasion.

Visiting stately homes, castles and other 'heritage sites', from Stonehenge to Second World War bunkers, is something of a craze for the English. According to the preservation organisation, Historic England, 73 per cent of English adults enjoy spending time at such places. That's 58.6 million visits a year, a figure that has been steadily rising since the turn of the century. If, as sociologists claim, national identity is forged by a shared history that is memorialised partly in places we can admire, then Newby Hall and its beautiful treasures ought to be near the top of the league of such identity-forming locations.

But is that true? While Newby can show off plenty of furniture and china made by those revered old Englishmen, Thomas Chippendale and Josiah Wedgwood, the most valuable artefacts that adorn its halls and salons are not English at all. The Gobelin tapestries are French, and, of course, the 2,000-year-old statues and busts are from the heart of the ancient Roman Empire. How then can Newby be said to help form the identity of the English? The answer lies not in *where* these objects were made, but in *how* and *why* they were acquired. That tells us a great deal about a peculiarly English outlook on life in the eighteenth century, and how certain values were born then which still influence who the English think they are today.

***

To understand what was going on, we need to see that in the eighteenth century the culture of the upper classes in England was influenced by two separate trends. One was purely English. The other was Europe-wide. And, the two came together as one. So first let's look at the English trend.

It had started with the Glorious, Bloodless Revolution of 1688–89, which we talked about at our last stop. Part of the agreement between the Whigs and the Tories – parliamentary descendants of the old rivals, the Roundheads and the Cavaliers – was, as you'll recall, that henceforth citizens would express any opposition through rational argument rather than armed rebellion. Tolerance of others was now a cherished principle of political and other aspects of life. The immediate evidence of this new tolerance was in the way that religious differences were now handled.

Over the previous 150 years, the mere sight of a citizen praying in a different way from his neighbour had opened up deep
divisions in English society, had brought torture and burning at
the stake for heretics, and was in part responsible for the slaughter
of a civil war and the oppressive regime of a dictator. It was the
sign of a new era, then, when in 1689 Parliament agreed the Act
of Toleration, which decreed that most Protestants outside the
Church of England were now free to practise their religion. It's
true that religious tolerance didn't yet go all the way; Catholicism
was still banned. Nevertheless, opposition to religious minorities was now expressed on paper or from the pulpit rather than
erupting in physical violence. Bishops who pressed Queen Anne
to prosecute heretics, found that nothing happened – the queen
'conveniently' kept losing the papers. Blasphemy remained a crime,
but magistrates and juries tended to find the accused 'not guilty',
regardless of the evidence. The philosopher John Locke wrote in
his *Letters on Toleration* that tolerance of the behaviour of others 'has
now at last been established by law in our country. Not perhaps so
wide in scope as might be wished for, but still it is something to
have progressed so far.'

Rational debate in politics, rather than violence and suppression,
became increasingly accepted as the way to settle differences. And
this predilection for reasoned argument spread beyond Parliament.
Something called 'public opinion' started to be considered.
Newspapers provided information to inform that opinion. This
new fashion for tolerant debate didn't happen suddenly however.
There were some spectacular bumps on the road.

In 1763, the dashing and profligate owner of a muckraking
newspaper, one John Wilkes, published vitriolic attacks on the
king's mother, whom he accused of adultery, and on the king himself for agreeing a humiliating peace treaty with the French. Wilkes
was prosecuted for seditious libel. He turned the case into one of
principle, claiming that civil liberty itself was on trial. Nevertheless,
he was convicted and kicked out of Parliament. In a complex series
of adventures over the next few years, he fled to France, fought
a duel, lived with a teenage mistress, returned to England, stood
for Parliament and was re-elected amid two days of rioting by his

supporters, was disqualified as an MP and reinstated several times, and ended up as popular hero, while the government's dealings with him looked increasingly silly. Finally, in 1774, he was elected Lord Mayor of London and entered Parliament as the unopposed member for Middlesex. His story is hardly peppered with rational debate, but Wilkes's final acceptance into English society was seen as a victory for freedom of the press, and that was a necessary adjunct to well-informed reasoned argument. Governments and MPs could no longer ignore this new 'public opinion'.

These were the purely English forces at work during this period: the growth of political and religious tolerance, rational debate, and a certain amount of freedom of expression.

The second, parallel, trend was not confined to the English, but was Europe-wide. It was represented by the architectural and artistic fashion known as neoclassicism. The educated classes in France, Italy and many of the Germanic states during the eighteenth century were embracing the culture of ancient Rome and Greece. Great churches and public buildings were often designed with a façade of towering columns, topped by a triangular capital. Their strong, unfussy lines, as recommended by the Renaissance Venetian architect Palladio, were seen to represent restraint, harmony and order.

The two trends, one an English preference for well-ordered, rational debate, and the other a pan-European fashion for well-ordered, balanced, symmetrical architecture matched each other. The English themselves were beginning to feel part of a broader international culture. That outward-looking trend had begun in the Elizabethan age, a time of exploration led by men such as Sir Francis Drake and Sir Walter Raleigh, and in the seventeenth century the systematic English colonisation of north America was in full swing. But now, in the eighteenth century, while exploration and colonisation continued under men such as Captain James Cook, others who could afford it were striking out in foreign lands for no other reasons than pleasure and education. It has been estimated that by the 1760s, around 12,000 English folk a year were touring continental Europe, and that over the next twenty years that figure shot up to 40,000. Now, the English weren't just imposing their ways on foreign lands, they were accepting and absorbing culture and ideas from other people and other civilisations.

The Grand Tour, like that undertaken by William Weddell in 1765–66, was the most extreme version of this eighteenth-century foreign holidaymaking. For the privileged young men who undertook these long trips, it was an adventure. Travel books warned them of lodging houses afflicted with fleas and bed-bugs, of food that would upset their stomachs and of roads where accidents and robbers lurked around every bend. But it would be worth it for the education, and maybe too the promise of romantic encounters in exotic locations.

For Weddell, like many of his young contemporaries, the Grand Tour was life-changing. On his return to Newby, Weddell devoted himself to things of beauty. His collection of marble generals and elegant goddesses exuded noble simplicity and calm grandeur. And when he refashioned the house inside and out to accommodate them, he did it in a way that reflected the spirit of the age. He didn't turn Newby into an exact replica of some ancient Roman building. He adopted – with the advice of Robert Adam and others – distinctly English designs, but ones that were inspired by the classical world. Bright simple, rounded shapes on salon ceilings, and, outside, a four-square façade with symmetrical arrangements of windows. It was all well-balanced, just as rational argument and polite, tolerant behaviour should be.

The events of the Glorious, Bloodless Revolution had ensured that the values of the Age of Reason took a strong hold in England. And in fact, the English came to be regarded as leaders of the new culture. The French writer, Voltaire admired the English. 'I will acquaint you with the character of this strange people,' he wrote after his visit here, 'an unaccountable nation fond of their liberty, learned, witty, despising life and death, a nation of philosophers.'

***

But the Age of Reason also had a strange, chaotic underside to it. Behind the order and courteous etiquette at its forefront, there was something surprising, something very disorderly and anything but polite within eighteenth-century English society. We saw it in the mildly pornographic prints in the bedroom and bathroom at

Newby. And young William Weddell, for all his aesthetic sensibilities, knew all about it too.

Weddell was a leading member of the Society of Dilettanti. This was a London dining club for wealthy young men, whose stated aims were to study and propagate an interest in the arts of the ancient classical world. And to join, you had to have done the Grand Tour. But this wasn't all that Society members got up to. According to Prime Minister Horace Walpole, it was 'a club, for which the nominal qualification is having been in Italy, and the real one, being drunk.' A painting by Sir Joshua Reynolds portrays a group of dilettanti paying glassy-eyed attention to a learned guest, who is showing them an illustration of a Grecian vase, while another young Society member is waving a lady's garter, and one of his mates is toasting it with a glass of red wine. To be fair, young Weddell was more towards the Grecian vase rather than the lady's garter end of the dilettanti spectrum. But it is clear that the Age of Enlightenment was not just an age of polite reasonableness, it was a time of boisterous drinking, whoring, bawdy jokes and other rakish behaviour. The two strands seem to be mutually exclusive. How then do we explain their co-existence?

In part, the laddishness of some dilettanti may have been the kind of rebelliousness we see in any age when the young kick out against the confining, respectable values of their elders. But there was more to it than that in the eighteenth century. Tolerance – an essential element of rational, polite behaviour – didn't mean simply that religious minorities were no longer persecuted as they once were. Tolerance of what others say and do can also mean permissiveness. And in eighteenth-century England, tolerance came to imply that a bit of sexual licence, social mayhem, and even a dissolute lifestyle might be OK too.

What makes this 'anything goes' counter-culture so significant in the eighteenth century is that after a while it spread way beyond a boys' night out phenomenon and was taken up in mainstream upper-class England. It became fashionable for the ladies and gentlemen of polite society to show off by dressing down, and they would turn up at the great houses of their friends in the garb of a chambermaid or a manservant – or at least in a well-cut version

The Dilettanti Society in action, portrayed by Sir Joshua Reynolds. The young members are more interested in the wine and the lady's garter – held up by the chap in the back row, left – than in the lecture on a Greek urn.

of these simple clothes. In the 1760s, Queen Charlotte, wife of George III, was seen strutting about in a kitchen-maid's apron (and, unlike her husband, she was not insane). And there were more outrageous goings-on. Masquerade balls became the thing. At a masquerade, otherwise respectable upper-class folk might spend an evening cross-dressed or even wearing nothing at all except a less than disguising face mask and a couple of strings of pearls. Fondling of strangers was permissible at these dos – and not just by the men. Harriette Wilson, mistress of the Duke of Wellington, wrote, 'I love a masquerade, because a female can never enjoy the same liberty anywhere else.' And so it was that eighteenth-century English society – as Reynolds's dilettanti illustrated – could be polite, rational and well ordered on the one hand, and rebellious and permissive on the other.

To some extent, this is also what happened in another eighteenth-century club, the House of Commons. It may be ironic, but tolerance does much to explain the adversarial politics that we witnessed on our stop at Westminster. Boisterous conduct and politeness somehow live side by side. What the House of Commons has demonstrated over the past 250 years is that you can afford to shout and jeer if you know full well that no one's ever going to draw their sword or throw a punch. And when the division bell has sounded and the votes have been counted, you may well end up having a friendly drink in the Members' Bar with the very MP that you'd mocked in the Chamber an hour before. To foreigners, it may seem odd. To the English themselves it's a source of pride in being different.

***

Eccentricity, a touch of madness, as Shakespeare observed, is an English peculiarity. We see it at Newby in Robert de Grey Vyner's hobby of collecting chamber pots. The bizarre behaviour of our upper classes has often delighted the English. A visit to many a country house will reveal the accuracy of P.G. Wodehouse's presentation of the titled and wealthy as odd, impractical, out-of-touch and just funny. Woosterish, in fact. Even in the twenty-first century, the upper classes, though they struggle to throw off this image, can never quite manage it. Witness the official Newby guidebook. In its introduction, the present proprietor of the Hall describes the place as having 'the atmosphere of a lived-in family home'. It's an endearing remark, but it's wonderfully ludicrous as well. Has Mr Richard Compton never been in the average suburban semi or well-kept council house? The Newby guidebook puts him right back in the eccentric, out-of-touch category.

But we love it. To be eccentric, slightly crazy even, is quintessentially English. As we all know, 'Mad dogs and Englishmen go out in the midday sun.' Social historians argue that this tendency of the English to be oddballs is part of our long tradition of political liberty and tolerance, which allow us to value the nonconformist. There's a practical logic to this. If you live in a totalitarian state, any sign of strange behaviour can get you branded a subversive. So – unless you're brave enough to be Pussy Riot in Russia – you tend to keep your head down and not do anything out of the ordinary to get yourself noticed by the secret police or their informers. The English, however, by and large haven't had to worry about that in recent centuries and so can feel free to be daft sometimes or just different. It's a freedom that is born of tolerance. It came to the fore in eighteenth-century England, and has survived to this day. So long as oddballs or rebels act in a peaceable way, we don't mind. We tolerate them. In fact, we quite like it. It's what the English do.

***

As the eighteenth century wore on, England's relationship with Europe was changing. It was less one based on the peaceful absorption of culture and philosophy from friendly neighbours, and more one of violence. The country had become involved in a long series of continental wars. So did that mean that tolerance of others was slipping out of the English character? To find out, we're heading 280 miles south, and we're going to board a battleship, where a 5ft 4in disabled sailor spilt his last drop of blood and became England's most celebrated military hero.

12

HMS *VICTORY*, PORTSMOUTH

'ENGLAND EXPECTS ...'

IF WE CONTROL THE CROSSING FOR TWELVE HOURS, ENGLAND IS DEAD.

NAPOLEON BONAPARTE (1769-1821)

Elegance, excitement, brutality, heroism and death have surely never been brought together in one place as they are on the decks of HMS *Victory*. The bulging curves of its black and cream hull, the delicate balustrades of its tilting stern and the dark crouching lines of its massive guns, its near vertical stairways descending to the surgeons' bloodied tables: if you want to get your children hooked on history, bring them here.

HMS *Victory* is a vital clue in our search for the roots of Englishness. More than any other place in England, this ancient battleship still generates English pride much as it did 200 years ago, when Horatio Nelson was shot dead by a French sniper on its quarterdeck during the Battle of Trafalgar. Back then the very survival of England as an independent state was at risk. If Nelson and the English fleet had failed that day, then the country may well have become – in Napoleon's words – 'a mere appendage of France'.

At first sight from the quayside of Portsmouth's Historic Dockyard, *Victory* looks odd. It's as though two ill-matched structures have been forcibly married. There's the war machine, with its rows of cannon barrels thrusting out at us beneath masts and yardarms and enough rope work to stretch the length of a marathon.

And then, bolted on the back, there's a Georgian house whose tiny windows, miniature mock pillars and statuettes of Grecian gods could belong in an elegant square in Bath, except that this house is toppling backwards like an enchanted gingerbread cottage. And the contrast is no mirage. As we're about to discover, it reflects the truth about life on board.

Across the gangway we go, duck under a low beam and we're back in 1805. One of the many wonderful things about this ship is the way that the National Museum of the Royal Navy, which has been charged with looking after it since 2012, doesn't present it as a museum. They've done away with anything that might get in the way of our appreciation of what life was like on board in the early nineteenth century. Today, there's not even an explanatory sign to get in the way of our time travelling. Instead there are well-informed guides on each deck to answer our questions and help us feel what it was like here 200 years ago.

The first guide I meet is Catherine on the quarterdeck. She's in her 20s, wears dark glasses, is Canadian and is excited by *Victory*'s story. She leads the way into the gingerbread cottage bit of the ship. Here, because *Victory* was the flagship, both Nelson himself as the fleet's overall commander and the ship's captain Sir Thomas Hardy had their quarters, one above the other. And it's Hardy's seaborne world off the quarterdeck that we enter first. In the small cabin, hanging from a rail, is what looks like a wooden rowing boat with curtains draped over both ends. This is the captain's bunk. It's an elaborate version of a hammock. 'These cots were always made to measure especially for the officer who'd sleep in it,' explains Catherine. 'This one's extra long. Captain Hardy was over six feet tall. The curtains were always embroidered by wives or girlfriends. Oh,' she adds, 'and if you were killed in battle, the cot would become your coffin.'

'That must have guaranteed a few sleepless nights,' I say. Catherine nods.

Next door, the captain's 'day room' is enormous, spanning the full width of the ship, and it's bright, lit by a line of windows along three sides. This is where he worked at a rosewood desk placed on a small Persian rug. The floor of the cabin is black and white squares. 'It is

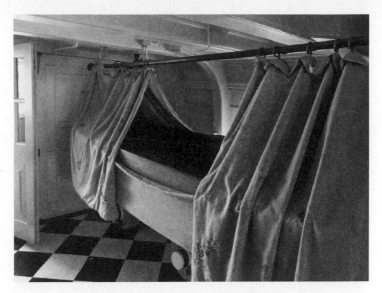

The swinging cot made specially for Sir Thomas Hardy, *Victory*'s captain.

in fact canvass that has been stretched and painted,' says Catherine. 'The idea was to imitate the marble flooring of the captain's elegant residence back in England. To make him feel at home.'

I'm just about to go and explore one of the gun decks when I notice a panelled door – brass handle in the middle – which would seem to lead out to thin air on the side of the ship.

'Ah,' says my guide, 'that leads to the seat of easement. You can open it and have a look if you like.' I do, and there inside is an eighteenth-century naval officer's loo, neat and clean. The main difference from a similar facility today is that the distance between your bottom and the water is somewhat longer here on *Victory* – about 30 feet to be precise, straight down to the ocean waves. 'There's another identical one on the opposite side of the cabin,' Catherine points across to a matching door, 'so you could choose which one to use according to the wind direction.'

Out of respect for Admiral Lord Nelson, I withhold further comment.

'Those who weren't officers,' she adds, 'weren't quite so fortunate. Eight hundred men had to share just eight "heads", which

– as I'm sure you know – is the technical term for such places on board ship. Have a look now at what life was like for the ordinary seamen.' And she directs me down a flight of narrow wooden steps.

They're steep and I soon discover that I need to climb down backwards, as you would a ladder. At the bottom it's dark, and the beamed ceiling is so low that I have to stoop. Most of the space is filled by two ranks of massive black cannon, girded with thick ropes, their barrels pointing out through small portholes along the ship's side. Black leather fire buckets – each decorated with a crown and the twirling letters GR – hang ready alongside bulky ramrods. This is one of *Victory's* three gun decks – a name that tells you only part of their function. As well as being the battle stations, they are also where the sailors ate, slept, and did everything else in their seaborne lives.

A small group of visitors is crowded around a young man with slicked back hair, who is describing the scene here at the height of battle. He's so excited, you could believe he'd served in Nelson's navy himself.

'When the gun was fired,' he says, giving a tug on an imaginary fuse and dodging sideways at the same time, 'it shot backwards with great violence – six feet in one second! If you didn't get out of the way, it could kill you! Then one of the crew would perch on the gun port to clear it and load it again. You had to be careful, because the barrel would be red-hot. They would try to cool it down with a sponge dipped in seawater. Otherwise the gun could split and explode with dreadful consequences! Imagine what it was like down here with thirty-odd of these mighty cannon blasting away and jumping backwards. At any moment, an enemy cannonball might rip through the deck, sending splinters of wood and metal in all directions. The place would have been full of blinding smoke and dust, and the noise would have been deafening! And I mean deafening. If a sailor survived the terrors of battle, he'd be left deaf for the rest of his life.'

Anthony – that's our enthusiastic guide – explains that during the campaigns of the wars against the French at this time, 90 per cent of the deaths on board *Victory* and similar naval vessels weren't from enemy shot. Most died from disease or the inevitable accidents that occurred in stormy seas, including shipwrecks when a badly wounded vessel limped on before sinking to the ocean bed.

And who were the men who risked their lives like this? More than two hundred of them on *Victory* at the time of Trafalgar didn't want to be there at all. They had been press-ganged. These men would have been going about their lawful business on land when they were grabbed by the thugs of the press gang, who got paid for every man they delivered to a naval vessel like *Victory*, where they were forced to join its crew. The rest on board were volunteers. What was the incentive? Pay was relatively low – the equivalent of £1.18 a month – but a volunteer got to share in any treasure taken from a captured enemy vessel. And if you were in debt, which in 1805 meant you could be thrown into a debtors' prison, the navy would protect you. Many seamen were very young. Forty per cent were under 24, and *Victory*'s crew included a boy of 12. They slept here on hammocks, slung alongside each other over the guns. That allowed each man overnight just 15in between his two neighbours.

In the middle of the deck, between the sets of guns, is a giant stove whose ovens could bake 80lb of bread while copper pans boiled 250 gallons of stew at the same time. The cooks were usually sailors who had lost a limb in an earlier battle and so were relegated to this lighter duty. There was a superstition on board that it was unlucky to whistle. An exception was made for the cooks, who were encouraged to whistle all the time, thus proving to all who could hear them that they weren't spitting in – or eating – the food.

Punishments on board were harsh. Any sailor caught drunk, who was insolent to an officer or who neglected his duties was taken up to the quarterdeck, stripped to the waist, tied to an upturned grating and given between twelve and thirty-six lashes with a cat-o'-nine-tails, a whip made from nine knotted thongs. The whole of the ship's crew were ordered to stand on deck to witness it. A seaman who stole from his mates was made to 'run the gauntlet' past his fellow crewmen, who beat him with knotted ropes. Men convicted of serious offences such as mutiny or desertion, were hanged from the yardarm.

Desertion was a problem, as we can readily appreciate. When a ship like the *Victory* put into port, the men were not allowed ashore for fear they'd never be seen again. To keep them entertained, local prostitutes were brought on board, known – with thinly veiled decency – as 'wives'. The gun decks, where no such thing as privacy existed, was thus on occasion the scene of more than eating, sleeping and fighting.

***

At the stern end of the upper gun deck of *Victory,* immediately below Hardy's cabins, are the admiral's quarters. The contrast between the living spaces of officers and men is stark: cramped and dark battle station cum lodgings for 800 sailors, and a spacious, sunny, Georgian mansion for just one man. But as we'll soon discover, cannonballs and musket shot were great levellers of social class.

In layout, Nelson's home at sea matches Captain Hardy's quarters on the deck above. The guide here is Hilary. 'Nelson didn't have a hanging cot like Hardy and other officers,' she says and leads the way into the small cabin where he slept, or tried to. 'He was an insomniac,' she says. 'He would often spend the night pacing the decks, or he would try to get some sleep in an armchair. But the problem with anything resembling a hammock for him was that, because he'd lost one arm, he couldn't climb into it without help. So here, you see, he had a more conventional bed.' It's not quite like a bed we'd recognise. It's boarded in with wooden panels on three sides, with a thick curtain that could be pulled across the front, all to keep out the cold drafts that would whistle through the cracks and gun ports of *Victory* on a stormy night.

There's something else here in Nelson's bedchamber that's even more bizarre to our eyes. There are two giant black guns, one standing next to each end of his bed. I jump to the conclusion that they've been placed here – out of context – because *Victory*'s curator couldn't find room anywhere else.

'Oh no,' says Hilary. 'This is exactly where they were kept, because when it was time to fight the enemy every part of the ship became a battle station. Come through to the day room and I'll show you.' And there in the light and spacious quarters, amid shiny brown walnut table with matching chairs and silver candlesticks, close to Nelson's polished desk and standing like insults on another red-patterned Persian rug, are two more brutal black guns.

'Several of the windows doubled as gun ports,' explains Hilary. 'When the ship went onto battle alert, this whole area – the admiral's quarters, and the captain's above, too – were transformed in just six minutes. All the furniture was cleared out, the rugs were rolled up and even the wood and glass partition between here and the dining room was removed.' She walks over to the bank of windows at the stern. 'Three of the window frames could be dropped down,' she explains. 'The gun crews swung the cannon into place pointing through the openings. These guns were called "stern chasers" because they could bombard any enemy ships in pursuit. So the place where Admiral Nelson, minutes before, had been writing his dispatch became one of *Victory*'s vital gun stations.'

***

Nelson's talents, bravery – and sometimes wayward character – had surfaced early in his career. He was born in 1758, the son of a Norfolk clergyman, and he joined the navy at the age of 12. By 20 he was a captain. Over the next few years, he served in the West Indies, the Arctic and the seas off Canada. Then for five years, after he'd argued with his superiors at the Admiralty, he was confined on half-pay to dry land. But when war against France broke out in 1793, he was back to pacing the decks of his own ship again. He would always put himself in the front line, and was wounded several times. At the Battle of Calvi in the Mediterranean, a flying splinter of shrapnel took out his right eye, and at Tenerife his left arm was shattered and had to be amputated almost up to his shoulder. His finest moment before the Battle of Trafalgar came at the Battle of the Nile in 1798, when he destroyed Napoleon's eastern fleet.

In the same year, he began his romantic entanglement with the wife of the British ambassador to Naples, Emma, Lady Hamilton, who three years later gave birth to their daughter, Horatia. As in his private life so in his professional career he tended to disregard the rules that others took for granted. On at least two occasions he won resounding victories by disobeying orders – most famously at the Battle of Copenhagen in 1801, when, ordered by the fleet commander to retreat on sight of the enemy's vessels, he put his telescope to his blind eye, said, 'I see no ships,' and proceeded to inflict 6,000 casualties on the enemy. By 1803, he was in command

One of the many ways Nelson
was commemorated is in this
figurehead from the 120-gun
HMS *Trafalgar*. The wine used
at the ship's launch in 1841 was
originally from HMS *Victory* in
Nelson's time.

of the Atlantic fleet and aboard HMS *Victory* was chasing an armada
of thirty-three French vessels all around the ocean.

The danger that England faced in the opening years of the century cannot be overstated. Napoleon Bonaparte, now Emperor of
France, along with his Spanish allies, threatened to invade England.
'The Channel,' he pronounced, 'is a ditch which will be crossed
when someone has the boldness to do it.' Napoleon had built
2,500 gunboats and had recruited 165,000 men into what he
called 'An Army of England', which he based along the French
coast opposite the Straits of Dover. On a clear day, people near the
Kent beaches could see the French troops drilling. 'Foggy weather
and some luck,' said Napoleon, 'will make me master of London,
of Parliament and of the Bank of England.'

The English worked themselves up into a frenzy of patriotism.
Pamphlets were circulated suggesting that Napoleon 'promises to
enrich his soldiers with our property,' and 'glut their lust with our
wives and daughters'. There'd be no more roast beef of old England,
and the English would be forced to eat black bread and vegetable

soup. 380,000 men flocked to join local Volunteer groups. People were nervous and panicky in the south-east of the country. One evening in Colchester, it was thought the French invasion fleet was sighted on the horizon. One resident wrote, 'The volunteers were flying to arms ... The officers were scampering out to gallop home to their camps ... Women were running out of their houses screaming murder.' It was a false alarm. During this period, seventy-three Martello towers, circular forts with guns on top, were built overlooking the Channel in Kent and Sussex, and by 1805 around 800,000 men were performing some sort of military service. That was one in five of males aged between 15 and 55, and the number was 50 per cent in the most threatened areas along the south coast.

In August 1805, Napoleon made ready for the great invasion. The French fleet now stood off Cape Trafalgar near the coast of Spain 25 miles west of Gibraltar. Napoleon ordered it to proceed to the English Channel, where it would protect and reinforce the invading army that he had standing by around Boulogne. 'If we control the crossing for twelve hours,' Napoleon boasted, 'England is dead.' HMS *Victory*, Nelson, his guns, his fleet and his men were what stood in the way. The French must be defeated at Trafalgar.

***

Nelson, among his many other qualities, was a brilliant tactician. On 20 October, the eve of battle, he summoned his captains to a briefing. Each came across in a small rowing boat and climbed up a ladder onto the quarterdeck of *Victory* and down to the admiral's quarters. There, over charts laid out on his dining table, Nelson expounded his plan. The fleet would split into two columns and sail directly towards the Spanish and French, who were spread into an arc. The two attacking columns would be led, one by HMS *Royal Sovereign* commanded by Admiral Collingwood, and one by Nelson's *Victory*. These two would take the full force of the enemy's guns. After the briefing, Nelson recorded the captains' reactions. 'Some shed tears,' he wrote, 'all approved, "– it was new – it was singular – it was simple".'

The next morning, the Admiral's quarters were cleared, *Victory*'s 104 guns were primed and the stocks of gunpowder and ammunition made ready. Nelson gave orders for signal flags to be raised up the mast with a message for the fleet; it has never been forgotten: 'England expects that every man will do his duty.' Over on *Royal Sovereign*, Collingwood – in a fit of pre-battle nerves – remarked, 'I wish Nelson would stop signalling, we all know what to do.'

At noon, *Victory* shook as the first cannonball was blasted from its gun decks. Within seconds, the air was thick with smoke as hundreds of heavy cannon began their thunderous action. Nelson smashed through the centre of the enemy line and found himself alongside the stern of the French flagship *Bucentaur*. *Victory*'s guns devastated the French ship, killing 197 men outright. But it was not a one-sided fight. The enemy's cannonballs and grapeshot ripped through *Victory*'s bulkheads, sending shattered shards of iron and wood hurtling through the lower decks. Fifty-seven crewmen were killed on *Victory* alone and another 102 were injured. In the few spare moments when the firing died down as the ship manoeuvred to a fresh position, men would carry their fallen comrades down the three flights of steps into the bowels of the ship to the Orlop deck. There, the surgeon and his assistants struggled amid the chaos of screams to do what they could for the wounded, as the ship again began vibrating and rocking with the blast of the 100 heavy guns recoiling and jumping on the decks above.

Today, we can still get some sense of the dark, oppressive atmosphere of *Victory*'s primitive hospital. After backing down its precipitous stairways, I find myself stooping, almost crouching, beneath its shoulder-high ceiling and screw up my eyes to make out by dim lantern light the crude tools laid out on the surgeon's bench. The guide steps forward out of the gloom. Her name's Caterina; to my amazement, she's Spanish. 'How does it feel to be …' I hesitate and smile to soften the blow, '… the enemy?'

'Actually I'm from Cadiz' she replies. 'Our city was never conquered by Napoleon and we fought alongside English soldiers.'

She picks up a partially rusty saw. 'Eleven amputations were carried out during the Battle of Trafalgar,' she says. 'Seven legs and four arms. No anaesthetic of course. The surgeon's greatest skill was his speed. He would try to cut through the flesh and bone as fast as possible. But your chances of surviving the operation were only fifty-fifty,' she adds. 'Infection was common, and there was no way of treating it.'

Back on the quarterdeck, Nelson and Hardy saw through the smoke that *Victory* and the following column of ships had managed to smash a gap in the enemy line. The rest of the English fleet poured through. The French were overwhelmed. The fighting lasted four and a half hours. Nelson's plan worked. By 4.30 p.m. it was all over. The French were defeated.

But now, news of a more devastating kind was transmitted by signal flags across the fleet. At the height of the battle, a sniper positioned up in the rigging of an enemy vessel had picked out the man in admiral's uniform, aimed his musket and hit Nelson in the left shoulder. The ball continued its course, cutting through his lung and a major artery before entering his spine.

The spot where that happened is marked today by a small brass plaque screwed to the quarterdeck. It says simply: 'Here Nelson fell. 21st Oct 1805'.

In great pain, he was carried down to the darkness of the surgeon's deck, while the deafening explosions of the guns continued to shake the ship. But there was nothing that could be done to save him. He whispered to the man who had been his friend as well as his comrade, 'Kiss me, Hardy.' Some have said that his last words were in fact, 'Kismet, Hardy,' – kismet meaning 'fate'. After three hours, Nelson died.

***

In all, nearly 500 men were killed across the whole fleet, and more than 3,000 French and Spanish sailors lost their lives. The battle had been won not only by Nelson's plan and its daring execution; a key factor was the speed with which the disciplined gun crews had been able to fire their cannon. Able Seaman Benjamin Stevenson, who was on HMS *Victory* that day, wrote to his sister:

> We had a very hard engagement with them. There was constant fire. But thank God we had the good fortune to gain the victory. After the prisoners came on board, they said that the Devil loaded the guns, for it was impossible for man to load and fire so quick as we did.

Seventeen enemy ships had been captured and another was left blazing out of control. Not one of Nelson's twenty-seven ships had been lost. And with the French fleet now crippled, Napoleon had no choice but to abandon his planned invasion of England.

It was reported that late on the afternoon of the battle many of the victorious sailors across the fleet were in tears. They had heard the news of their commander's death. Nelson was not without his faults – he could be vain, awkward and sullen at times – but his confidence, courage and charisma meant he was worshipped by those who served him. The *London Times* wrote: 'We do not know whether we should mourn or rejoice. The country has gained the most splendid and decisive victory that has ever graced the naval annals of England; but it has been dearly purchased.'

King George III, tears pouring down his face, said, 'We have lost more than we have gained.'

Nelson's body was brought back to England preserved in a barrel of brandy – some of *Victory*'s sailors claimed they had toasted the great man with a glass of that same liquor, and that while Nelson's body was unsullied, the brandy was not. His funeral ceremonies lasted five days. Hundreds of thousands of people lined the Thames to see the river-borne cortège sail from Chatham to Greenwich, where it lay in state for three days. Then, watched by another massive crowd, a funeral procession consisting of thirty-two admirals, over a hundred captains and an escort of 10,000 soldiers took the coffin from the Admiralty to St Paul's Cathedral, where a four-hour service was attended by the whole royal family. The sailors charged with folding the flag draping Nelson's coffin instead tore it into fragments and each took one as a memento.

Nelson's permanent memorial surpasses in magnificence that of any other hero in English history. The largest square in London, with its fountains and stone lions, overseen by the splendid neoclassic National Gallery, is named after the decisive battle that Nelson won at Trafalgar. And in the middle, a single column rises into the sky, its pedestal decorated with four bronze panels, each cast from a captured French gun. On top, 170ft above the streets of London, stands a statue of Admiral Lord Nelson in full naval uniform. He's looking south-west over the rooftops towards Portsmouth and his beloved HMS *Victory*.

***

Every nation needs its heroes. And they tell us a lot about what that nation reveres in its history. Nelson was and to some extent remains a symbol of England's pride in its naval prowess. At the same time, the story of Nelson and HMS *Victory* is a powerful reminder that this is an island nation, which unlike countries in the rest of Europe cannot simply be invaded by crossing a land frontier.

The wars against Napoleon and post-revolutionary France had the impact that most wars have. They united the nation in fear and hatred, and that was particularly so in this conflict – partly because the fighting was marked by two of the greatest victories ever won by the English, at Trafalgar and, ten years later, at Waterloo, and partly because the country was at war for so long, twenty-three years in total. But most of all, it was because – as in the First and Second World Wars in the next century – the very existence of England as an independent nation was threatened. The country, its people, traditions and culture were almost overcome by a ruthless foreign power. Once England had triumphed against Napoleon and survived, English people treasured all the more the Englishness that they had so nearly lost.

But there's a puzzle here. By the time of the Battle of Trafalgar in 1805, England was no longer a separate country. For 100 years, since the Acts of Union in 1706 and 1707, England had been combined with Scotland to form Great Britain. And Wales had been incorporated in the reign of Henry VIII. So is it correct to talk about Nelson as an English hero? Shouldn't we now, and during the rest of our journey, be talking about British identity and not English?

One clue to the answer is to be found in Nelson's famous signal to the fleet: 'England expects every man to do his duty.' He did not say, '*Great Britain* expects every man to do his duty.' That was partly because a French invasion was a threat – in the first instance at least – to England, rather than to Scotland or Wales. But also, following the Acts of Union, no one in Scotland, England or Wales wanted to see the identity of the different nations wiped out and absorbed into some new Britishness. In fact, forty years after the Union, the Scots and the English were fighting each other with bloody intensity. If anything, the creation of Great Britain made the Scots and the Welsh accentuate their differences from the English. This was a reaction against a tendency of the English to regard Britain as an extended version of England. They would say 'England' when they meant 'Britain'. Remember, we saw that *The Times*, in reporting the Battle of Trafalgar, spoke of 'the naval annals of England'. This confusion between British and English is something we shall return to on our journey. It has helped form whom the English think they are today.

***

The peace that followed the final defeat of Napoleon would soon be followed by rapid change. A revolution was on the way. Not a sudden, violent, political revolution, but a technological revolution, the like of which the world had never seen. This was a revolution in the way people made things. It was a revolution in how and where they lived. And it was also a revolution in the speed with which people could now move about, a speed that would make the era of HMS *Victory* look like the age of the snail. And who led this revolution? The English. To find out more, we're going next to a shed in north Derbyshire. It's a big shed. I can smell it and hear it already.

13

Barrow Hill Roundhouse, Derbyshire

STEAM, IRON AND INGENUITY

WE SELL HERE, SIR, WHAT ALL THE
WORLD DESIRES TO HAVE. POWER.

MATTHEW BOULTON (1728–1809) AT
HIS STEAM ENGINE FACTORY

Grimy brick walls 8ft high line both sides of the road for half a mile. They're punctuated at intervals by gateways, mostly boarded up. I spot one with steel mesh across it, so pull the car over and get out to see what's on the other side: Nothing.

Actually that flatters the place. Emptiness is neutral. But the odd pile of rubble and the sort of nettles and scrubby shrubs that used to be found on a city bombsite might indicate that something once precious has been destroyed here – a factory maybe or some other industrial works. Heaped against the mesh gate on the other side are huge rocks, presumably to stop you ramming your way through, and there's a sign on the brick wall that says, 'Security Cameras Are In 24 Hour Operation On This Site.' Who on earth is going to want to get in there? What kind of place is this, where desolation has to be fortified against intruders?

Welcome to Works Road, Staveley, Derbyshire.

Geoff had warned me that Barrow Hill Roundhouse would be difficult to find among the forgotten ruins of England's once mighty industrial empire. And I'm not exactly sure what I'm looking for. The only roundhouse I've ever come across before is the Roundhouse Theatre at Chalk Farm in north London. What I do know is that the Chalk Farm Roundhouse and the one at Barrow Hill both started out life as railway engine sheds. Barrow Hill still is one. It's *the* place, Geoff says, where you can get some feel for the in-your-face power of the Industrial Revolution.

Back in the car, I peer around for one of those brown heritage signs. After several hundred yards I find one and follow it up a black gritty track till it dumps me among some heaps of discarded iron junk at a dead end next to a dark brick block of a factory. Or is it a disused warehouse? I must have taken a wrong turn, and I'm about to reverse out when one of the junk piles catches my eye. It has an old tarpaulin tied over it as if somebody cares about it. And thrusting up from under one end of the cover is a rusty smoke-stack chimney. A tall guy appears from behind it and waves at me. It's Geoff.

I wind my window down, and grin at him. 'So where's the roundhouse?' I shout. He nods over at the factory block. 'Doesn't look very round to me,' I say. 'I thought it was going to be like the Chalk Farm Roundhouse. That's round.'

'It's round inside,' replies Geoff, nodding again towards the building's uncompromising square exterior. 'C'mon.'

Once I've parked, we've shaken hands and exchanged headline news, Geoff leads me into a neat little cafe hidden inside one end of the building, where amid spotless plastic table-cloths, ketchup bottles and walls full of shiny black engine plates we sup mugs of tea.

Geoff is something of an expert on the railways. What he doesn't know about their history wouldn't fill a British Rail sandwich menu. Tea finished, we head into the vast shed, and I can now see why it's called a roundhouse. It's laid out like a star with all the engines ranged around the outside, each pointing in towards the middle. And in the centre there's a giant turntable.

'It's just a neat way of getting twenty-odd locos into a confined space where they can be worked on,' explains Geoff. 'They can move in and out without you having to shunt all the others around.'

A model of Barrow Hill roundhouse. Each locomotive enters left and moves onto the turntable in the centre, which then delivers it to a vacant slot around the outside.

We're alongside a black, shiny locomotive. The first thing that hits me is the smell. Sulphur, carbon, garden bonfires. Then it's the noise. There's a sudden shrill hiss, loud enough to make your ears pop, as clouds of white steam spurt from somewhere over our heads. When it stops, a slow *clang*-atty *clang*-atty *clang*-atty echoes off the brick walls of the building, like a metal dragon breathing. 'It's the pump filling the air brake,' says Geoff. After a few seconds, it stops, and there's a strange silence, full of our anticipation at what ear-splitting noise will next assault us.

The sheer size of the loco we're looking at is intimidating. Its driving wheels are as high as my head, and the whole locomotive rises to around 15ft. I pace out its length: nearly 20m, I reckon. Every bolt and pinion is sparkling, every square inch of its green and black paint gleams and glints.

'By any standards,' I say to Geoff, drumming out the words, 'this is a thing of elegance and beauty. I can understand why someone would want to preserve *this.*' I run my hand along its hard, cold side, then glance across to the far corner where two young men are working on a battered blue diesel engine. Pointing at it I add, 'Though why anyone would want to keep that thing going, I can't understand.'

'Bloody diesels!' chips in a voice from behind my right shoulder. It's a chap in a faded blue boiler suit, his words forced out between teeth clenched on an empty tobacco pipe. 'I couldn't help overhearing you,' he says, removing the pipe now to give added vigour to his speech. 'Bloody diesels! I wouldn't give 'em house room. They were the death of the railways. The real railways that is.'

We introduce ourselves. He's George, and we soon discover that he's part of a team that owns, cherishes, adores and proudly shows off the giant loco now towering over us.

'OK, George, 'I say, 'so why do you do it?'

'What? Smoke?' he says holding up his pipe.

'No, spend your time caring for an old loco.'

'You might as well ask me why I bother breathin',' he replies, and he turns to stroke the thick, bevelled spoke of one of the creature's wheels. 'Well, I'll tell you. I fell in love with 'em when I was 8 years old. The first time I saw an engine – it was a Standard Class 9F 2-10-0 – snorting and raging down the track at 80 miles an hour, I said "Bloody Hell!" It was that exciting. And from then on, I used to go and stand on a railway bridge near our house whenever I could. And I used to watch the Glasgow express roaring down the track straight underneath me. When you saw it head-on, sparks skittering in all directions, it seemed to jump from side to side. Sometimes I thought it'd bounce right off the rails and smash into the houses. It's been a lifetime's love ...' He says these last words slowly, as though it's a phrase well used over the years to sum up how he feels. 'You couldn't help but be excited about it.'

'The romance of steam,' I say, though it sounds feeble after George's outburst of worship.

And another voice behind me thinks so too: 'Romance! There weren't much romance when I started work at Barrow Hill during the war, I can tell you.' It's another chap in boiler suit. He takes off his peaked cap and gives it a light punch.

'During the war!' I exclaim.

'Aye, that's right,' he says. He must be knocking on for 90. He's slim, sprightly and unwrinkled. I'd have put him at 60, tops.

'Now then, Roy,' says George, 'you tell 'em what it was like on the footplate back then.'

'In 1943,' says Roy, shifting his weight from one foot to another, 'I was 14 and a half. By rights, I should have been 15, but they needed the labour, so they set me on cleaning out fireboxes.' I imagine him standing on the footplate and sliding his shovel into the firebox to clear out the debris: wrong. 'They gave me an overall and told me to climb inside,' he explains, leading us over to the huge green loco. And he shows us on the footplate the size of hole he had to clamber through. It's an oval about 18in by 12in.

'You had to put one arm in first,' and he stretches his right hand up towards the roof of the roundhouse to illustrate, 'then get your head in next, and somehow slide your other shoulder through and pull the rest of you in after. And that's where we spent us days, inside there, on all fours in the dark and the dust, scrozzling over the fire grates, clearing out the soot and the cinders.'

Promotion for him and his mates, Roy explains, was strictly by seniority. There was no question of getting on by shining at your work. It was advancement according to a strict hierarchy. He'd eventually become a locomotive fireman. Roy then gives us a long and loving account of the run from Butterley near Ripley in Derbyshire, and how each curve and gradient required a precise amount of coaling and adjustment to the pressure. 'If you don't get it right,' he adds, 'the 'ole engine can explode. It'd kill men as well as disable th' engine.' He talks about it as though it were yesterday.

* * *

The Industrial Revolution, the shift from a world mainly of farms and countryside living to one of factories and towns, was the most fundamental change in the 1,600 years of our journey. At first, the innovations were so gradual they were hardly worthy of the word 'revolution'. But the pace of change shot up into top gear with the birth of the railways, a generation after the Battle of Trafalgar.

The first technological breakthroughs had come in the eighteenth century. At a time when William Weddell of Newby Hall was touring Europe and collecting beautiful statues and tapestries, others of his fellow countrymen – most of them from less privileged backgrounds than Weddell – were devising new, more efficient ways of working. James Hargreaves's spinning jenny enabled one worker to spin as much yarn as a dozen people had done with a conventional spinning wheel. Thomas Newcomen's steam engine could power a pump without the assistance of a horse. Henry Cort's rolling mill speeded up the production of iron. And many other English innovators, such as Josiah Wedgwood and Edmund Cartwright, took practical steps that resulted in less human labour being needed in order to produce more things that people wanted to buy.

The most revolutionary of these innovations was turning coal into energy by means of the steam engine. But again, improvements at first were very slow. Newcomen had built his steam pump back in 1712, but it needed a large amount of coal to drive its piston. That meant it was only of use close to the source of coal itself, so it served to pump water from the bottom of deep mines. Almost a century passed before there was any significant improvement. In 1804, a Cornish engineer, Richard Trevithick, mounted his new high-pressure steam engine on wheels, and the curious ironworkers at Merthyr Tyddfil in South Wales watched agog as it moved itself along a set of tracks outside their foundry with neither man nor horse hauling it.

Robert Stephenson was the Englishman who took the railways to the next stage. He realised the need for a fast, light locomotive. The result was the *Rocket*, the first engine to pull carriages full of passengers along tracks. His success reached its climax one mild autumn day in 1830. It was at the grand opening of the first rail passenger service in the world, on the Liverpool & Manchester Railway. With elaborate ceremony, no fewer than eight locomotives and their carriages proceeded between the two cities. The Prime Minister, the Duke of Wellington, had his own train on a separate track. The other seven, led by Stephenson's *Rocket*, carried a large delegation of MPs, lords and other dignitaries along a parallel rail.

The *Rocket* was so called because it could reach a previously unimaginable speed: 35mph. During that September day between Liverpool and Manchester, one of the many surprises was that the world's first railway passengers survived the ordeal. Or most of them did anyway. It had been commonly believed that anyone travelling at more than 30mph would suffocate because of the pressure of the air rushing past their faces. But *Rocket's* passengers – brave souls! – were relieved to find, as they hit top speed, that they were suffering nothing more serious than ruffled hair

Rocket was designed by Robert Stephenson. It wasn't the first steam locomotive, but because of its innovations – including a single pair of large driving wheels – it was chosen to lead the opening of the Liverpool & Manchester Railway in 1830.

and a rosy bloom to their cheeks. But there were other terrors awaiting them.

At a scheduled stop halfway between Liverpool and Manchester, many of the world's first train passengers – no doubt overexcited by their experience – ignored warnings from railway officials and, when they spotted the Prime Minister, the Duke of Wellington, got out of their carriages and walked along the railway track in order to greet him. One of these foolhardy folk was the former cabinet minister, William Huskisson. Huskisson had fallen out with Wellington over the issue of parliamentary reform, and now wished to get back in his good books. He approached the Duke's carriage and shook hands with him through the open window. Too late, Huskisson turned to see the *Rocket* rattling and hissing towards him. He panicked and tried to scramble up beside the Prime Minister, but the door to the carriage swung open and left Huskisson hanging in the path of the oncoming locomotive. He ended up beneath its wheels, and his leg was mangled. Those who had seen the accident carried him to one of the other trains. Stephenson himself jumped onto its footplate and oversaw Huskisson's journey to a nearby hospital. The unfortunate man died a few hours later.

The sight and noise of the first locomotives, smoke and steam belching from them, must have been more terrifying than any of us in the twenty-first century can imagine. And in 1830, many foretold that England with railways would be a world without birds and horses. Cows would yield no milk, hens wouldn't lay and the earth would be consumed in a general conflagration. It was certainly true that the planet would never be the same again. John Ruskin saw a railway viaduct built across his favourite view of the otherwise idyllic Derbyshire dales, and wrote, 'The valley is gone, and the gods with it; and now, every fool in Buxton can be at Bakewell in half-an-hour, and every fool in Bakewell at Buxton.' Today's opponents of the HS2 high-speed rail link through the Chilterns will sympathise.

But the railway did much more than cart fools about. It carried coal – in vast quantities, quickly and cheaply – from the pits that were being sunk all over the Midlands and the North to the iron foundries. The same locomotive that delivered the coal could then transport the iron and steel that the foundries produced, iron and steel that was turned into everything from lamp posts to ocean liners, from the breathtaking Crystal Palace to a million domestic cooking ranges. Where the railway was, there were jobs, and millions of those whose forebears for centuries had worked on the land now flocked to cities. The railway meant bricks made in Bedford could build houses in Manchester. Cherries and cabbages picked in Devon could be eaten fresh in London. You could mail a letter in Birmingham for it to be read the next morning in Newcastle. The posting inn, where for centuries horse-drawn coaches had stopped overnight, became redundant. In times of peace and prosperity, people no longer had to live near where they worked, and an old word was forged into a new meaning: 'commuting' was born. In times of war, troops could be shifted quickly to ports of embarkation.

The steam locomotive changed everything. It was truly a revolution. And Works Road, Staveley, site of the Barrow Hill Roundhouse, was once at the heart of it, bustling with the noise and rush of wealth-producing men and machines. Coal, iron and steam made a powerful team here. Go out into the street wherever you are right now in England and look at the nearest cast-iron manhole cover. If it's more than a couple of decades old, the odds are you'll see the name 'Staveley' on it.

***

I'm starting to look at the engines of Barrow Hill in a new light – a dirtier, greasier light. For a start, I can see they weren't all built to roar down the track at frightening speeds with a fancy nameplate on the side. Many – like the squat little black loco whose cab we're clambering into now – just pootled around for the whole of their lives in the same freight yard, shunting trucks about. In an age when a spacecraft destined for the outer edges of the solar system, or a message to your friend in Australia, can be launched by the touch of a single clean little button, the controls we see in the cab here before us are utterly foreign. They are dirty, clunky pieces of iron, in inconvenient places, whose operation relies entirely on physical strength. Wheels and levers are directly linked to valves, gears, and brakes.

As I climb down from the footplate of the shunting loco, I almost bump into a stocky middle-aged man, close-cropped hair, grubby hi-viz jacket. 'All OK, gents?' he asks.

I'm guessing from his enquiry that he's got something to do with running Barrow Hill, so I nod and say, 'Quite a place you've got here.'

'Yes, I'm very proud of it,' he replies. 'If there's anything you're particularly interested in, just let me know. I'm Mervyn Allcock, the general manager.'

We introduce ourselves, and I leap in. 'Could I ask how you got involved in Barrow Hill in the first place?'

I'm often amazed at the reaction you get when you interview a total stranger. Sometimes the reply is just a dreary, self-centred ramble that makes you regret you opened your mouth. But every now and again your reward is precious. As it is with Mervyn.

'This place is a lifetime's passion for me,' he says, immediately talking at full steam. 'I used to be in computers and then became a professional musician. I'd known the roundhouse here as a kid, and I loved it then. But in 1989 I heard it was going to be demolished, and

I thought to myself, "This place is a piece of Derbyshire's history, a piece of England's history, in fact." It was built in 1870. It was essential to the coal industry and the iron and steel industry, to the whole economy of the region. And I thought to myself, "I'm going to save it." I managed to get the demolition order stopped, and I got together with other like-minded folk and over seven years we raised £350,000 to restore it. We put a new roof on. Now it's Grade II listed.'

'So how do you keep it going?' I ask.

'We run it as a business,' he says. 'We charge a rent to all the railway preservation societies here and the commercial companies that service their engines and rolling stock. I look around on a day like today, and it makes me feel very proud.' And at that moment he does look around.

'May I ask you,' I say, 'why trains? What's the big attraction of trains?'

'A train,' he replies, 'is raw power. A train is a promise of adventure. A train is going to take you somewhere. I started out just wanting to save the place, but now ... well, I shall keep doing this job till I die.'

I feel humbled by this man's commitment and enthusiasm, by his love of what he's made of his life. Without a tinge of embarrassment, he adds, 'I want to leave behind my mark on the world for the next generation: Barrow Hill, the last working roundhouse in the country.'

Geoff and I shake his hands and wander off. Outside we come across a bloke who's staring across the tracks and shaking his head. He turns and hails us with a 'Mornin'.' He's in his 50s, I'd guess, and is wearing a padded camouflage jacket, a blue woolly cap, and a dangly earring. He takes out a small notebook and gives a sigh, the sort that invites conversation.

'How're you doing today?' I open.

He repeats the sigh and shakes his head. 'There's a new lot arrived again,' he says, looking over towards some modern railways coaches in grubby blue and white, all parked up with nowhere to go, the dullness of their immobile existence relieved only by the unpromising words 'Restaurant Buffet' on one of them.

'How do you mean?' I ask.

'The bogies,' he answers, scanning the first line of carriages and writing something in his notebook.

'The bogies?' I repeat with a puzzled frown. 'You mean where the wheels are fixed on the train?' I add, deciding that jokes about nasal congestion would not be well received. He turns and gives me a look, as though I'm daft or foreign. Geoff's wandered off and left me to it. 'Do you mind if I ask,' I say, 'why are you writing the numbers down?'

'It's to put on my Facebook page,' he explains in the tone you'd use to explain to an untidy child what a coathanger's for.

'Sorry to be nosey, but I'm not sure why you'd put them on Facebook.'

'Somebody out there, in cyberspace,' – he raises his eyebrows – 'is going to be interested. There's always new units coming in and out here. It's a full-time job keeping up with all the different types of bogies on 'em. You wouldn't believe it.' He's shaking his head and sighing again.

I peer across at the wheels and their mountings beneath the carriages in front of us. 'Forgive my ignorance, but they all look the same to me.'

'See that one on the left,' he says, 'that's a BR1 bogie, but then the one on the right's a BR10.'

I study the two arrangements of springs, axel ends and rods for several seconds. 'Sorry,' I say, 'I'm still struggling to see the difference.'

He puffs out a pitying breath. 'The BR10's got no horns on the end of its tap casting!' he exults.

'Is that good?' I ask.

'It's different,' he replies. 'There are forty-seven types of bogie. And that's not counting all the new ones coming in now from China and Estonia. Globalisation, huh! All this international trade, hah, they never think about the impact on the railway bogie now do they?'

I haven't got a reply to that. So instead I ask him, 'Do you get down here often?'

'Not often enough,' he replies, putting biro and book in the map pocket of his combat jacket. 'Not often enough.' And he moves off, no doubt to observe some rare Asian species of axel coupling at the other end of the yard.

This, of course, is a fine example of English eccentricity, well able to compete with the chamber pot collector of Newby or any of Shakespeare's mad English folk. And in one of those strange coincidences that happen sometimes when you set out looking for answers, rather than just looking, I stumble a few minutes later on the explanation of why being harmlessly crazy is such an English thing.

I find myself chatting to three young men, each with a long-lens camera hanging round his neck. I'd heard them speaking a language I didn't recognise. So, of course, I'd gone over to talk to them. They're Polish. Do they have anything like Barrow Hill back home? 'No,' replies one of them and continues to explain in faultless English that more Polish people are becoming interested in trains, especially steam locomotives. But it's something new, adds the second guy. 'For my father,' says the third, 'it would have been unthinkable. Under the communists, if somebody had been seen writing down the numbers of trains, the police would be suspicious. They would take you away.'

So the Hastings' factor is at work among the old railway sheds of England. Eccentricity and loco-restoration have both benefited from the freedom from oppression that we've enjoyed in this land from 1066 right up to the twenty-first century.

***

The great twentieth-century historian George Macaulay Trevelyan wrote, 'The railways were England's gift to the world.' They were born in England, and some of our ancestors made their fortunes exporting them all around the globe. To Argentina and India, to South Africa and Canada, and to every continent, engineers from places like Barrow Hill went to build hundreds of thousands of miles of track and to run steam trains on them.

But in what way did the Industrial Revolution and especially the railways mould how the English see themselves? We'd expect – because these towering achievements that changed planet earth for ever were conceived and put into practice by English minds – that there'd be a fundamental impact on our identity. But is there? It's true that the craze for preserving old steam engines is an example of eccentricity born of English freedom. But also hasn't it got a lot to do with a romantic yearning for a golden age of mechanical engineering when men could feel the power of the machine directly through the levers gripped in their hands, rather than as now sitting in a sterile office tapping a tiny electronic screen? Even the admirable Mervyn, founder and manager of Barrow Hill – though he's devoted his life to preserving a piece of English history – confesses that his love of the place is to do with the might and beauty of the steam locomotive.

Something has been lost. And we know it. England was once the manufacturing heart of the world. During the first half of the nineteenth century, exports of manufactured goods increased by 500 per cent, and even at the time that Trevelyan was writing in the mid-twentieth century, manufacturing made up 50 per cent of our economy. Today that figure is only 11 per cent and only 2.5 million people are employed in making things. Nowadays it's what the Chinese, the South Koreans and the Japanese do, not the English. And of course the great staples of the first industrialisation of England – textiles, coal, iron and steel – have all but disappeared from our land. Buy a good-value sweater today and the label will probably say 'Made in China.' Our coal industry collapsed during the Thatcher years, and anyway is condemned today for destroying the planet. And much of what remains of our steel industry is owned by an Indian conglomerate.

The tradition of innovative English engineers is, however, not dead. A new breed of English inventors is treading in the footsteps of Cartwright and Newcomen. Not all the new ideas have been world changing. Clive Sinclair's pocket calculator in 1972, and James Dyson's bagless vacuum cleaner in 1983 were simply useful. However, there are other recent English innovators who can claim to rival their nineteenth-century forebears. There's Frank Whittle, who invented the jet engine in 1937; Tim Berners-Lee, who is credited with devising the World Wide Web in 1989; and a team at Bath University who in 2007 developed the first self-replicating 3D printer – the full impact of which has yet to be seen. And we shouldn't forget that, though not an invention, the existence of the so-called 'God particle', the Higgs boson, was first predicted by an Englishman, Peter Higgs.

Now it's true of course that England today, among the other industrialised nations of the world, has nothing like the near monopoly on innovation that it did during the Industrial Revolution. Nevertheless, there does exist in the twenty-first century a sense that the English have a particular skill in combining imagination with engineering. The English still often see themselves as a nation of inventors. However, before we pat ourselves on the back with too much vigour, there's something lacking. And it was Geoff who pointed it out to me as we admired the mighty engines of Barrow Hill. 'These days, we've lost the power, or the will, to follow up on innovations,' he said. 'We invent something, or make an important scientific discovery, but then leave it other countries to exploit it.'

Geoff's observation is borne out in a recent survey by the global management consultancy firm PwC. The results don't refer to England, but to the UK. However, since the majority of the UK's economic output is generated in England, we can take PwC's conclusions as a criticism of the English. PwC says:

> From a UK perspective, companies are far less likely to focus on product innovation than their international competitors. Also, despite a clear competitive advantage in the UK's university sector, a significantly lower proportion of UK companies plan to collaborate with academics over the next three years. They're failing to exploit this key resource.

The English led the world in the Industrial Revolution. Today the spirit of Barrow Hill has been lost.

***

As we observed when we first arrived at Barrow Hill, the massive changes that took place in the late eighteenth and throughout the nineteenth century were as much a social revolution as an industrial one. The population of England doubled between 1801 and 1851, and people fled the countryside for work in the towns. Many ended up packed together like battery hens. It's difficult for us to imagine today what life was like in the vast, spreading slums of England's great industrial cities. So come with me to Birmingham and back in time when four children had to share a bed, listening to Dad – drunk again – fighting with Mother downstairs.

14

THE BACK TO BACKS, BIRMINGHAM

ENGLISH MONSTROSITIES

OH ENGLAND IS A PLEASANT PLACE
FOR THEM THAT'S RICH AND HIGH,
BUT ENGLAND IS A CRUEL PLACE
FOR SUCH POOR FOLKS AS I.

CHARLES KINGSLEY (1819–75)

Lurid lettering in pink, green, and yellow proclaims in both Chinese symbols and fat, cartoon English letters 'Anytime Snacks'. Shifty-looking men in baseball caps and short leather jackets with guilty cigarettes in cupped hands wait for Ming Moon ('Blackjack Roulette Slots Restaurant Late Bar') to open. Delivery vans and taxis pack the road in a slow-moving, polluting jam. A young guy on the corner is balancing a placard on a pole that says 'Subway' over a garish picture of a BLT and an arrow to direct potential customers.

I'm standing on the corner of Hurst Street and Inge Street in the centre of Birmingham, waiting for the National Trust guide. I've signed up for the 3.15 p.m. tour of the Back to Backs, a restored remnant of an old slum that thrived – or rather struggled through cholera, rats and domestic violence – here for 180 years.

A small exhibition behind the National Trust office round the corner, where I bought my ticket, had given a preview of what life used to be like here. It's the sort of thing we're all vaguely aware of, but the bald statistics still shock. In the mid 1800s, life expectancy was 29 years and 9 months, compared today with 81 years for women and 76 for men. Early Victorians spent 57 per cent of their meagre income on food, while we eat far, far better on 11 per cent of our fatter earnings. *They* could afford nothing at all for transport or recreation, while *we* fritter away 41 per cent of our wealth on cars, Xboxes and foreign holidays.

Here's the question for this stop on our journey. Given that our identity as a nation comes from our shared history, what did the poverty and misery of these slums do for us? How – if at all – has our sense of who we are today been formed by a century or more in which vast wealth was created but was not shared by many?

* * *

There are six of us waiting on the corner by the time Heather, our National Trust guide, arrives. A retired couple, two young parents with a baby strapped on dad's chest, plus me. Heather – cocooned against the afternoon chill in an extra-thick green sweater – leads us down a narrow, tunnelled entry into a brick-built courtyard. Before us, three battered prams sit at regular intervals in the middle of the yard. There's a line of terraced houses along one side, and brick lean-tos on the other, with metal buckets outside. And washing hangs from a line, extra-large knickers, faded floral skirts, collarless shirts.

'This whole area of central Birmingham,' explains Heather, 'was a vast slum where thousands of people lived during the nineteenth and early twentieth centuries.' In its noisy, cluttered heyday, the little courtyard where our tour begins was shared by sixty people. It was where the women did the washing, and where the kids played. Back-to-backs, we learn, were like terraced houses with neighbours on each side, but then with another row of houses fixed behind them facing the other way. So there could be no windows on three sides of your house. The ones we're going to see were built around 1830. The National Trust has restored four of them to the state they would have been at different periods in the life of the place.

As Heather leads us into the 1840s, I'm expecting to be shocked by the squalor. But the door of the first house looks freshly painted in conservation green. And inside, there are glowing embers in the large open fireplace, and the table is laid for a meal. Willow-pattern crockery, I note, like my great-auntie Phoebe used to have.

Heather tells us that a Jewish family lived here. They'd moved from London's East End. He was a watchmaker. It doesn't look very slummy to me, so – since we seem an intimate group – I venture to say, 'It seems quite big, this room. Where I was born in the East Midlands, the old terraced houses had living kitchens only half this size.'

'Well, you have to remember this was the *only* room downstairs,' says Heather. 'And the Levy family who lived here were among the better-off working class. You see, when these places were first built, they weren't in the run-down state they got into later. But nevertheless, if you notice, there's no oven, and there was no water supply, either inside the house or in the courtyard. There would have been rats, and death from cholera was common. But it got even worse here in later years.'

Next, we're off upstairs. It's like climbing a twisted pile of tea chests, and I wonder how Mrs Levy carted babies up and down on a dark winter's evening, out of range of the nearest candle, with kids playing under her feet, and without the benefit of a Mothercare papoose? The answer, I suppose is – it depends what you're used to.

There are two bedrooms, one on the first floor and another, up more precipitous stairs, in the attic. Here at the very top, three beds share space with a watchmaker's bench and several chamber-pots. On one of the beds is a pair of knitted socks, long enough that they'd chafe the top of your thighs, and the feet are so big they look like they'd fit over your boots. The young man in our group bends over to examine them. The older woman next to him laughs, 'What would you look like in these? And they must have been so uncomfortable.'

'Well,' says Heather, 'Just keeping warm in winter was a big problem in these houses.'

***

We move across into the house next door. The National Trust has made a passageway through, so we don't have to retrace our steps and meet head-on the next tour scaling the staircase. The bedroom here is where the Oldfield family lived in the 1870s, and it's much smaller than the one we've just left. Its two double beds are almost touching and are separated by a makeshift screen of a brown blanket hanging from a length of string stretched across the room.

'So that's as much privacy as you'd have had?' I ask.

'It's worse than you think,' replies Heather. 'The Oldfields had ten children. After Mrs Oldfield's death – she died of tuberculosis at the age of 52 – and once five of the children had left home, Mr Oldfield decided to take in lodgers – a young man named William Holder and his girlfriend, Ann Hawkfield.'

'And they slept where?' I ask.

'The lodgers were in the bed behind the blanket-curtain,' she continues, 'and then there were four Oldfield children in the other bed a couple of feet away. Two at the top, two at the bottom.' It's a distressing image. We shake our heads, tut and sigh, but otherwise are silent.

'I'm going to play you a tape,' says Heather. 'Although it talks of a childhood in the early twentieth century, it wouldn't have been much different in the 1870s.'

There's a click and the voice of an elderly man echoes round the tiny room.

'There was twelve of us in our family. Six boys and four girls as well as our mother and dad. The house was so small we was really, really crushed. There was no room, so we kids had to stay outside, in the yard or out in the street by the lamp post. But we loved it being outside. We had to eat on the hoof. And when we came in, we had to go straight to bed. I always had to sleep at the bottom …' We all look down at the iron bed frame next to the hanging blanket. 'Dad was often drunk. He'd spend all the food money then blame Mother for losing it. We kids used to lie awake listening to them fighting downstairs.'

***

In the little living room, down more near-vertical stairs, there's a workbench in front of the window, where Herbert, the father, made a living to support them all. We're being watched. An eye is peering up at us from the bench top. In fact, several eyes. Herbert was a glass eye maker.

'The Victorians loved stuffed animals,' explains Heather. 'That might have been for a stag or something of that size.' The young mother in our group picks up one that has a sharp piece of wire poking out of the back. 'For a teddy bear,' explains Heather. 'Open the drawer on the side of the bench,' she adds.

I do so. If you have never seen a tray full of human eyes all staring up at you, it's disturbing. You think they're about to blink any moment, and you could swear they're making furtive glances. Eyes in their own home – the faces of your family and friends – mean life, smiling, understanding, crying. But torn from their human heads, they're like evil little creatures that have escaped from the underworld.

'Herbert did artificial eyes made-to-measure,' Heather continues. 'It was one of the industries Birmingham was famous for. Craftsmen like him would match the colour to your good eye, and they boasted that even your partner couldn't spot the difference.'

It's time for a more thorough look around the courtyard. First, we crowd into the stone outhouse where the women from all eleven families around this one yard would have washed their clothes.

'Each family had to bring its own coal supply,' says Heather, pointing to what looks like a stone kiln with a large copper bowl embedded in the top. 'And of course the women had to carry in their own water from the supply out in the street. Then, when they'd finished, they had to scoop out the dirty water – there was no drainage pipe – and throw it into the courtyard.' Next she gets us all to turn around to examine a big iron-framed mangle with wooden rollers that would convert your fingers to butcher's meat if you weren't careful.

Outside again in the courtyard, Heather tells us, 'As well as being where women did the washing and children played, this was also where the outside privies were. There were only half a dozen shared by all sixty residents.' Some of them got knocked down over the years, as the houses themselves were gradually demolished. Today one of the old 1840s loos has had its door removed so we can see it. It's a wooden plank with a hole in it – like the one Nelson and his sailors used on the *Victory*, except that here the source of evil smells did not get blown away on the wind before disappearing into the depths of the ocean. Instead it was held in a large bucket confined beneath the bench, and there it stayed day after day. No running water, no drains, and no rolls of super-soft tissue. Heather explains that the job of emptying the sloshing buckets just before they overflowed fell to a group with the quaint title 'night soil men', who came around once a week like modern refuse collectors.

Birmingham's back-to-backs didn't suddenly disappear with the arrival of some more enlightened age. By the 1930s, the houses clustered around this little courtyard were no longer bustling with the noise of eleven families laughing, crying and squabbling together. Old people living alone were now the norm here. And it was not until 1966 that Birmingham City Council condemned these slums as unfit for human habitation. Even then they were not torn down. Though some of the little houses were boarded up, others that faced out on to the street struggled on for another three decades as shops. One of these has been kept for us to look at. Its rooms are bare, its walls covered with blotched and stained paper peeling at the edges. There are jagged holes in the ceiling plaster where the rain has leaked in. There's a smell of mould. This is the grim reality of the slums, unpalatable and unrestored by the National Trust, and I'm left wondering if this is closer to what all the old houses looked like back in the 1870s when the four children shared that bed alongside the torn curtain.

***

The Back to Backs is a rarity: a historic place open to the public that tells us about England's poor. I estimate from reviewing lists of England's heritage sites that around 90 per cent of them are either upper class or military in origin, stately homes or castles. Of the remainder, there are one or two workplace sites, such as the Arkwright textile mill at Cromford in Derbyshire for instance, or the National Coal Mining Museum at Wakefield in West Yorkshire, and we might include Barrow Hill. But there are only a handful which – like the Back to Backs – tell how those on the bottom rung of society lived away from the mill, the mine or the beet field. A negligible number compared with the 1,500 or more great houses of the wealthy and titled that we can visit

So the statistics are back to front. The overwhelming majority of us have ancestors who led ordinary, even meagre existences, while the overwhelming majority of the historic sites we've preserved relate to people who led extraordinary and rich lives.

How has this misfit come about? It's partly because the big well-built homes have been more likely to survive and be passed down through generations of titled families. On the other hand, medieval hovels fell down or burned down with distressing regularity, and the brick-built slums of a later age lasted only until growing prosperity and a social conscience required them to be 'condemned' and bulldozed, like the thousands of dwellings around the Back to Backs.

But the fragility of the homes of the poor is only part of the story. There's something else happening here, which has got more to do with the way we see ourselves through our history. Could it be that there's no market for historic sites that are downbeat, and tell of a life of misery? Perhaps we shun those that have no trace of heroism or beautiful craftsmanship. Maybe we find places like the Back to Backs shameful? Shameful, because it doesn't fit with our proud sense of who we are, to admit we allowed terrible things to happen in our past.

I might not have thought too much about this, except that the National Trust – usually sticklers for historical accuracy – seem to have fallen short of that principle at the Back to Backs. It can certainly be praised for preserving the rotted appearance of the last couple of rooms we saw, and its conservation department has done a wonderful job of gathering together artefacts and recordings – some of them very personal – to represent the various time periods. And of course, as you'd expect, the National Trust guide was knowledgeable and thorough. However, much of the nastiness and squalor that would have existed back in the mid-nineteenth century has been glossed over. Paintwork would have been mucky brown and chipped, woodwork would in places be rotten, and there would have been filthy bits of litter in the courtyard corners. Furniture would have been stained and its upholstery dirty and torn. The people who lived here in the later nineteenth century had barely enough money for food, never mind to repair and paint. And there would have been so many folk crowded into the same communal areas like the yard, bickering and fighting for space, that it's unlikely that anyone would take responsibility for keeping it all clean. We were told that rats and cholera were rampant during the nineteenth century. Rats and cholera don't thrive where all is scrubbed, painted and sparkling. Instead of this squalor, the privy we were shown more resembled a suburban garden arbour with its comfy wooden bench than the stinking, slimy – and I'm sure clumsily-used – reality. All the doors and windows in the courtyard had been painted the kind of shiny conservation green that's common in genteel Cotswold towns. And inside, the rooms – with the exception of the last one, the later shop - looked as though a team of housekeepers had just been through them. The overflowing fruit bowl, the willow-pattern table setting, the comfortable, restored furniture, the welcoming fireplace might almost tempt the Interiors Editor of *House Beautiful* to book it for next month's cover feature.

So why hasn't the NT shown the old slums in the battered, littered, untidy, dirty state they were back in the later nineteenth century? The explanation can't be that this would contravene health and safety laws, which wouldn't allow spilt cabbage leftovers on the staircase. There is much more that could be done – or left undone – within the law. Paintwork could be left faded and peeling. It's not difficult to imitate dirty floors and worn furniture without using real dirt. What would have struck us about the place, if we'd been transported in time to the Back to Backs of 1870, would have been the smell. Foul water, rotting food, smoke, musty dampness, human waste. You can recreate smells these days, artificially and safely. So why hasn't the country's leading manager of historic sites done any of this?

In the little museum attached to the Back to Backs, I spotted an information board on which was written – without further comment – a telling quote from some unnamed Birmingham grandee. It must date from around the time of the millennium, when the National Trust started the campaign to rescue the last of the old slums. It reads, 'the people who lived in those hovels were made to exist under the most impossible conditions. I am at a loss to understand what the reasoning is behind preserving these monstrosities.' The implication is that the 'monstrosities' are a shameful reminder of an all too recent past – something we should feel guilty about, perhaps, best swept under the carpet and forgotten. We've seen many times on our journey how – in the words of social psychologists – 'memorialising' our past in places and objects helps form our view of who we are as a nation. So is it too much to suggest that – leaving professional historians on one side for a moment – there's a tendency among the rest of us to ignore those bits of our history that make us feel the English might not be quite as heroic, tolerant or caring as we thought?

If that's the case, it's a pity, because the truth of our history – and of our national identity – is always more complicated and intriguing than any dust- and stain-free living room could ever imply.

***

Those in the nineteenth century who lived in conditions much more comfortable than the slum-dwellers of Birmingham were split in their attitudes towards poverty.

On the one hand, they regarded its privations as some sort of punishment for fecklessness. For the previous 250-odd years, England had had a fairly generous welfare system. Ever since the Poor Laws of Elizabeth I's reign, paupers had been able to claim relief in the form of cash from local ratepayers. In the early part of the nineteenth century, the French political thinker, Alexis de Tocqueville remarked, 'The English poor appear almost rich to the French poor.' But the costs of the system rose along with the population, and in 1834 the old charitable system was dropped. The poor were regarded as – in twenty-first-century jargon – 'benefit-scroungers.' In that year, the New Poor Law decreed no more cash handouts. Instead, the only assistance would be provided in workhouses. And conditions inside those workhouses were kept deliberately unpleasant. The food was monotonous, the labour hard and even the 'respectable poor' – i.e. the sick, disabled or elderly – were humiliated by being made to wear a uniform. Families were split up. One elderly man told a newspaper, 'As long as I can arne a sixpence anyhow, they sharn't part me from my wife.' That was the idea. The New Poor Law was not welfare, it was a deterrent. The workhouse represented the lowest rung of poverty. The residents of the back-to-backs earned their sixpences, but their lives in the cramped, disease-ridden slums were little better. And those who went out to work in factories, in mills or down coal mines faced a daily gruelling routine for pay that hardly met the cost of food.

However, not all the more privileged Victorians regarded the lowly masses in society as sinners to be punished. Benjamin Disraeli, a newly elected MP in 1838, said the Poor Law 'disgraced the country', and a group of paternalistic Tories argued on moral grounds that conditions in factories should be improved. One such MP wrote after a visit to a mill, 'I heard their groans, I watched their tears.' The campaign brought about the Factories Act of 1833, which made it illegal to employ a child below the age of 9, and decreed that the under-12s should not work more than nine hours a day. That may seem thin gruel to us, but in 1833 it represented an improvement. I say 'represented', because in practice the factory inspectors could be bribed or bullied into ignoring the new regulations.

Some at this time tried to improve living and working conditions. This was an age when trades unions were born – not as it happens in the textile mills or iron foundries, but in the old world of agriculture. In 1834, six Dorset men, led by a farm labourer and Methodist preacher named George Loveless, formed a friendly society in an attempt to stop their wages being cut. The men were prosecuted for illegally administering oaths, and were sentenced to seven years' transportation to Australia. Loveless wrote:

We raise the watchword Liberty
We will, we will, we will be free!

He, and his fellow society members, soon were. A public outcry brought them home. They were the Tolpuddle Martyrs.

Some reformers believed there was unlikely to be any change unless political power itself was shared with the masses. The Chartist Movement, founded in 1838, demanded that all men should be entitled to vote in a secret ballot. Even after the medieval limitations on who could vote had been relaxed with the Reform Act of 1832, only around one in ten of the male population was allowed the ballot. The Chartists also wanted Parliament to be open to all men, and for MPs to be paid. Their charter was

In 1848, the year of violent revolutions across Europe, 20–25,000 Chartists gathered on Kennington Common, London. It was regarded as a dangerous moment by those in power. Cavalry and infantry were mustered, cannon were wheeled out, rifles were issued to Post Office clerks and 170,000 special constables were sworn in. The demonstrators were trapped, the rain pelted down and the threat to English political stability – along with Chartism itself – petered out. The photograph is one of the first known examples of a crowd scene.

signed by 1.2 million people and, throughout the Midlands and the North of England, workers came out on strike in support of its principle. There was widespread rioting. Some Chartists started to form themselves into revolutionary militias, and to collect weapons, including home-made bombs.

The year 1848 saw violent revolution spread across Europe. In Paris, fifty-two insurgents were shot dead on the barricades, 1,500 noblemen were killed by a mob in Poland, sixty-seven protesters were mown down in Milan, and there were other bloody uprisings in the German states, in Denmark, Hungary, Switzerland, and elsewhere. It might have been thought that conditions in England were ripe for it too. But it did not happen here. Why?

It was not unknown for social unrest in nineteenth-century England to end in blood on the streets and grieving families. The most infamous such incident was the Peterloo Massacre in

Manchester in 1819. A vast crowd had gathered to protest against famine and unemployment. The cavalry were called out, and in the charge that followed eleven people were killed and many hundreds were injured. In 1842, during a series of strikes in Staffordshire, Yorkshire and Lancashire, troops shot dead six rioters in Halifax and another four in Preston. But these were relatively atypical events, and – more significantly – there was never anything approaching an attempt to overthrow the government by force.

So did the English tradition of moderation and compromise in political life, established by the Glorious Revolution of 1688–89, play a part in maintaining the stability of the country? Perhaps so. Parliament did just enough to head off real trouble. Although the Chartists' desire for universal male suffrage wouldn't be met for another three quarters of a century, Parliament – undemocratic as it still was – wisely brought in some modest improvements to the legal minimums for working conditions in mines and factories. Once it was clear that the violent upheavals that had shaken the rest of Europe had bypassed this country, *The Economist* magazine, founded in 1843, wrote, 'Our disturbances, trivial and partial ... only served to show ... how thoroughly sound at core is the heart of our people, how unlimited is our personal liberty.'

There's a dash of wishful thinking in that comment. Nevertheless, the facts can't be denied. The slums of Birmingham and other great cities, of which the Back to Backs is only one tiny remnant, would never become the breeding ground for violent revolution. Instead, England – and the other British home nations – chose gradual change within the law. The English preference for moderation and compromise rather than political revolution delayed the arrival of full democracy and at the same time prevented change that might have cleaned up the daily lives of a majority of its lower-class citizens. The English, sometimes, have been prepared to pay a high price for stability and safety.

But at the same time, that English desire for a peaceful, predictable way of life allowed another very English phenomenon to take root, a phenomenon still seen on our streets today: the unarmed Bobby. In 1829, the Home Secretary, Sir Robert Peel established the Metropolitan Police in London. Until then, any outbreaks of mass violence had been dealt with by calling out the army. But there was a desire for a less confrontational alternative. So Peel didn't give guns to his new force – it was going to be policing by consent, not by fear and threats. And he kept police pay at the same level as that of an ordinary working man, so officers shouldn't feel superior to the rest of the population. There was of course plenty of crime in the slums of Victorian England's big cities, from 'dipping' – pickpocketing – to the brutal murder of prostitutes, but the governing classes chose to deal with it not by terrorising its citizens but by trusting the majority of the poor to behave themselves. Peel himself said, 'The police are the public and the public are the police; the police being only members of the public who are paid to give full-time attention to duties which are incumbent on every citizen in the interests of community welfare and existence.' 'Bobbies' (Which other nation has an affectionate nickname for its police officers?) were so called because they answered directly to the Home Secretary, Sir Robert 'Bobby' Peel.

***

Victorian England would remain a nation of social extremes: a few wealthy and powerful, and many poor and disenfranchised. Those at the top, by and large, were there because their fathers were rich and titled. But there was a difference now. With talent, luck, courage and determination, it was possible for those from nearer the bottom of the social heap to climb.

The man who embodied that dream was William Armstrong, born on 26 November 1810 at No. 9 Pleasant Row, Shieldfield, Newcastle-upon-Tyne, the son of a quayside corn merchant. When Armstrong died, ninety years later, he was by today's standards a multibillionaire. But he was also a lord, an engineer, an inventor, a philanthropist, an imperialist and a businessman. He was a Victorian. His story tells us much about an age when the English looked to the future but lived in the past. And this paradoxical way of behaving gave the English one of their strongest characteristics. It was a lesson in survival. To find out more, we're going next not to a factory or workshop but to a castle. Now, what's a castle dating back to before the Norman Conquest in 1066 got to do with a self-made Victorian industrialist? Well, let's go and see.

15

BAMBURGH CASTLE, NORTHUMBERLAND

FORWARDS TO THE PAST

THE HISTORY OF ENGLAND
IS EMPHATICALLY THE
HISTORY OF PROGRESS.

THOMAS BABINGTON MACAULAY (1800–59)

It was when I got out of the car and stopped to look up that I first smelled a rat. I was standing below the walls of Bamburgh Castle in Northumberland, surrounded by bag-laden families and coach parties of retirees, pulling on their rain jackets and rounding up their kids, ready to go and take a tour of what can claim to be England's mightiest medieval fortification. I'd first seen it from 3 miles away as I drove north along the coast road. It had loomed ahead of me on the horizon like a giant at rest, silhouetted against the morning light atop a bed of land floating out on to the North Sea. As I got closer, I could make out its four-square keep, its turrets, battlements and grey-streaked stones, 100ft up above the fussy little red roofs of Bamburgh village's houses on one side and the grassy dunes and sand-blown beach on the other. The castle's walls stretched for over 500 yards across a rocky mound, and it was easy to see how in the Middle Ages whoever controlled Bamburgh Castle controlled Northumbria. It was an intimidating sight.

You may now be wondering if this chapter has been put in the wrong place. 'What's it got to do with the Victorians?' you may be asking. All will soon be clear. And it's to do with that rat I'd smelled when I parked the car below the walls. I sensed something about the grand and massive castle before me that didn't square with its history.

Bamburgh is the biggest castle in a county that has more of them than anywhere else in England. There are eighty here, a tenth of England's total. And Northumbrians over the centuries have needed their castles. The first fort here was built by the Anglo-Saxons on the sea-facing rock at Bamburgh. Then the Normans soon discovered this was the most turbulent region of their new kingdom. When an army of 700 sent up here by William the Conqueror was massacred, William seized Bamburgh Castle and made it the headquarters from which he would control the rebellious Northumbrians. But for the next 350 years it was the Scots who were the real trouble, and this castle faced and usually withstood countless brutal assaults from over the border from the north. Then, during the Wars of the Roses, in 1464 Henry VI was besieged here by a Yorkist army. During a prolonged artillery bombardment, the king fled as the ramparts and towers came crashing down in a storm of smoke. It was a fatal moment. Bamburgh entered the record books as the first castle in England to be destroyed by gunpowder and shot. From then on, it fell into decay, and a painting in 1776 shows only the square Norman keep still standing intact, surrounded by a few shattered walls and the wreckage of masonry.

So you can see why I got suspicious. I'd read that the castle had been 'restored' by the Victorian industrialist, William Armstrong. But 'restored', I'd assumed, meant fallen building material carefully put back in place, shaky walls discreetly fortified, and surviving stonework scraped clean. In other words, I'd expected to find ruined roofless walls, half-wrecked barbicans and broken archways, all hinting at the many past dramas enacted here. But that was nothing like what I could see now.

It was the huge, not-very-medieval clock face with gold numbers and hands on one of its corner towers that first alerted me. And then, as I looked along its high boundary walls, I saw that the stonework – though in the requisite shades of grey – had been constructed from neat, standard-sized blocks with what are clearly machine-cut edges. There's not a dent or a hole or a crumbled line from a siege engine, a cannonball or a sapper's pack of gunpowder, to be seen. Some of its windows – you're right, real castles don't have windows, they have arrow-slits – look like they've come from a suburban Victorian villa. It's clear – Bamburgh Castle hasn't been 'restored'; it looks like it's been built afresh.

***

Along with several score other visitors, I walk beneath a rounded archway and on up a narrow road to where a dozen or so small cannon have been positioned with their black barrels poking through the battlements towards the open sea 100 feet below. Line after line of white breakers are hitting the shore, and tucked in against the castle's wall there's an emerald green field, flat and freshly mown with a brownish square in the middle. It's a moment or two before I recognise its purpose. It makes the castle itself – as the guidebook observes – 'possibly the biggest cricket pavilion in the world!' 'Quintessentially English', reads the picture caption.

I turn back and see straight ahead of me within the castle's walls an open area laid to lawns criss-crossed by small paths. On the left are various grey stone buildings. And my heart lifts for a second or two when I spot the keep. This is the original Norman fort, built 850 years ago, a four-square stone tower 100ft or so high, sitting on the highest point of what I have to call the 'modern' castle. And I'm delighted to spot a bit of genuine ruin here. Weatherworn, and all the better for being so, the broken apse wall is all that remains of the Norman chapel. In its centre, a 5ft-high bell hangs on a gibbet, its base dangling inches above the ground – not exactly where it must have been at any point in its history. A sign explains it once lived a useful life in the clock tower, but was moved here because 'its constant chiming irritated the fourth Lady Armstrong and villagers alike.'

Next to the keep is the doorway leading to the staterooms. The false buttresses, prissy little glass windows and especially the straight lines are poor imitations of the genuine medieval or Tudor articles. I join the throng pressing to see inside and wander through a series of rooms packed with curiosities: a sedan chair, a boneshaker bike and a New York pianola. And there are enough suits of armour, glinting swords, 10ft-long pikes, crossbows, battleaxes and muskets with bayonets fixed to keep a medium-sized civil war going for several years.

There are two kinds of room. Some resemble cathedral crypts. Fat round, brown sandstone pillars support fans of vaulted ceilings, above bare stone floors and wide draughty staircases, the sort of places that could be hired out for shooting a vampire movie. Other more comfortable salons have lead-canopied stone fireplaces and elaborately carved dark wood-panelled walls surrounding bulging leather sofas, polished oak floors and several of those globes that look like they would open up to reveal a drinks cabinet.

The exception to this pattern of Dracula haunts and gloomy drawing rooms is the King's Hall. This is magnificent by any standards. It's the size of the nave in a large parish church, and in design is a cross between a theatre auditorium and a gentleman's club dining room. High on its walls, above the top of the wood panelling, hang gigantic gilt-framed portraits of bewigged kings, crinolined duchesses and sly youths leaning against trees with dogs at their feet. At one end there's a proscenium arch above what could be a stage set for an episode of Downton Abbey.

But the glory of glories is above our heads. Bamburgh Castle's King's Hall has what looks like the most elaborate and spectacular hammer beam roof you could hope to find anywhere. A series of wooden half-arches leap from near the top of the side walls and end in two lines of suspended columns, dripping with carved cur- licues and each pair framing another series of arches and intricately decorated timber beams supporting delicate posts and more carved columns rising to the peak of the ceiling at the very pinnacle of the Hall. If you think this sounds contrived, you'd be right. No one could but admire the craftsmanship of the wood-carvers. But it's a fake. Hammer beam roofs were a way in the Middle Ages of supporting a ceiling that was wider than any tree trunk that could be sawn into a cross-beam. But the elaborate hammer beam ceiling in Bamburgh's King's Hall doesn't actually support the roof at all. It's just for show. By the time it was built in the 1890s, structural engineers had long since developed methods of reinforcing roofs with cast iron, which in this case could be cleverly hidden behind a mock façade of carved wood.

***

So Bamburgh Castle – despite its millennium-long history – is, in the way we see it today, a largely Victorian creation, the brain-child of William Armstrong. So, who was he? Why did he build this mock castle at Bamburgh? And what does this tell us about English identity?

He's been called England's 'forgotten genius.' But that does little to indicate the range of his talents and activities, and it ignores what today seems a darker, more controversial side to the man. William Armstrong was not born to great wealth or privilege, but nor was his childhood in Newcastle in any way disadvantaged. The Armstrongs were middle class. They could afford to send him to a private school. In his teenage years, young William developed a fascination for machines and anything to do with engineering, but his father insisted he should become a solicitor and packed him off to London to train. He then came back to Newcastle, where he practised law for the next eleven years. But engineering was his real love, and in his spare time he invented a water-powered piston engine to drive a crane. Though he was still an amateur, his work was far from amateurish and at the age of 36 he was elected a Fellow of the Royal Society. Within a year, he had resigned from his lawyer day job. He had seen a business opportunity in his invention and was building a factory to manufacture his hydraulic cranes. Four years later he was employing 300 men and had adapted his hydraulic engine to power moveable bridges.

What made Armstrong a genius was the flexibility of his mind. In 1854, at the time of the Crimean War, he picked up *The Times* newspaper one day and read that the army was having difficulties with its heavy guns. They were too weighty to be manoeuvred quickly, their range was limited and they were inaccurate. Within a year, Armstrong had devised a cannon with a strong, rifled barrel made from wrought iron with a steel inner lining, designed to fire a bullet-shaped shell rather than a ball. Armstrong decided he would make no money from this invention himself. He gave the patent to the nation, and set up a separate company, in which he had no financial stake, to manufacture his gun exclusively for the British government. In 1859, his altruism was rewarded with a knighthood.

But disputes followed. The rival arms manufacturer, Whitworth and Co. managed to persuade the country's military leaders that Armstrong's artillery was unreliable, and the government stopped ordering his guns. He then had to fight to regain the right to supply his weaponry elsewhere. That done, by the early 1860s, he was selling his guns to both sides in the American Civil War.

His business was expanding into new areas. As well as manufacturing artillery and all manner of hydraulic equipment – including the mechanism to raise Tower Bridge in London – Armstrong turned his attention to warships. His factory at Elswick, on the Tyne just west of Newcastle, now stretched for three quarters of a mile along the river, and by 1871 employed 27,800 people. A shipyard was added to its other factories. The first vessels made there were torpedo cruisers for the Austro-Hungarians, to be followed by the 11,000-ton battleship HMS *Victoria* for the British navy, launched in 1887. That same year, the queen made him Baron Armstrong. He was the first engineer to become a member of the House of Lords.

William, 1st Baron Armstrong outside the Hancock Gallery, in Newcastle. (Photograph by Clem Rutter, Rochester, Kent. www.clemrutter. net)

By this stage in his life, although he still remained in control of his companies, he'd left the management of day-to-day business to others. Lord Armstrong now devoted much of his time to his own engineering plans, to philanthropic works and to building. On the moors north of Newcastle he erected Cragside, the first house in the world to be lit by hydroelectricity, and he planted 7 million trees on its estate. He founded the College of Physical Science, now Newcastle University. Then in 1894, he bought Bamburgh Castle, by now in a ruinous state. It was to be his last great project before he died aged 90 in 1900.

***

The rebuilding of a ruin that has a long, venerable and historically important past, if it were carried out today, would be regarded as vandalism, regardless of whether that rebuilding was an accurate recreation of what the place looked like at some point in its history. And Armstrong's 'restoration' of Bamburgh Castle can't even be said to be accurate, with its clock tower, its machine-cut building blocks, and the surface of its bulwark walls as flat and polished as the bonnet of a brand-new Rolls-Royce car.

But we mustn't judge past generations by our own values. The Victorians didn't think what Armstrong did at Bamburgh was unacceptable. The question for us is: why was that? What does that tell us about their relationship to their history, and their sense of who they were? And has any of that been passed down to us today?

The first thing Armstrong did after acquiring Bamburgh Castle was to employ the architect Charles Ferguson to design the rebuild, and oversee the huge amount of work needed. Ferguson's speciality was the neo-Gothic style. Neo-Gothic buildings – also called 'Gothic revival' – were imitations of medieval architecture. The fashion had begun in the late eighteenth century in a few large houses, but during the early nineteenth century, neo-Gothic – rather than the neoclassic we saw at Newby Hall – became the fashion in the design of new churches and great public buildings. Its distinctive features were pointed arches, rib-vaulted ceilings, flying buttresses, long windows with intricate tracery, pinnacles, spires and often elaborately carved decoration. One of the many famous examples is St Pancras Station in London.

The Victorians' appetite for building surpassed that of any generation before them. There was no city or town that didn't acquire some neo-Gothic structure in its streets. Over 6,000 parish churches in England, that's 80 per cent of the total we have today, ended up with a pseudo-medieval Gothic appearance. For some that might mean minor alterations to windows, floors, walls or ceilings. But a staggering 3,765 brand new churches, in Gothic Revival style, were consecrated during the height of the craze in the forty years up to 1875 – 1,000 alone during the 1860s. And it's impossible to estimate the number of suburban houses and town halls that were built in a dim, dark forbidding echo of the Gothic, nor how many railway stations, waterworks, schools, colleges, hospitals, law courts, even factories and warehouses, were designed to look like something vaguely medieval, even though they might be constructed from industrial-age red brick.

Now here's what puzzles me. Why would a forward-looking people like the Victorians adopt an all-pervasive backward-looking fashion?

The overriding philosophy of the day was the glorification of progress. Many Victorians saw the story of their country as one of steady improvements in technology, morality, democracy and even hygiene, reaching a pinnacle in their own time. In the words of the great historian, thinker and Whig politician Thomas Babington Macaulay, writing in 1848, 'The history of England is emphatically the history of progress.' Given such an uncompromising attitude, we might have expected the Victorians to choose a style in their architecture that celebrated their many achievements. Today, for instance – despite the acid criticism of Prince Charles – leading architects design public buildings which use and exploit the strengths and advantages of modern construction materials, with a result that they believe expresses the spirit of the age. Buildings like the Velodrome, Birmingham Library or the Museum of Liverpool.

So, why did the Victorians – men like William Armstrong, the very embodiment of the technological age – turn to the style of a period when the power of kings was often absolute, when countless numbers suffered an early death from bubonic plague and dysentery, and when technology meant no more than a single-blade horse-drawn plough or a crossbow? In other words, why did they revere a time when their beloved 'progress' had yet to achieve much at all?

There's no doubt there were trends in Victorian England that go some way at least to explain this contradiction. Take, for example, all those neo-Gothic churches. The Church of England was undergoing a revival and wished to stress spirituality rather than the modern works of man, and places of worship that looked ageless – or at least ancient – were a reminder that the Christian religion had existed for many, many centuries, long before the steam engine or hydraulically operated bridges.

Gothic Revival also chimed with the views of those Victorian intellectuals and artists who were unhappy with what progress had delivered. There were practical utopians like William Morris, who believed that rapid industrialisation had dehumanized work, had turned the men and women in mills, mines and factories, like Armstrong's Elswick, into mere extensions of machines. Morris and his fellow devotees of the Arts and Crafts movement sought to revive ancient skills, such as handcrafted furniture making, which they felt had been lost, and they developed designs what echoed what they saw as a simpler past, before the Industrial Revolution. And with a different means of expression but a similar theme, authors such as Charles Dickens and Elizabeth Gaskell, brought to public attention the misery of poor people hidden in sprawling cities, and what they saw as the sometimes unprincipled greed of wealthy factory owners. The popularity of Dickens's work showed that the recognition of the downsides of industrialisation was not confined to a few idealists.

These movements in Victorian society – the Church's need to encourage a spiritual life embodied in an earlier age, the intellectual yearning for a more human, pre-industrial, golden past, and the popularity of realist literature – all help explain why a backward-looking style of Gothic Revival architecture took off in such a big way in the nineteenth century. They are all, in different ways, reactions *against* industrialisation. But why did the industrialist magnates themselves – the owners of railway companies, or those who built water supply systems for cities, men who had benefited from, who lived by, and who believed wholeheartedly in progress and industrialisation – also embrace a style of building that idolised a primitive, pre-industrialised, unprogressive age?

It's possible that part of the explanation lies in the fact that they were self-made men in a culture where birth and ancestry still counted. Part of Armstrong's own motive for rebuilding Bamburgh Castle, for example, may be that he wanted to award himself at least the trappings of a long and noble heritage. But as we've seen, Armstrong, who was typical of many a captain of industry, was not a man who lacked self-confidence. So there's likely to be more to it than that.

One explanation is this: even the great Victorian industrialists knew that their life's work was not appreciated by everyone and could provoke a dangerous backlash. As we saw on our stop at the Back to Backs, the lower classes didn't always tug their forelocks, say 'Thank you, Sir,' and put their noses back to the company grindstone. England suffered bouts of social unrest, which on occasions erupted in violence. There were strikes and riots and subversive mass movements like Chartism. The country had avoided the attempted revolutions that had spread like a forest fire across the rest of Europe in 1848 and the William Armstrongs of England wanted to keep it that way. The Industrial Revolution had brought a habit of fast change, uncertainty and a feeling that if something doesn't work it can be fixed. It wasn't just engineers and businessmen who felt that, it was an example that social reformers, revolutionaries and even anarchists might follow too.

So all those neo-Gothic railways stations, waterworks, town halls, suburban houses and thousands of churches were erected – at least in part – to remind England's citizens that some things don't change. English values, all had their roots in England's long history: Christian worship, tolerance, politeness, a class structure and especially Parliament and democratic institutions. It's significant that the most famous and magnificent neo-Gothic building in England is the Palace of Westminster, home to the House of Lords and the House of Commons, rebuilt after a devastating fire in 1834.

This, then, was the message of the Gothic Revival. It reinforced a sense of tradition that was needed not just by the clergy, a few romantic intellectuals or nouveau riche industrialists, but by the whole country. The very term 'national identity' was coined by the Victorians. Disraeli wrote, 'Nations have characters, as well as individuals.' National identity is, as we've seen, based on a people's shared history. The Victorians knew that, saw the traditional way that England did things was at risk in an age of rapid change, and with buildings – spiritual, workaday, high and modest – that spoke of that history, they attempted to shore it up.

***

So, did the Victorians have a lasting effect on the English image of who they are? The hundreds of thousands of Victorian pseudo-medieval buildings are well built. Many have survived and will do for years to come. They're with us, almost wherever we turn. We may lament the way the Victorians couldn't resist forever meddling, reconstructing or even demolishing our medieval past, instead of leaving it for us to study and enjoy as it's come down to us. It was almost as though they felt they could do medieval better than the people of the Middle Ages. The many neo-Gothic buildings are still today a reminder of what the Victorians stood for.

The very word 'Victorian' has been incorporated into the English language as a term of mild abuse, meaning 'overly conventional,' 'straight-laced', 'humourless', 'snobbish', 'narrow-minded' and 'prudish'. These words are not entirely justified by the facts. It's a myth, for instance, that the Victorians put little curtains around piano legs for fear young men would be reminded of female limbs. Nevertheless, respectability and snobbishness were common characteristics, largely among the middle classes.

Industrialisation had brought a rapid growth to the numbers of English people who were wealthier than the working class, but could not aspire to mix with the titled upper class. And the members of this expanding middle-class needed to distinguish themselves from those below while aping what they saw as the respectable values of those above them. They did it by creating a private world inside the home, a world of tea-drinking and fireside pleasantries. The Victorian middle classes hid themselves away from the unmentionable horrors that lurked beyond their suburban neo-Gothic houses. Fallen women (Victorian respectability required euphemisms), wealthy men with mistresses, and a working class who – heaven forbid! – enjoyed their pubs and the comedy and song of the music halls.

Victorian values reinforced the class-system in England. In 1848 – the year that saw revolutions across Europe – the Victorian poet Frances Alexander published in her *Hymns for Little Children* the well-known verse 'All things bright and beautiful'. Children all over England were thus taught:

> The rich man in his castle,
> The poor man at his gate,
> God made them high and lowly,
> And ordered their estate.

In the 1960s, at my Nottinghamshire grammar school, we were still singing it without batting an egalitarian eyelid. And we'd then go home and watch one of the funniest sketches ever on TV, in which John Cleese, Ronnie Barker and Ronnie Corbett represented the three classes, and Ronnie Corbett delivered the unforgettable line, 'I know my place.'

Victorian age class consciousness became so entrenched that it would not be seriously eroded until after the Second World War. And some would say that class divisions are still part of Englishness today. And what's more, the idea of moral respectability, summed up in the word 'Victorian', persisted in much of middle-class England right up to the 1960s, when the older English value of permissiveness resurfaced and elbowed it to one side.

***

The concept of progress does, however, survive in the England of the twenty-first century. Not in the strict Victorian, Whig sense of the relentless march of improvement throughout history. We're all too aware now that progress could mean the destruction of our planet through climate change or nuclear explosion. But we can't help but recognise today that, while there are many things we dislike about our society, our age is better than Victorian times, because we're much less likely to get tuberculosis and more likely to survive cancer, our workplaces are safer, our houses less

From this *Tatler* magazine photo of 1908, you could be forgiven for thinking
fourteenth-century sumptuary laws, governing what each social class could wear,
were still in force. The caption says, 'Lady de Bathe with Lord Dalmeny.' *Tatler* didn't
think the chap in the trilby and rain mac was worthy of a name.

rat-infested, everyone has a vote, racial abuse is illegal, and …
well, you can continue the list yourself. And with that recognition
comes a feeling of superiority, be it ever so slight, as well as a hope,
at least, that our children and grandchildren will see even more
improvements in health science, tolerance, equality and the other
things on your own list.

But perhaps the greatest contribution of the Victorians to English identity was in the way they demonstrated that tradition and long-held values can survive an era of terrifying change. That's something that the English understand. The rate of technological change in the twenty-first century is exponential compared with that in the nineteenth century. But we've learned that beneath the surface rush of the digital age, with its unstoppable expansion in the ways we work, communicate and entertain ourselves, there are certain values that we should hold to be timeless – values such as the rule of law, personal freedom, democracy and non-violent political debate, all of which remain because we think they're worth keeping, just as our English forebears did.

***

Everything we've learned on our last three stops in Victorian England was intertwined with a massive institution which we've hardly yet mentioned: the Empire. What did it do for the English character? To find out, we're going next to a place now best known as the birthplace of the Beatles and for its two football clubs. But Liverpool was once the Venice of the world. Its story, and that of the Empire it served, is one of contradictions: outward-looking but self-obsessed; where both slavery and racial tolerance have thrived; brutal and at the same time charitable. So to make sense of it, let's go to Merseyside.

16

LIVERPOOL DOCKS

BY JINGO!

REMEMBER THAT YOU ARE
AN ENGLISHMAN, AND HAVE
CONSEQUENTLY WON FIRST PLACE
IN THE LOTTERY OF LIFE.

CECIL RHODES (1853–1902)

If all you saw of Liverpool was Great Howard Street where it runs parallel with the River Mersey near the old Stanley Dock, you'd think it was a city lost to humanity. In a dreary line, like giant discarded boxes waiting amid litter for the bin-men, stand the old warehouses. Their grey, pockmarked sides punctured with rows of gaping black holes, their roofs like battered lids.

I park the car on an abandoned bit of land covered with couch grass and thistles to take a closer look. The square structure across the road, twelve storeys high, has its former function spelt out in the brickwork 80ft above me: 'Tobacco Warehouse'. To the right is a towering concrete wall, blank but for the broken lettering, 'White   omkins & Courage Grain Silo'. The nearby Atlantic Café on the corner of Dublin Street has boards over its windows, and The Bull pub is bricked up.

Next to it, another derelict warehouse has remnants of smashed glass in its ranks of window holes. Grubby bushes are sprouting from the cracks in its sides, and its brickwork is mottled with fire-blackened smears and white-encrusted mould. The wrecked building is defended behind a 10ft-high wall with castellated turrets every

A mile or so from the bright, bustling, restored Albert Dock, acres of desolate dereliction.

five yards, as though this were some sort of ridiculous knights-in-shining-armour castle. On a rusted iron gate, rubbish bursting out from behind, a torn poster proclaims 'Heaven'. Not a Liverpudlian joke, but an ad for 'The best after-hours club in Liverpool'. There's no one here to read it, except me. The area's deserted.

Back in the car, I head south and after a mile I'm looking at three buildings that could be from a different planet. Gone are the redundant industrial leftovers. These structures sit amid lawns and trees, their pale grey stonework exuding a busy dignity. My eye is drawn to the roof of the first. It's an elaborate collection of stepped towers, reaching up to two huge domes, one capping a massive clock face, and both topped with giant metallic birds, wings spread, about to take to the air. They're the liver birds, and this is Liverpool's most famous landmark, the Liver Building. When Liverpudlians travelled the world and sailed back up the Mersey, and they saw the liver birds, they knew they were home. Today, on the promenade between the building and the waterfront, tourists are snapping each other on their smartphones alongside life-sized statues of the Beatles, while office workers with briefcases or clutching folders of important papers are rushing to their next meeting.

The second building a few yards further along the dockside, has all the grandeur of an old French Riviera hotel. It's the Cunard Building, once headquarters of the company that ran ocean liners heading to New York and Boston, and now one of Liverpool's most prestigious office addresses.

Completing the trio, is a huge neoclassical edifice, all shining white stone, colonnaded façade, massive domes and an intimidating entry beneath a tall, pointed arch. It's as pompous as any town hall in England's great industrial cities. But this is not a town hall. It houses the Port of Liverpool Authority. It's had two names during its century or so of existence, both understating its splendour, one with cut-it-down-to-size simplicity – the Dock Office – and the other with the lilting rhythm of a nursery rhyme – the Mersey Docks and Harbour Board.

These fine buildings are known as the 'Three Graces.' They're proud testimonies to the wealth and might of this city, founded on the British Empire. Or I should say 'the *former* wealth and might, founded on the *former* British Empire.' The giant derelict warehouses we first saw, show what became of both Liverpool and the Empire in the later twentieth century.

***

But there's a third stage to the history of Liverpool. A couple of hundred yards on from the Three Graces is the Albert Dock. I've got rid of the car now, and am walking with the wide waters of the Mersey on my right – I can see the black hull and red funnel of a ferry chugging across to Birkenhead. When the end of Empire following the Second World War brought the end of Liverpool's role as a great trading nation, the sad dereliction of the docks prompted a campaign to preserve its architecture, to renovate some of the old, redundant brick warehouses and even to give them a new life. And so, after a six-year programme of restoration, the Albert Dock was reopened by Prince Charles in 1988. And once I've walked across a swing bridge with shiny iron railings, there it is laid out before me.

Imagine St Mark's Square in Venice on one of those days when it's flooded by the waters of the lagoon. And, instead of the baroque decoration of the Venetian marble buildings, picture them in mottled light red and grey brick. And replace Venice's colonnades of stone in your mind's eye with rows of sturdy iron columns painted a vibrant orangey pink. And as I walk along the edge beneath the shaded arcades behind the columns, I discover that the Albert Dock, like St Mark's Square, is packed with hundreds of tourists sitting at restaurant tables, meandering around the many souvenir shops and crowding into one of the country's finest art galleries. The Albert Dock is home to Tate Liverpool.

If you find it a bit far-fetched to compare Liverpool with Venice, a closer look at the Albert Dock's shops, restaurant and quayside proves you have a point. They're Liverpool through and through. There's plenty of celebration of Liverpool's most famous sons for instance. From The Beatles Story ('an atmospheric journey through the lives, times, culture and music of the Fab Four') where people are queuing to get in, to an image of the Sergeant Pepper album cover in - wait for it – 15,000 jellybeans. And outside the Comedy Central Club, a middle-aged couple – he in shorts and a blurred blue tattoo crawling up his arm, she with purple hair down to her shoulders – are sipping flat white coffees and sharing a bowl of chips topped with a slurp of ketchup. It's 10 a.m..

The industrial history of Liverpool is never far away here. A heavy hook is hanging from a metal gibbet 6ft above a bunch of lads swigging bottles of lager and oblivious to the threat hanging over them. It's one of the original swing cranes, once used to hoist bales of cotton and sacks of sugar cane off the sailing ships just back from the Caribbean. Elsewhere, old iron frameworks of cranks and cogs for hauling in the sailing ships have been positioned at intervals along the arcades to remind us of the city's working past.

But likening Liverpool to Venice isn't quite as fanciful as you might imagine. Venice was once known as the 'Mistress of the Sea', ruling a trading empire that reached its height in the late Middle Ages. Compare it with this: In 1852, one local Liverpool writer proclaimed,

> The commerce of Liverpool extends to every port of importance in every quarter of the globe. In this respect, it far surpasses

the commerce of any city of which we have a record from past times, such as Tyre, Venice, Genoa, Amsterdam or Antwerp, and fully equals, if it does not surpass that of London and New York.

An early twentieth-century historian summed it up thus: 'All seas lead to Liverpool.' It was the trading hub of the British Empire.

***

The British Empire – sending millions of people across the globe to fight, trade, rule and to settle for good – had a profound effect on many nations: the Scots, the Welsh, the Irish, the people of India, Jamaica, Australia and countless other countries, as well as the English themselves. In Victorian times there was a tendency to regard the *British* Empire, at its heart, as an English institution. Prime Minister Disraeli called it, 'The Empire of England.' And a popular history, published in 1898, was titled *The Building of an Empire: the story of England's growth from Elizabeth to Victoria*. Much of Liverpool's story is the story of Empire, and of radical changes to the way the English thought of themselves.

The Victorian writer of that history in 1898 was right to point out that the foundations of Empire had been laid in the reign of Queen Elizabeth. Explorers such as Sir Francis Drake, Walter Raleigh and Henry Hudson, disappeared over the horizon in small ships and weren't heard of for several years, until they returned to announce they'd sailed all the way around the globe, navigated the length of the West African coast, or had tried and failed to find a sea passage across the north of America. And in 1600, Queen Elizabeth granted a charter to the East India Company to pursue trade in the Indian subcontinent and China.

During the seventeenth and eighteenth centuries, explorers reached most of the world we know today, and a new phenomenon began: migration. Not in the sense we understand it today when many want to come to Europe. But the other way – a tide of migrants began to leave Europe. Ordinary citizens from England, as well as from Spain, Portugal and France undertook risky and uncomfortable journeys over the oceans to go and live in the Americas and other newly found lands. British settlers in such places were directly governed – in so far as anywhere up to six months away by sailing vessel could be directly governed – from London. All of this vast new empire meant trade. Raw materials such as sugar, cotton and tobacco were shipped in to Liverpool and other ports, and the products of English workers' labour were exported back to the colonies.

But there was a dark side to this trade that brought distress and death to millions. In the eighteenth century, Empire could mean slavery. Liverpool played a leading role in this sorry drama. Its harbour on the estuary of the River Mersey was big enough for ocean-going sailing ships to manoeuvre in and out. And it was handy for the cloth-making districts of South Lancashire whose products could be rapidly transported here and shipped off to buyers in Spain and the Mediterranean. But it was the notorious triangle of trade that took Liverpool from small harbour town to booming city port.

Almost the whole of one side of the Albert Dock is today occupied by two museums: the Maritime Museum, recounting Liverpool's links to the sea, and the Slavery Museum. It's there I go now to learn how the triangle worked. An exhibition of images and captions starts by looking at the first line of the triangle. On the wharves of Liverpool, goods such as cloth, guns, ironware and salt were loaded onto ships, which then set sail for West Africa. There, slave-traders had captured men, women and children at gun-point or had bought them from African chiefs. The captives were force-marched, hands tied, necks yoked together like cattle, for many miles to the coast. When the ships arrived from Liverpool, their cargoes were off-loaded, and were exchanged for a combination of cash and the slaves. This human cargo was then pushed below into the ships' holds. And in these cramped and insanitary conditions, with barely enough food to keep them alive, the slaves were transported – in the second line of the triangle – across the Atlantic to the West Indies. Those who survived the several months' voyage were then sold in the Caribbean to the highest bidders at auctions. Their new owners forced them to work on plantations growing sugar, coffee and tobacco. And in the third line of the triangle, these products were bought by the Liverpool traders and shipped back in the same vessels to be sold in England.

It was a highly profitable business. By 1770, Liverpool was driving it. The new wealth of the city attracted workers from all around the British Isles and beyond. Between 1700 and 1801, Liverpool's population grew from less than 6,000 to 78,000.

However, by the end of the eighteenth century, the movement to abolish slavery was gaining strength in England. Abolitionists pointed out that the people of Liverpool might not see the black slaves on their own quaysides, but the wealth of their city depended on this immoral trade. One Presbyterian minister wrote in 1797, 'Throughout this large-built town, every brick is cemented to its fellow brick by the blood and sweat of negroes.' And in 1808, after years of determined campaigning by the MP and evangelical Christian William Wilberforce, trading in slaves – though not slavery itself – was declared illegal across the Empire. It brought an end to the triangle. Some in Liverpool were furious – but not all. Many people in the city had been persuaded that buying and selling fellow human beings was wrong. And anyway, the economy of Merseyside had begun to diversify by then. Metalware from Birmingham, pottery from Staffordshire, steel from Sheffield and especially local textiles were being carried on horse-drawn boats via the new canal system to the Liverpool dockside to be exported to the now rapidly expanding Empire.

After Napoleon's defeat at the Battle of Trafalgar in 1805, Britain was in command of the seas. Her naval power guaranteed international open trading with forty-three individual colonies, from New South Wales in Australia to Jamaica in the West Indies, and from the Cape Colony in South Africa to much of Canada. Again, Liverpool soon benefited. And it was in this period that the city invested in a mighty project to capitalise on the new opportunities: the Albert Dock.

***

To get a different view of the Albert Dock, I decide to take to the water. Not quite in the risky manner of a nineteenth-century timber trader, but on board *Skylark*, a thirty-eight-seater pleasure boat berthed just outside the dock itself. I'm the first to arrive for the next trip, and that gives me chance to chat to *Skylark*'s skipper, Keith. He's in his 60s, his neat shorts and a dazzling white shirt are matched only by his smile. 'Born and bred here,' he tells me. 'Man and boy Liverpudlian.' Salthouse Dock, he explains, where we are now, was – as its name implies – where salt was brought in by canal boat from places like Droitwich in the West Midlands, ready to be loaded onto ships and sent around the world. Today, it's still where canal craft gather. 'Purely for pleasure these days,' says Keith. We are joined by a dozen fellow passengers, and Keith performs the obligatory safety demonstration. 'You've no need to fret,' he reassures us. 'There's plenty of life jackets, and I'll dish 'em out to everybody.' The sun's shining, the water's like a mirror, and Keith tells us, not for the last time in the next forty-five minutes, 'I love this place. I really love it. The water's in my veins.'

We start off under the old iron bridge that separates Salthouse Dock from the Albert. And now, looking from water level at the long line of quaysides above us, there's not the slightest hint of anything Venetian about them. From low down here, you're more conscious of the dirt-stained dock walls below the iron columns. And you're well away from the very twenty-first-century Costa Coffees, fish and chip cafes and T-shirt shops. Now the dock looks more like the workplace it once was. I can imagine the scene as one nineteenth-century visiting New Yorker described it from his ship moored here: 'Thousands of men … measuring packages, invoicing goods, shipping merchandise; the tramp of horses, songs of stevedores, and shouts of sailors.'

Keith, over the loudspeaker – he's at the helm now – tells us that this was the world's first enclosed commercial dock. 'Before that,' he explains, 'the old wharves had lots of problems. The warehouses weren't big enough to hold all the cargo being off-loaded. So it was often left standing on the quayside where it was easy pickings for thieves. And the warehouses themselves were made of wood. They often caught fire. So the Albert Dock was a bit of a revolution. It was enclosed by a wall, so thieves couldn't get in, and there was plenty of storage for all the tea and sugar and other cargoes, in these grand old brick fire-resistant buildings. And aren't they beautiful? Just look at them. I love this place. I really love it!'

The Albert Dock was the brainchild of the engineer and architect, Jesse Hartley. Construction began in 1841, and five years later the official opening ceremony was performed by Queen Victoria's consort, Prince Albert. It was the first structure in the country to be built entirely of cast iron, brick and stone. Today, the dock forms the largest collection of Grade I listed buildings anywhere, and it's a World Heritage Site. The twentieth-century art historian, Nicholas Pevsner wrote: 'For sheer punch there is little in the early commercial architecture of Europe to emulate it.'

***

It's fitting that the Albert Dock is a bizarre mix – Victorian industrial practicality and the soft echo in its columns of ancient Greek civilisation. The Empire often brought together unexpected bedfellows.

On an innocent level, commerce and charity often went hand in hand. Those politicians and entrepreneurs who ruled or made their fortune in the Empire saw themselves as having duties as well as trading interests. They thought they had an obligation to spread English values – such as tolerance, democracy and the rule of law – while at the same time generating vast wealth from commerce with the colonies. Sometimes quite ordinary citizens took it upon themselves to go and spread the word of God to the natives in obscure parts of the Empire. In 1816, Robert Moffat, a man of little education and no theological training, went on behalf of the London Missionary Society to live among the Bechuana people of southern Africa and stayed with them teaching and preaching Christianity for the next fifty years. During this period, missionaries set up clinics and schools in many African and Asian colonies with money from their supporters in England. The mix of trade and good works in the Empire was summed up by one of the most famous and controversial of imperialists, Cecil Rhodes: 'Pure philanthropy is very well in its way but philanthropy plus 5 per cent is a good deal better.' It's clear that it was the '5 per cent' that attracted Rhodes.

The days of Empire often seemed to bring out the worst in the English, and Rhodes was typical, for instance, of a blend of arrogance and self-interest that surfaced in England's imperial age. The colonies, he said, would 'provide a dumping ground for the surplus goods produced in our factories.' He saw nothing conceited in pronouncing that the English 'are the first race in the world, and that the more of the world we inhabit the better it is for the human race.' Rhodes was not alone in expressing such views. That inveterate admirer of England and Empire, Thomas Macaulay, summed it up, without the slightest curl of an embarrassed toe, 'England is so great that an Englishman cares little what others think of her, or how they talk of her.' And this wasn't just the code of an elite. One Victorian school textbook taught children that the English were 'the greatest and most highly civilized people that the world ever saw.'

This kind of nationalistic bumptiousness can make us snigger and shudder today, but it had a very serious, dark side to it that stained the long history of Empire. Many of the people who found themselves subject to colonial rule were abused in every way imaginable. The 1808 William Wilberforce Act had made trading in slaves illegal, but it was not until 1833 that slavery itself was banned throughout the Empire, and even then not in India. That took another ten years. But this wasn't the end of forced labour. Slavery continued in all but name. Plantations across the Empire, in Fiji, Natal, Burma, Ceylon, Malaya, Guiana, Jamaica and Trinidad, still needed cheap labour. The answer was to ship in East Indians as 'indentured' workers. This often meant they were treated just as inhumanely as African slaves had been. They were in effect prisoners, were paid a pittance and were punished if they slacked at work. By the time the system was banned in 1917, 2.5 million Indians had been indentured.

But even this release didn't spell the end of violent abuse in India. Two years later, on the afternoon of 13 April 1919, a crowd of at least 10,000 men, women and children gathered in an enclosed square in the city of Amritsar. The local colonial administration regarded it as a dangerous protest against the arrest of prominent Indian leaders. Soldiers arrived and sealed off the only exit from the square. Without warning, the troops opened fire on the crowd. We still don't know exactly how many were killed, but one official report put casualties at 379 dead and 1,200 wounded. Many of them had nothing to do with the protest and were there to celebrate a spring festival.

The most puzzling contradiction of Empire for us today is how its rulers could see Christian civilisation and brutal racism as compatible. What happened in Ireland during the Great Famine between 1845 and 1852 helps explain the thinking of some Victorians. During these seven years, approximately 1 million Irish people died and a million more emigrated. At the height of the famine, the colonial administrator Charles Trevelyan gave orders that further relief aid from the imperial government should be cut off. He described the famine as an 'effective mechanism for reducing surplus population'. The real evil is not the famine, he wrote, 'but the moral evil of the selfish, perverse and turbulent character of the people'. The famine, he concluded, was 'the judgement of God'. On 27 April 1848, he was knighted for his services.

***

There was a strange moral blindness among Victorian imperialists. William Armstrong, whom we met at our last stop, was once asked if he had any regrets about inventing a better gun that had killed so many. He replied, 'If I thought that war would be fomented, or the interests of humanity suffer, by what I have done, I would greatly regret it. I have no such apprehension.' This kind of overweening arrogance produced an unquestioning 'my country, right or wrong' nationalism, a jingoistic patriotism. The very word 'jingoism' was born at this time. A popular song during the Crimean War went, 'We don't want to fight, but – by jingo! - if we do, the Russians shall not have Constantinople.'

The English believed they were unbeatable. And, so strong was this feeling of invulnerability, that on those occasions when they were defeated, they still managed to convince themselves that in some way or other they were victors. This twisted logic became embedded in the English psyche in 1854 with the Charge of the Light Brigade. In the second half of the nineteenth century, other nations had joined the scramble for empire – France, Germany, Belgium, Russia, Japan and the United States – and the competition between them to grab land sometimes erupted into armed conflict. It was at the Battle of Balaclava during the Crimean War – in which Britain was in alliance with France against Russia – that 673 cavalrymen rode into the 'Valley of Death'. They were ambushed by 5,000 Russian artillerymen and massacred. Only 200 cavalrymen returned. A muddled order had been given and had been blindly obeyed. Alfred Lord Tennyson, inspired by the event, wrote what remains to this day one of the best-known works of literature in the English language. Here are verses 2 and 6.

> Forward, the Light Brigade!
> Was there a man dismay'd?
> Not tho' the soldier knew
>   Someone had blunder'd:
> Theirs not to make reply,
> Theirs not to reason why,
> Theirs but to do and die:
> Into the valley of Death
>   Rode the six hundred.

> When can their glory fade?
> O the wild charge they made!
>   All the world wondered.
> Honour the charge they made,
> Honour the Light Brigade,
>   Noble six hundred.

If you didn't know, you might imagine this was a victory, rather than a ridiculous and tragic cock-up. Tennyson's popular version fails to take proper account of the stupidity and the waste of life, and it ignores the pain, the severed limbs, the cries of agony, the smell of death. Yes, the soldiers were brave, but as a French general who witnessed the charge, said, '*C'est magnifique, mais ce n'est pas la guerre. C'est de la folie.*' – 'It's magnificent, but it's not war. It's madness.'

But it wasn't quite as 'mad' as the Frenchman thought. It's difficult for us now to comprehend the sheer organisational and military skill required to administer and defend a quarter of the earth's landmass and a fifth of its population when military spending for most of the nineteenth century was around 2 to 3 per cent of national income, little more than today. The belief, encapsulated by the Charge of the Light Brigade, that it is not dishonourable to be defeated so long as you go down fighting had a practical benefit. It was vital to the survival of the Empire when so many territories around the world needed to be defended against any rebellion among their native residents or against competing imperial powers by relatively small numbers of soldiers. An army that disdains death can terrify an enemy.

The tradition had a profound effect on English character and behaviour. At its worst, it was used to send hundreds of thousands of soldiers in the trenches of the First World War to wholesale slaughter. At its best, stripped of the blunder and blindness of the Light Brigade's charge, it has given Britain's armed forces today a deserved reputation as one of the most disciplined and courageous in the world. And at its most idiosyncratic, it is reflected in the English public school maxim, 'It matters not to win or lose, it's how you play the game.' Today it allows the Saxon re-enactor we met at Hastings to say, 'In our hearts, we English always win… even when we lose.'

What's more, the Light Brigade's combination of bravery and self-belief, which was celebrated back in England by a proud and tearful public, reflected one of the most famous of English characteristic: the stiff upper lip. The idea that, even facing death, an Englishman (this is sexist because it's a sexist belief) betrays no emotion nor panic, stays calm and earns the respect even of his enemy.

At its height, the Empire made up the largest association of countries the world had ever seen. To have amassed such a huge realm, and to continue to rule and defend it, made the English feel mighty, and that was the origin of their overbearing self-belief and the arrogance of men like Rhodes. But although we find so much today to condemn in Empire, we should also recognise that – in the days before computers, instantaneous communications or air travel – just running it was an extraordinary achievement. It wasn't just that the Empire was defended by relatively small numbers of soldiers and sailors. The Diplomatic Service consisted of only 150 men throughout the second half of the nineteenth century, compared with 6,000 diplomats and foreign office civil servants now. The Colonial Office in 1903 employed just 113 clerks. However else the Empire is remembered, it did bring out one positive English quality: a talent for administration.

***

The period of most rapid growth in the size of the Empire came in the second half of the nineteenth century. And expansion brought more trade. In 1869, the Suez Canal was opened, making the passage to and from the British Raj, which covered modern-day Pakistan and Bangladesh as well as India itself, faster and more economic. And Liverpool merchants cashed in. These were the halcyon days of the Albert Dock.

But such days were short-lived. The Albert thrived for no more than half a century. From where we are now, on board *Skylark,* the old dock's limitations are clear. It's roughly the size of Trafalgar Square with two narrow water entrances, both spanned by cast-iron swing bridges like the one we've just passed beneath. The dock was built to accommodate sailing ships with a cargo capacity of no more than 1,000 tons. But Hartley's design hadn't anticipated the impact of the steam engine, and by the turn of the twentieth century only 7 per cent of vessels coming in and out of Liverpool were still under sail. However, although the Albert Dock went into decline, many of Liverpool's other docks were kept busy, ones where the much larger, steam-powered ships could enter to load and offload their cargoes. Keith explains how each dock had its own speciality: the Queen's for fish; the Old Dock for West Indian and African business; the King's for ships coming and going from America and the Baltic. All of these we see from *Skylark*'s deck as we move along short canals and beneath the iron bridges that connect them. They have a much more open feel to them than the Albert. Today their warehouses are converted to luxury flats, and one's even a casino. Liverpool at one time or another has had no fewer than forty-three separate docks. And by the early 1900s, one third of the country's exports and a quarter of all imports passed through the warehouses we're looking at now. Liverpool merchants owned one third of the country's ships and no less than one seventh of the total registered shipping in the world.

***

We're now in the Wapping Dock, and Keith directs us to look over to the left, where a metal-coated spire rises over the old warehouses. 'That's the Norwegian church,' he explains. 'Lots of fellers from Norway came over on ships carrying timber. They fell in love with our own beautiful scouser girls, married them and never went back.'

Liverpool was a multicultural city long before the rest of England. In 1877, a local magazine wrote, 'Everything around us tells us of far-off countries and foreign ways, and in our midst are constantly natives of so many distant lands.' The influx of people had started early in the city's history. Its growing prosperity in the eighteenth century had been a magnet to people from Wales and Scotland as well as other parts of England. By far the biggest contingent came from Ireland, driven from home by poverty and famine; the Scouse accent today owes much to the Irish, who by 1851 made up over 22 per cent of Liverpudlians. And there were Africans and West Indians here, at first freed slaves and then later ships' crew members who, along with many Chinese and Filipinos, decided to stay. And then there were those who ended up here by accident. They were the immigrants from central Europe and Russia who when they saw the thriving wharves and magnificent buildings on the docks at Liverpool thought they must have reached New York, got off at the wrong stop, and settled here. The American novelist Herman Melville – author of *Moby Dick* – admired Liverpool's racial tolerance: 'Three or four times, I encountered our black steward, dressed very handsomely, and walking arm-in-arm with a good-looking English woman. In New York, such a couple would have been mobbed in three minutes; and the steward would have been lucky to escape with his whole limbs.'

During the days of Empire, more than at any other time in its history, England was outward-looking. It wasn't just sailors, traders and soldiers who learned about the world beyond England's shores. Colonial administrators, academics, parliamentarians, journalists, novelists, artists, businessmen, tourists, transported criminals and many others did too. And the people of Liverpool, Bristol, the East End of London and the rest of England's trading ports didn't have to travel at all to rub shoulders with others of different creeds and colours. As a result, one of the most valuable legacies of Empire came with its impact on the English language. Exposure to almost half a billion people speaking hundreds of different languages and dialects enriched the way the English speak. So, today for instance, without realising we owe a debt to the Hindi and Urdu people, we use words such as 'avatar', 'bungalow', 'cushy', 'dinghy', 'guru', 'jungle', 'loot', 'mantra', 'nirvana', 'pyjamas', 'shampoo', 'thug', 'veranda', 'yoga' and many more.

***

Liverpool's decline as a great trading city paralleled that of the Empire itself. With the end of the Second World War, the Empire soon collapsed. The very English value of political freedom could no longer be denied to colonies whose soldiers had fought and died alongside those of the home nations. And besides, the blows that the war delivered to the home economy meant that the costs of administering and defending a global empire could no longer be supported. India – the 'Jewel in the Crown' – became a self-governing state in 1947, to be followed by the rest of the colonies over the next decade.

The Empire – as much as any other force in England's history – had brought out powerful characteristics in the English. By the turn of the twentieth century, they saw themselves as the greatest trading nation ever, ruling the most expansive realm, even surpassing that of ancient Rome. The self-belief and self-confidence of the English erupted in the most jingoistic nationalism, and blinded them to the immorality of the systematic racist brutality that was used to support commercial profit and obedience to rule from London. And the certainty of the English that they were undefeatable generated a macho militarism. However, at the same time, the imperialists persuaded themselves that they were benefiting those they ruled by spreading the values of Christian civilisation. And it's true that it was the English who took the lead in abolishing slavery (though of course forced labour continued), while an outsider could praise the people of Liverpool for their racial tolerance, and thousands of Christian missionaries set up schools and hospitals in needy regions of the Empire.

All the contradictions in the English character during the age of Empire can best be explained in one word: arrogance. You can only believe that brutal racism and brotherly love can exist side by side if you're conceited enough to think that you are a nation that can do no wrong. While other elements of English identity – a preference for political stability, for instance, or respect for the rule of law – had developed over many hundreds of years, the peculiar national characteristics that emerged at the time of the Empire were forged over the relatively short period of a century. So would the identity created by Empire persist? Would these new English characteristics survive the end of Empire in the middle of the twentieth century? How would they be affected by two world wars? We shall come back to look for answers shortly.

***

But on our next stop, we're going to consider one particular question. Would the macho battle cries of Empire drown out the increasingly loud demands of many women back home? They wanted equal rights.

It had been a point of special pride for the Victorians to claim that the English parliamentary democracy led the world. It was self-delusion. The English may have been first, but voting rights had been stuck in the Middle Ages for 400 years. True democracy requires every adult citizen to have the right to choose those who make the laws. But it was well into the twentieth century before 50 per cent of the population, women, got the vote. Did their struggle influence who the English think they are? To find out, let's go to a racecourse where a 40-year-old woman was trampled to death beneath the hooves of a horse. And England today still can't make up its mind whether she was a hero or not.

17

Epsom Downs
Racecourse, Surrey

....

RETURN TICKET TO DEATH

....

THE QUEEN IS MOST ANXIOUS TO
ENLIST EVERYONE WHO CAN SPEAK OR
WRITE TO JOIN IN CHECKING THIS MAD,
WICKED FOLLY OF 'WOMAN'S RIGHTS'
WITH ALL ITS ATTENDANT HORRORS.

QUEEN VICTORIA (1819–1901) IN 1879

The weather is so bad they've named it twice.

For the technically minded, it's called an 'explosive cyclogenesis'. Sounds like a prototype version of a car bomb, a sort of bike bomb. Its other name, for the benefit of non-technos, is 'Petra'. Meteorologists have this compulsion to give hurricanes and other bouts of foul weather cosy names. Why, I don't know. As I rush from the house to the car through the torrents of driving rain, I'd be happy for it to be named Storm No. P67Y84, or something equally impersonal. But the bureaucrats in some Euromet Centre christen them alternately boy-girl-boy-girl as the tempest season progresses. Once upon a time, they chose only girls' names. Then somebody pointed out that this was discriminatory against 50 per cent of the world's population. Men had as much right to share the humiliation of being used to denominate something nasty. Today's explosive cyclogenesis, though, is a girl, and in fact, we're only getting her tail end.

Petra is concentrating her efforts on trashing the Basque Country in northern Spain.

I throw myself into the car, splashing water everywhere from my hat and coat. We're off to the races. To be precise, Epsom Downs Racecourse in Surrey.

At Epsom on Derby Day in 1913, a 40-year-old woman stepped on to the track and ended up beneath the hooves of Anmer, the king's horse. She died four days later. Her name was Emily Wilding Davison. She was a suffragette, making a protest in the fight for women's right to vote. I want to answer the question, did the bitter struggle by women to win equal rights with men do anything to modify the macho characteristic that Empire had brought out in the English?

***

Today, through the frantic thrashing of the windscreen wipers, I suddenly make out a small dirty river straight ahead. It seems to be flowing under a railway bridge. I stop to allow the van in front to launch itself into the water before beaching itself on the other side. Once it's clear, I tell myself, 'Go for it, I guess.' And after a satisfying five-second whoosh, I'm in Epsom High Street.

There are five races at Epsom today. It's the Spring Meeting and the third race is a practice outing for horses and riders who'll be running in the Derby itself in a few weeks' time. What I'm aiming to do is stand at Tattenham Corner, the famous bend just before the final straight on the Epsom Downs course, just as Emily Davison did before she stepped out into the path of the horses. The course today will be less crowded, so I should be able to position myself in the exact spot where the tragedy happened.

There's an unsolved mystery about her death. No one knows whether she committed suicide or whether it was a reckless accident. Emily Davison had earned a First in English at Oxford, though because she was a woman it couldn't officially be awarded to her. The campaign to recognise the right of women to cast their vote was launched in 1867, and at first was conducted peacefully. It got nowhere. Then along came Emmeline and Christabel Pankhurst, who decided that militancy and even violence were the answer. In 1906, Emily Davison joined them. Over the next few

Emily Wilding Davison.

years, she chained herself to the railings of government buildings, smashed windows, attacked a police barricade with an axe, tried to assault the Prime Minister and on three occasions broke into the Houses of Parliament.

She was imprisoned five times, and it was in jail that the bravest of her protests took place. She barricaded herself in her cell. She was hosed down with freezing water, handcuffed and straitjacketed. Later, like other suffragettes in prison, she went on hunger strike. The response of the prison authorities was brutal. They force-fed her. Emily described what happened:

> While I was being held down, a nasal tube was inserted. It is two yards long with a funnel at one end. The end is put up one nostril one day, and the other nostril the next. Great pain is experienced during the process, both mental and physical. The drums of the ear seem to be bursting, a horrible pain is in the throat and the breast. If the doctor doesn't think the fluid is going down sufficiently swiftly, he pinches my nose with the tube in it and my throat, causing me great pain.

She records that she was subjected to this treatment on nearly fifty occasions. By the time she came to Epsom on Derby Day in 1913, repeated brutal treatment had affected her health, perhaps psychological as well as physical.

***

Today, once I've found somewhere to park the car, I'm soon leaning on a balcony railing, peering through the misty downpour at the finishing post, and studying the 'racecard' I've bought (actually a forty-eight-page booklet) and making marks on it with a pen as though I know what I'm doing, which – as you'll have gathered – I don't. But something does catch my eye. The name of the very first horse here, in the first race, is Liberty Lady! And this on the day I've come to search for memories of a woman who fought for a basic freedom. Liberty Lady! If I were superstitious, I'd think it was a good luck message. I should go and place a bet on her, but I don't because I don't know how to do it and I don't want to look stupid.

A commentary starts blaring from the loudspeaker above my head, and I take it that they're off, though I can't see any horses anywhere. Soon everyone's yelling, and the race is over. It was won apparently by a horse called Cadeaux Pearl ridden by Kieran Fallon – even I've heard of him – in a time of fifty-seven seconds. Liberty Lady comes in tenth. Sometimes stupidity pays off.

I decide to take advantage of the fact that the rain, which keeps alternating between typhoon and just plain old heavy stuff, is more of the latter at this moment. But that's still enough to deter most of my fellow racegoers, so there's just me and a few press photographers there to see Cadeaux Pearl and Kieran arrive at the little ring in triumph. I'm within autograph-hunting range of the celebrated jockey, and for a moment I consider offering him my racecard and a pen. But instead I content myself with the thought that there's something satisfying about being up close to a famous person who's got splodges of mud all over his face. Besides he's busy chatting to a bloke in a trilby and astrakhan coat, who's clapping him on the back.

However, all this is displacement activity. A distraction, allowing me to put off the moment when I have to brave the elements and get to Tattenham Corner.

***

Epsom Downs is unusual. The track isn't a stretched circle like other racecourses. Its layout resembles a gigantic horseshoe whose two ends have been bent outwards. And as you stand, as I do now, opposite the winning post, you can see the final straight, but before that the track swings in from across the hilly downs and some-where over the horizon. The punters in the grandstand have to watch the start on a gigantic TV screen. Where Emily met the flailing hooves of the king's horse is about a third of a mile over to my left where the track curves away. So I've got to walk across the downs to get there, and what's more, she was on the inside of the bend, so I've somehow got to cross the track.

I ask various men in official Epsom hoodies how to do that, and either because I've wandered into the members' enclosure so they assume I'm posh or because it's starting to pelt it down with rain again and they don't want to stand around talking to me, they each point in a different direction then rush off before I can discover that they didn't really know the answer at all. So – knowing no better - I head for the gap in the rails where there's a sign in big green letters saying 'Keep Off The Course'. I have to be careful once I've passed it, because there are racehorses cantering about – or whatever it is they do when they're going quite fast though not at full speed trying to win. I guess they're getting ready for the next race, and are making their way round to the start. They're tall and formidable creatures, horses. You definitely do not want to get anywhere near their hooves when they're trying to reach somewhere on the other side of you. And it strikes me that Emily, born in 1872, had grown up in an age when horses were as com-monplace as cars are now. She would surely have known exactly what the risks were when she slipped under the rail that day.

I make it safely to the other side, pull my flat hat down over my eyes, and march on – straight into a wall of hailstones – up towards Tattenham Corner. When, after about two hours (yes, I know it couldn't have been that long, it just seemed like it), I reach the point where the track starts to bend, I stop and peer round. The hail has now given way to sleety rain, which appears to be coming at me horizontally from the direction of Wales, 140 miles away.

I realise for the first time that apart from two hooded guys with garden forks stabbing at clods of turf kicked up by the horses in the last race, there is not another soul in sight. When Emily was here, the crowds were six deep at the side of the rail, and of course it was a sunny day.

'Is this Tattenham Corner?' I shout to one of the two turf-stabbers.

He's either fed up with his task, or else he feels solidarity with me as a fellow storm victim, because he spends a good five minutes explaining that it all depends how you define Tattenham Corner. The pub of that name is further back on the road across the track, but on balance he reckons, as far as spectators are concerned, the Corner is several hundred yards further on. So I take a firm grip of my hat, which is now sodden and sitting like a half-cooked pancake on the top of my head, and off I trudge again, the sleet slapping against my glasses, my feet sliding sideways in the mud every second step.

***

After five minutes, I take stock. And I realise that, whereas Emily and the 1913 crowds could get right up to the trackside rail, today you're kept behind a second and a third rail six or seven yards from where the horses will race by. There's nothing to indicate this is Tattenham Corner, but I head on a few yards further to where another hooded and anoracked course employee is stationed. We greet each other, again like fellow sufferers. He's a young guy. I like him, because he's curious about things. He asks what I'm doing standing in the rain on such an awful day, and I tell him I'm researching the death of Emily Davison.

'Oh yes,' he says, 'I remember now. She was a suffragette. But I didn't know it happened right here. So it was suicide, was it?'

'Well that's the mystery,' I reply. 'Nobody's sure. There are two theories. Suicide. Or that she was just trying to make a protest, maybe by trying to pin a banner on the king's horse.'

Sam turns – he's told me his name now – and, pointing over to the far side of the course, shouts, 'They're off! They'll be here any moment.'

It's slightly downhill round Tattenham Corner, the point where the jockeys get the first glimpse of the finishing post, so they'll be travelling – today as in 1913 – at around 40 miles an hour. The clutch of speeding horses and riders comes into view. And three things occur to me in the next few seconds: First, the noise. Hooves are often said to thunder, but it sounds to me more like ten bass drums being thumped at once. You could imagine that the ground beneath your feet is vibrating. Secondly, there's the chaotic motion of the horses. A car going past at 40 miles an hour is unremarkable, because it's a smooth movement. But a horse is rocking, literally. Its long nose is pumping up and down, its whole body pivoting like a piston with every stride. And its legs - with those lethal hooves – are flying up, back and even outwards. And thirdly, in a race, like the Derby, you have to multiply that image ten or fifteen times, till you have a towering mass of pounding horseflesh coming at you, moving unpredictably as the jockeys edge their mounts this way and that to gain an advantage. It's over and they're past us in a flash.

'Wow,' I say, nodding my head, 'it's exciting!'

'Yeah,' says Sam, 'I know. It always gets me.'

We turn our backs to the wind and the rain, and I put it to Sam, 'So, what do you reckon, could she have brought the horse down safely and fixed a banner on its side?'

Sam shakes his head. 'Well, you've seen for yourself, it'd be odds on you'd be killed or badly hurt. She must have known that. It's got to be suicide, hasn't it?'

'Well, there's evidence both ways,' I reply. 'For instance, when she caught the train from Victoria Station to Epsom that morning, she bought a return ticket. And another thing, she told friends she'd see them at a suffragette meeting the following evening. Nobody said she behaved like a woman who knew she was about to die. She seemed her usual self. And apparently she had a suffragette flag pinned inside her coat where she could whip it out and place it on the king's horse.'

'It still doesn't make sense to me,' says Sam.

'Sure. We do have first-hand evidence to help us decide,' I say 'A Pathe News cameraman was filming from across the other side of the track, probably up there.' I point to a little hillock which today has a garden seat on top. 'Of course, it's a very grainy black and white picture, and the shot is pretty static. But it's recently been

Derby Day 1913, Tattenham Corner. Emily's hat is still tumbling, the King's horse is on its back, and many in the crowd, looking towards the finishing line, have missed what's happened.

cleaned up and you can see it on the Internet in slow motion at the crucial moments.' I've watched it before I left home, and I describe it to Sam. Emily slips under the rail and onto the track just as the leading horse gets level with her, and then she stands there on the turf waiting for a moment or two. When the first group of horses has gone through, she dodges round the last one, and there's a slight gap before the king's horse, Anmer, which is pretty much on its own. You can see Emily in her long dress, wearing a light coloured hat. As Anmer gets closer, she raises her left arm slightly and appears to drop her head. It's difficult to make out what she means to do next. It could be that she steps forward straight into the oncoming horse. Or it could be that she moves slightly to the left as though she intended to grab its reins as it went by. You can't tell for sure. But whichever it is, the horse falls and Emily is tossed by its hooves. She's flung in a rolling somersault through the air, arms flailing like a rag doll for several metres, her hat flying off. The horse gets up and races on riderless. The jockey's lying on the ground. He was knocked out. Then the crowds all rush onto the track to go and help the two of them or just to gawp.

'Was she killed outright?' asks Sam.

'No. She was taken to Epsom Cottage Hospital. She had to be protected by police from angry punters who'd lost money on Anmer.'

'Jeez,' says Sam, 'that's terrible.'

'I know. She never recovered consciousness. People sent hate mail to her in hospital. One letter said, "I hope you suffer torture till you die," and somebody else wrote, "I should like the opportunity of starving you and beating you to a pulp."'

Sam shivers, 'You just can't believe it, can you?'

'The country was split. Some thought she was a monster. Others a heroic martyr. She died four days later. 50,000 people watched her funeral procession in London.'

'I suppose we'll never really know what she really meant to do,' he says. 'What happened to the jockey?'

'Herbert Jones. He was the Kieran Fallon of his day. He suffered concussion and a few broken ribs, but he always said he could never get Emily's face out of his mind.'

'That's like train drivers,' observes Sam, 'when somebody kills themselves jumping in front of their train.'

'That's right. Herbert Jones committed suicide himself some years later.'

'Terrible story,' says Sam shaking his head, and as the rain starts pouring again. We nod to each other, and Sam gets back to his work, prodding the lumps of turf back into place.

***

There can't be much doubt that when Emily Davison set off for Epsom, her intention was to carry out a protest of some sort, and it's difficult to believe that, at that stage, she intended to kill herself. You can't ignore the return ticket, or her up-beat behaviour beforehand. But then how do we account for an act which, she must have known, was almost certain to lead to her death or very serious injury, just as surely as if she'd stepped straight in front of a car going at 40 miles an hour?

The only explanation that fits all the evidence is that she acted on impulse, and at the very last moment decided to kill herself. If she'd told anyone what she was going to do, we don't know about it. It could have been that she'd arrived at Epsom intending for instance to plant the banner on the king's horse while it was being paraded before the race, or something else far less risky than what actually happened. Her mother – and who would know her better? – seemed to think it was a last-minute, split-second decision. She wrote, 'It must have been some sudden impulse and excitement.' And the notion of suicide had been in Emily's thoughts before. When she was in prison, she once threw herself down a 30ft drop onto wire netting. She survived, and wrote afterwards, 'The idea in my mind was one big tragedy may save many others.'

I look around the spot where she died. From here, gorse bushes half-shield a distant view of the grandstand. Thick black clouds lurch across the sky. If it weren't for the white rails alongside the course, this could almost be a Scottish moor. But on that sunny June day in 1913, thousands of people here were drinking, picnicking, laughing, shouting together to urge on the horse they'd put their money on, 'Go on girl! Go on girl! Get up there!' The atmosphere would have been frenetic. And that too might have contributed to her sudden decision to kill herself. So the evidence points to a quick flash across her mind. Now was her chance to do something spectacular which the whole country would know about, and which she felt would shock the nation into giving women the vote.

***

So did Emily Davison's death hasten the day when women won the right to vote?

It's hard to claim her act had any direct impact. This was 1913, and when war broke out the next year and the men went off to die in the trenches, the women took over many of the jobs on the home front. The war changed the role of women for ever, and in 1918, they got to vote for the first time. Even then, though, it wasn't universal. It was only for those over the age of 30 who owned property or whose husbands owned property. Full voting equality took another 10 years.

I cross back over the track, empty of horses now, and find myself this time among the other non-badge-holding members of racing society who have left the warmth of the bar since the rain is no longer driving full force across the concrete slope in front of the grandstand. There are bunches of young men in tight-fitting suits and loosened ties, as though they've bunked off from the office for the day, splashing plastic pint mugs of lager about, laughing and barging into each other. And there are lots of young women, some with blokes in tow, others in girl-groups. They've adopted a uniform. Long hair, short jackets, spray-on jeans and the highest stiletto heels it's possible to wear without dislocating an ankle. They lark about, taking photos of each other on their smart phones in grinning startled poses. One, with raven black elbow-length hair and a tight blue top pinched in at the waist, screams, 'Cheryl! Cheryl! What's she like!' Cheryl is draping herself round the neck of a young man with a hazy smile.

I wonder if I'm the only spectator here today who's given any thought to Emily Davison and her death at Tattenham Corner.

I watch a couple more races, standing at the winning post, then decide to leave and beat the traffic. Pausing just before the gate, I spot a full-size statue of horse. There's a plaque on its plinth.

GENEROUS
Winner of the Derby 1991
Presented to Epsom Racecourse by his owner
HRH Prince Fahd bin Salman
bin Abdul Aziz Al Saud
Unveiled by Her Majesty Queen Elizabeth II
10th June 1995

Emily Wilding Davison was the only woman to lose her life in the struggle to win votes for women. And this is where it happened. And yet, there's a statue to commemorate a horse, but no such memorial to remind people of the historic sacrifice of a human being struggling for democratic rights.

***

The day after this field research trip to Epsom, I decided to write an article for the *Guardian* Women's Page, and it was published the following Monday under the headline, 'Why is there still no memorial for Emily Wilding Davison?' It seemed to me an unarguable miscarriage of justice for this hero to be so ignored. I could not have guessed at the reaction. I was shocked. By mid-morning, within hours of the article being published, there was a long train of comments on the *Guardian* website. Twenty-two people were going at it, back and forth, chucking insults at each other. Opinion was split roughly 55:45 *against* the suffragette and *against* the idea of a memorial to her. Most of the comments, as far as I could tell, came from women, and none from some outraged male voicing anti-feminist views. I was amazed that readers of the *Guardian* Women's Page weren't united in their demand for recognition of the suffragette's heroic sacrifice to win them the right to vote.

But what also shocked me about the debate I'd unwittingly set off was the language. E-tempers flared across the net. Almost all those who commented jabbed out insults accusing each other of 'stupidity', of being 'irrational', they called each other 'you bloody people', with one writer claiming an opponent was guilty of 'the most disgusting and false things I've ever seen written'. And there was even worse. Davison herself was described in terms ranging from 'silly' to 'moron', and was even branded a 'terrorist'. It's difficult to understand the cause of so much venom and spleen. After all, readers of the *Guardian* are hardly likely to be fascist anti-democrats. And anyway, it's not as though Davison's death happened last week. It was 100 years ago. One of the less abusive writers picked this up. She wrote, 'I just googled the Tolpuddle Martyrs, who founded the concept of trade unions in 1832, and see that it took until 2000 for a competition to be launched to commemorate them in stone.' And the writer went on to suggest that the English like to put up statues to their ancestors, so long as they weren't rebels.

This may be so. And to extend the idea a little further, I wonder whether the present-day reaction to Davison's death means that the English still cherish the idea of non-violent political debate, of change through rational discussion and a rejection of anything that mixes democracy with bloodshed or extremism of any sort. It's one thing to do a bit of bad-mouthing, another entirely to think you can impose your views on others through acts of violence. That's the mainstream English view.

There's no doubt that a preference for political stability, that we first saw in England with the Bloodless Revolution of 1668-69, is still a powerful characteristic of English thought and behaviour in the twenty-first century. We often see it as the hallmark of a civilised society. But we should also recognise that it's had its downsides in our history. There have been times when our desire for a peaceful life could be mistaken for a lack of passion, even for apathy that could be exploited by those who supported the status quo, by those who had most to lose from change. The fight for the right to vote comes into this category. Women had to wait a disgracefully long time. And – something we often forget – so did the overwhelming majority of men too.

As we saw earlier on our journey, men who owned land outright which was worth at least 40 shillings a year, had been given the vote in 1429. It's extraordinary that after such a progressive early start, this limitation didn't change significantly for the next 400 years, by which time it was still only 3 per cent of the adult population of England who could vote. But pressure was mounting to extend suffrage. By the early nineteenth century, the voting system was clearly rotten and outdated. Industrial cities like Leeds, Birmingham and Manchester didn't have a single MP between them, whereas ancient boroughs such as Dunwich in Suffolk – population: thirty-two – sent two MPs to Westminster.

It had to change. The first Reform Act was passed in 1832. Note the words of the then Prime Minister, Lord Grey, who supported the new law only 'to prevent the necessity of revolution'. However, Grey made sure the Act did the minimum needed to satisfy that end. It gave the vote only to men in towns, and then only to those who occupied property with an annual value of £10. That still meant six adult males out of seven couldn't vote. And no women, of course. A second Reform Act in 1867 – the Tory politician Lord Derby shook his head and warned it would be 'a leap in the dark' – extended similar rights to those who lived in the countryside. But that still left three out of five Englishmen disenfranchised. Even the third Act in 1884, which gave the ballot to all male heads of households, still left 40 per cent of men voteless. And, of course, all women – whether duchesses or their maids – were still left out.

England – and Britain by this stage – lagged behind many of its neighbours. In France, all men were given the vote within three years of the Revolution of 1789. Greece followed suit in 1830. The Swiss government granted full male suffrage after the 1848 revolution there. And Germany did the same twenty-three years later. England and the other home nations were three quarters of a century later, with equal voting rights for all citizens in 1928 – and, just to show how recent that was, my own mother was already 19 years old.

The slow progress of reform here was partly because revolutionary violence seemed a little more distant, and little less of a threat than it was for our European neighbours. And there was something else too. By limiting reform, governments were also ensuring that the pace of change continue to be slow. While ever voting was restricted to men with property, men who had a stake in the country as it was, conservative rather than radical ideas were more likely to prevail. And history too played its part. In the mid-twentieth century, the left-wing writer George Orwell put it this simply: 'There's no revolutionary tradition in England.'

Now, I'm not advocating the violent overthrow of governments, or military coups, as acceptable mechanisms for change in England. Like most English people today, I value a political life where we can have robust debate without the fear that opponents will start to throw punches, pull out guns or erect barricades in the streets. But as a historian, I can recognise that sometimes the very English value of social and political stability has come with a heavy price. And I can also recognise and sympathise with the frustration that women like Emily Davison must have felt. She didn't start a revolution, and there's no evidence she intended to. But she had right on her side, and she was determined and brave. Just as Horatio Nelson was determined and brave. And for Emily the challenge was in some ways even greater than that faced by Nelson. She and her fellow suffragettes found the system was against them, and as an Englishwoman she had to do something very un-English to advance her cause.

***

Since I made my own pilgrimage to Tattenham Corner in 2012, there's been a slight change. If you go there today, you will find a small plaque fixed to the railings there at waist height. It's about 30in wide by 10in, and – without mentioning how Emily Davison died – it does note 'her lifelong dedication to women's suffrage'. I like to think my *Guardian* article may have played a small part in this minor victory. The plaque was unveiled just before Derby Day 2013. The Epsom Downs Racecourse management, by the way, rejected the idea of a minute's silence before the race began, because it was 'logistically impossible' to organise.

***

Thirteen months after Emily Davison's death, there began the bloodiest war the world has ever seen. Emily's death may not have done much to change the way the English saw themselves, but the First World War did. During the 100th anniversary commemorations, we remember it still as though it were yesterday. Come with me now. To reach our next stop, we're travelling back in time.

18

Imperial War Museum, London

....

Mechanised Slaughter

....

IF ANY QUESTION WHY WE DIED,
TELL THEM, BECAUSE OUR FATHERS LIED.

RUDYARD KIPLING (1865–1936)

The men are running in slow motion, bent forwards, rifles with bayonets fixed pointing at an enemy they can't see. You can hear them panting, short tense breaths. They're thin, athletic young men, no more than silhouettes against a dawn sky, where white ghosts are frozen in their own urgent dash. There's a stutter of machine-gun fire, then a howl, louder and louder, and the shriek of an incoming shell, its smooth note descending till it's swallowed by a rising chaotic rumble. The figure leading the men curves his arm in a 'Come on! Keep going!' gesture. There's no explosion. Just a fearsome roar. Then as it dies, the rat-tat of flying shrapnel, and the men, still running, fall, necks whiplashed, arms twisted, bodies crashing. We hear cries. In pain or shock, we can't know. The last man to fall, in a final defiant act, seems to throw something over his tumbling comrades, towards the unseen gun. For a few seconds, the bodies writhe in a rumpled carpet, legs fly up before being yanked back to the now blood-red ground. Then silence. There's no tense panting now. Only the ghosts of the men remain, still frozen in the dawn sky.

One minute later, it all starts again. The men are running in slow motion, bent forwards. There's the same deafening roar. The same cries of pain or shock. The same blood-red ground. The same ghosts left in the dawn sky. And one minute later, it starts again. And again, and again. The same deathly rigmarole, three hundred times a day.

We're in the Imperial War Museum, a ten-minute walk south of London's Waterloo Station. What we've been watching isn't a film. It's more like a *son et lumière*. But unlike the sound and light show we might sit and watch on a summer's evening, projected against the distant screen of a castle wall, this display is right in front of us, close enough that we could almost touch the shadows of the stricken soldiers. I'm one of a dozen visitors grouped before it, and a number of us stay to see it through several times. We don't speak. The display we've been watching, for all its two-dimensional limitations, is strangely moving, much more so than if it had been an accurate Hollywood performance. It's almost the first exhibit on the Museum's lower floor, which is devoted to what my grandparents always called the Great War.

The galleries here are dark. They're not big, open, square rooms as you'd see in an art gallery. There's just enough light to see the many uniforms, guns, letters home from Tommies in the trenches, and there are grainy black and white films, and photographs of men up to the knees in mud struggling with stretchers bearing their wounded or dying comrades. It's as though we're in a vast cellar – not a safe air-raid shelter, more a place where we're trapped, at the mercy of a hidden attacker. We weave our way around the dimly lit maze of exhibits, a disturbing nightmare where you can't find a way out.

What gives immediacy to the museum more than all else are the sounds. As we move around, among the other ghosts – we all whisper here, even the children – we hear the sudden, piercing rattle of machine-gun fire. Then, it's a thin whistle. In peacetime it would be a referee stopping play, but in wartime it's some lieutenant, not long out of school uniform, telling his men it's time to climb the ladders out of the trench, to go over the top, into no-man's-land, and charge against the enemy. We hear the echoing bang of an outgoing shell, and the distant crump as it lands. Then the screech of an incoming round, a half-second's silence before the explosion, the tings and clanks of flying metal on helmets and tanks, the muffled shrieks and the groans of injured men.

At one point on my journey through the war, I find myself in a trench. It's a yard wide and its sides stretch up a couple of feet above my head. Its floor isn't slimy with sludge, nor its walls crumbling, as they would have been in a real trench. A sign at its entrance tells us: 'The experience of trench warfare is impossible to recreate. But in the space you are about to enter, we have tried to give you a sense of the confinement and exposure to the elements that millions of men endured.' And again, it's the sounds as well as the shadows projected on the trench wall that hint at the ghosts of the men who fought in such places. You can hear the clink of tea mugs, of voices joking – 'Just like Mother makes, Alf,' of a man asking for news, 'What's happening down the line?' Suddenly we're in a thunderstorm, the rain hammering down. Then a more sinister noise: a plane flying over, a tank engine and then the bustle of men scurrying for safety when a gas attack is threatened. In the shadows, we see barbed wire, a sniper aiming his gun, men crawling. At the far end, life-sized photographs of real men back in 1916 together in just such a trench, crouching, leaning against a post, two with pipes gripped in their teeth, all with bayonets fixed to their rifles, helmets firmly down, waiting for that whistle to send them over the top. One man manages a tight smile for the camera.

At no point in the First World War galleries of the Imperial War Museum are there mannequins of soldiers. If we see a face, it's always on an original photograph or a grainy film. Even the uniforms – drab khaki, boots, webbing, knap-sack, ammunition belt – are mounted on empty metal stands, each with its helmet in the correct position, but a gap where the head and face would be. There are no lifeless dummies with blank faces posed around a gun, or with comic book expressions of horror at the moment of death. The Museum's curators have realised that to do this would be a pantomime, disrespectful, and that presenting the men of a century ago as spirits allows us to live with them in our imaginations.

But while the Museum's curators have made living ghosts of the men, they've chosen very real weaponry to show us. And the more I look at the heavy, curved lines of the massive shells and explosive mines, and at the steel and brass mechanisms of the gigantic, ponderous guns, the more I'm struck by the contrast between men and metal: iron and steel, still killers even when smashed into shrapnel, against the vulnerable flesh of men. It must often have felt like that in the trenches too. There must have been times when a soldier would feel he too was no more than an expendable cog in the killing machine, a number, no more.

***

The Imperial War Museum does more than create powerful images of life on the battlefields of northern France and Belgium 100 years ago. It also tells the story of how the war unfolded and, through artefacts and letters, explains the feelings and opinions of those who lived and died in it.

When war was declared in July 1914, volunteers flocked to sign up in the armed forces. The Secretary of State for War, Lord Kitchener appealed for 100,000 volunteers. Within weeks, he'd got 761,000. And by the end of 1915 almost two-and-a-half million men had joined up, one in three of those eligible. And 100,000 women, too, volunteered. Most believed – and historical evidence supports that belief – that they would be fighting against an autocratic regime which, unlike in England and in Britain, was anti-democratic.

The English, of course, weren't the only nation to go through the 'Great War'. Ordinary Germans, Russians and citizens of the Austro-Hungarian Empire suffered on the opposing side, as well as French, Belgians and – in the later stages of hostilities – Americans among the allies. And of course it was not an English army fighting, but the British army, with men – and women in nursing and support roles – from Scotland, Wales and Ireland going to war together. And 2 million men from the Empire – Australians, New Zealanders, Canadians and South Africans as well as 'natives' of colonies such as Nigeria – also fought, and many died. But the fact that the experience was shared does not undermine the way the war influenced the English sense of themselves. And, strangely perhaps, English soldiers in the British army saw themselves as fighting for English freedom, rather than British. The 27-year-old Rupert Brooke, who signed on as an officer of the Royal Naval Division when war broke out, wrote:

If I should die, think only this of me:
That there's some corner of a foreign field
That is forever England...

And there, he says, will be:

... dreams happy as her day;
And laughter, learnt of friends; and gentleness,
In hearts at peace, under an English heaven.

This kind of romantic, idealistic patriotism helped galvanise the war effort. It was in 1916 that the composer Hubert Parry turned William Blake's 'Jerusalem' into a stirring anthem that suggested that England was so special even Jesus may have visited it:'And did those feet in ancient time walk upon Englands mountains green?'

But this was a sentiment from an old world – a world of Empire – before the war, a world that would be shattered over the next four years, and with it any notion of romance in war. Many of the young men who were commissioned as officers had come from privileged backgrounds. At the public schools of England, they had been taught that it was their duty, and their honour, to defend their country. Lessons from the ancient classical world had been drummed into them:'*Dulce et decorum est pro patria mori*' – 'It is a sweet and honourable thing to die for one's country.' Wilfred Owen, who was in the trenches in early 1917, was not one of those public school boys, but he was well-educated and understood that culture of selfless sacrifice for country. His account of what happened one day in his war is one of the most shocking pictures of the reality of death in the trenches. His words are terrifying and touching:

Gas! GAS! Quick, boys! – An ecstasy of fumbling
Fitting the clumsy helmets just in time,
But someone still was yelling out and stumbling
And flound'ring like a man in fire or lime.
Dim through the misty panes and thick green light,
As under a green sea, I saw him drowning.
In all my dreams before my helpless sight,

He plunges at me, guttering, choking, drowning.
If in some smothering dreams, you too could pace
Behind the wagon that we flung him in,
And watch the white eyes writhing in his face,
His hanging face, like a devil's sick of sin;
If you could hear, at every jolt, the blood
Come gargling from the froth-corrupted lungs,
Obscene as cancer, bitter as the cud
Of vile, incurable sores on innocent tongues, –
My friend, you would not tell with such high zest
To children ardent for some desperate glory,
The old Lie: *Dulce et decorum est*
Pro patria mori.

The experience crippled Owen's mind, and within months he was diagnosed with shell shock, what we would call post-traumatic stress disorder. But by 1918 he was judged fit to return to active duty. He was awarded the Military Cross for 'exceptional courage'. He was killed in action one week before the end of the war.

Gas attacks and their terrible effects, which Owen describes, were especially feared. In the Imperial War Museum today, a sign explains that three different kinds of gas were used, each with its own peculiar form of torture. Chlorine could make you choke, turn blue and suffocate. Phosgene forced you to vomit so violently that you threw up gallons of yellow liquid for forty-eight hours. Mustard gas caused blisters on the skin that could burn down to the bone. Although only 3 per cent of victims died, the effects could last a lifetime. The gas masks that soldiers were supplied with weren't always effective. We can see them today in the museum, sinister and inhuman-looking. Captain Donaldson of the Royal Warwickshire Regiment described them as 'an appalling nightmare, as you look like some horrible kind of demon or goblin in these masks'.

By 1916, even the millions of volunteers were not enough, and conscription was introduced. In total around 6 million British men served in the armed forces. The Empire also made an enormous contribution: 1.3 million troops, including, for example, 827,000 from India. The combined forces of Britain and the Empire, however, were still predominantly made up of English soldiers. Of seventy-four divisions fighting at the front, fifty-two were English. At least three quarters of a million British Army soldiers died. Of those, 19,240 were killed on a single day, 1 July 1916, at the start of the Battle of the Somme. On that same single day, another 37,646 were wounded or went missing. One soldier wrote that he'd seen his comrades 'mown down like meadow grass. I felt sick ... and remember weeping.'

***

Soldiers were not constantly in the trenches. They were often back from the front line, awaiting their turn. Trench warfare, when it came, was hard physical work, severe discomfort and constant stress caused by fear of the dangers that day could bring, all punctuated by moments of fighting and death. But life in the trenches also included, in the words of one officer, 'relaxation and jollity and mere boredom'.

One of the strangest – we might say 'most English' – results of the death and suffering was humour. It was sometimes simple and innocent. It was sometimes cruel. And sometimes it was a cynical gallows humour. In 1916, the men of the 12th Battalion Sherwood Foresters, who were stationed on the Ypres Salient in Belgium, came across an abandoned printing press, and decided to produce and circulate a magazine among their comrades. They called it the *Wipers Times*, wipers being soldiers' slang for Ypres. Its speciality was comic stoicism. The German enemy were always 'the Hun' or the 'Boches':

If the Hun lets off some gas –
Never mind.
If the Hun attacks in mass –
Never mind.
If your dug-outs blown to bits,
Or the C.O.'s throwing fits,
Or a crump your rum-jar hits –
Never mind.

Spoof ads on the front page offered land for sale in No-Man's Land:'COMMANDS AN EXCELLENT VIEW OF HISTORIC TOWN OF YPRES. FOR PARTICULARS OF SALE, APPLY:- BOSCH & CO.'

Joke 'letters to the editor' read: 'Sir, Whilst on my nocturnal rambles along the Menin Road last night, I am prepared to swear that I heard the cuckoo. Surely I am the first to hear it this season. Can any of your readers claim the same distinction?' And, 'Sir, On taking my usual morning walk this morning, I noticed that a portion of the road is still up. To my knowledge, the road has been in this state of repair for at least six months. Surely the employees of the Ypres Corporation can do better than this.' It's the English sense of humour mixed in with the English stiff upper lip.

Sometimes, young officers treated the war as a schoolboy's jolly jape. On occasions they would start an attack by kicking a football into no-man's-land; the Germans, once they realised it wasn't a new kind of bomb, thought it dreadfully unmilitary. Siegfried Sassoon, who on other days wrote of the horrors of war, told a friend: 'I chased 40 Boches out of a trench... all by myself. Wasn't that a joyous moment for me? They ran like hell and I chucked bombs and made hunting noises.'

Sassoon, like some of the other war poets, could use a mirthless, ironic humour to condemn pomposity and ignorance. He wrote of the bishop, who in welcoming home a group of soldiers, warned their families that the men wouldn't be the same – they will be the start of 'a new honourable race':

'We're none of us the same!' the boys reply.
'For George lost both his legs; and Bill's stone blind;
Poor Jim's shot through the lungs and like to die;
And Bert's gone syphilitic: you'll not find
A chap who's served that hasn't found some change.'
And the Bishop said: 'The ways of God are strange.'

Robert Graves, who volunteered straight out of school, used a black sarcasm to attack those who gave the orders – the company commander, and here the sergeant major:

His Old Army humour was so well-spiced and hearty
That one poor sod shot himself, and one lost his wits;
But discipline's maintained, and back in rest-billets
The Colonel congratulates 'B' Company on their kits.

The idea that the mass of ordinary soldiers were heroes and that
their senior officers were all incompetent amateurs hiding away
from the action – 'lions led by donkeys' – gained credence and
still figures in the popular imagination today. But historians now
argue that the suggestion is not wholly justified. It's true that there
were some commanders, who valued the day when war had meant
leading a charge dressed in a red uniform and riding on horseback,
and who found it hard to cope with mechanised warfare. But there
were other generals who understood what was needed and delivered it. Among them, Sir Horace Smith-Dorrien, who had fought
in the Zulu Wars in 1878 and in the Boer War, and who soon after
the outbreak of war in 1914 saved the British Expeditionary Force
from catastrophic defeat by leading a resolute defence.

A wounded soldier is helped by his comrades after the Battle of Ginchy, September
1916.

That very English social characteristic, class division, didn't disappear amid the mud, blood and shared hardships of war. In the early years of the conflict, military rank tended to reflect the peacetime social hierarchy. Officers usually came from families who could afford to have them privately educated at public school. The public school ethos they brought to the trenches benefited the war effort. Those at the top of society had been taught that, while they were superior to those who served them, they also had a duty towards subordinates, an obligation to show courage and leadership. The young men from privileged backgrounds who suddenly found themselves lieutenants in the trenches knew that their job was to lead from the front. They were the first over the top, ahead of their men in the charge against the enemy. One result was that proportionately more young officers died than ordinary Tommies. Three out of four front-line officers were killed. By the end of the war, the pressure on numbers was such that one in three officers were from lower middle-class backgrounds and even some from working-class families. But they were still expected to adopt the upper-class culture. In the words of one non-commissioned officer, they had to behave like 'brave lads and real gentlemen.'

***

So, what was happening meanwhile away from the front, back in England? How much did those back home know and understand of conditions not just in the trenches but also in no-man's land under a rain of bullets and a storm of shells?

Parents, grandparents, wives, girlfriends and younger siblings would have chance to hear first hand from soldiers on home leave, or from their letters. Undoubtedly, sometimes, men would pour their hearts out and those back home would comprehend something of what they had been through. But psychological studies of veterans carried out over more recent years have shown that it's common for many returning veterans to repress their memories and not be able to talk about what they have been through. And others simply feel that they have endured a world so terrible and so different that those who have not seen and felt what they have won't understand. And sometimes the truth was concealed in order to spare the feelings of loved ones. Siegfried

Sassoon writes of the officer breaking the news of her son's death
to an elderly woman:

> … her weak eyes
> Had shone with gentle triumph, brimmed with joy,
> Because he'd been so brave, her glorious boy.

But then the officer

> … thought how 'Jack', cold-footed, useless swine,
> Had panicked down the trench that night the mine
> Went up at Wicked Corner; how he'd tried
> To get sent home, and how, at last, he died,
> Blown to small bits.

Newspaper reporting didn't help. It tended to accentuate the posi-
tives, in order to raise morale back home. As army chaplain and
medical aide Geoffrey Studdert Kennedy – 'Woodbine Willie' to
the men he handed out cigarettes to – wrote, tongue in cheek:

> I'm fighting like an 'ero,
> So the daily papers say.

Twenty million people went to cinemas and watched a documentary film called *The Battle of the Somme*. It lasts for an hour
and a quarter, and much of it is shot at or near the front line
before, during and after that long and terrible encounter. The 1916
documentary consists, of course, of black and white silent images
punctuated by captions showing a few words of commentary. A
local pianist in the cinema would be playing suitably patriotic or
respectful tunes according to the image on the screen. Much of the
film shows men marching, preparing vehicles and guns, with occasional wisps of distant smoke. The captions frequently tell us about
'A terrific bombardment of enemy trenches.' One short sequence,
filmed from inside a trench, has the men climbing out and disappearing over the barbed wire towards the enemy. One man falls to
the ground, apparently shot. Soon the scene changes to prisoners

being herded back, wounded men limping, some on stretchers, their mates struggling over the broken land to a field hospital. Caption:'Showing how quickly the men are attended to.'Then we see a body, clearly dead, doubled over in a trench, followed by the image of corpses on the ground – German, according to the caption.The final picture is of a column of soldiers marching past the camera, waving their helmets, and – from their open mouths, we can tell – cheering.'Seeking further laurels', proclaims the caption. Then just before THE END flashes up, there's a map showing the extent of the German retreat.

Of course, given the limitations of cinematography in 1916 – heavy hand-cranked, tripod-mounted cameras, fresh film stock needing to be loaded every few minutes – we cannot expect anything like the on-the-day, HD colour, full-sound television news reports which now bring the horror of the latest war into our living rooms every night.And the aim of the film was not journalism, but to rouse support for the boys at the front without so appalling the viewers that they would start to demand those boys be brought home. In balancing those objectives, it probably succeeded.And we have to remember that for cinema-goers 100 years ago these images were something new.Their senses, unlike ours, had not become numbed to televised suffering through the constant repetition of shocking images. So, while the 100-year-old documentary film *The Battle of the Somme* could not come close to conveying the dangers, the stress, the pain and the discomfort of the soldiers, it did give the families some clue as to what their young men might be going through.And that part truth, that glimpse through the curtain, best sums up what people knew back in England.

***

The First World War is the most striking example of how our national identity can be formed by how we today perceive our history, rather than how it was seen by those who fought, died, or lived through it. Our 'memory' of the Great War is not how most people felt about it at the time.

In 1914, the English regarded the Great War as a just fight for freedom against a land-hungry, anti-democratic tyranny. Millions volunteered to risk their lives in the struggle. They hated the enemy, and adored their country. H.G. Wells, the science fiction novelist, writing in the *Daily News* on the outbreak of hostilities, called it 'The war that will end war'. And even all the poets whose words have told us about the brutal reality of war, and who with irony mocked the generals and the uncomprehending bishops, still chose to fight, and most were recognised for their bravery. Their love of country, their patriotism was in no doubt. It was the system that was wrong. And even though Siegfried Sassoon and others in 1917 protested in public that the war was being 'deliberately prolonged', the anti-war movement, such as it was, didn't catch on. One reason for this was the popular anger against Germany. This came to head in 1915, when the Germans torpedoed the passenger liner *Lusitania*. Twelve hundred civilians, including children, were drowned. Back home, there were anti-German riots with German-owned shops set on fire. Feelings intensified five months later when the English nurse Edith Cavell was executed for helping Allied troops escape from occupied Belgium.

However, the kind of 'my country, right or wrong' patriotism that we saw at the start of the war in Rupert Brooke's romantic notion of dying in a 'foreign field that is forever England' faded as the war progressed. There arose a different kind of patriotism, one that looked ahead to a new world. Geoffrey Studdert Kennedy made it clear he hadn't volunteered so we could go back to the old pre-war England, which, he described as:

> ... cringin', crawlin', whinin'
> For the right to earn your bread,
> It were schemin', pinchin', plannin',
> It were wishin' ye was dead.
> I'm not fightin' for old England,
> Not for this child – am I? 'Ell.
> For the sake of that old England
> I'd not face a single shell.
> ...
>
> It's new England as I fights for,
> It's an England swep' aht clean.
> It's an England where we'll get at

Things our eyes 'ave never seen;
Decent wages, justice, mercy,
And a chance for ev'ry man
For to make 'is 'ome an 'eaven
If 'e does the best 'e can.

Kennedy's poem could be seen as a desperate way of trying to make sense of the senseless brutality without forsaking love of country. And once the war was over, it was as though the English were freed up to put the bad times behind them and work for that better 'new England'. The Imperial War Museum itself was opened by King George V, who proclaimed that the war was now consigned to 'a dead past'. Plans to celebrate – with Victory Balls, for instance – were stopped as inappropriate. The Cenotaph – 'the place of grieving', said Rudyard Kipling – was inaugurated. In one week, a million people visited the Tomb of the Unknown Warrior in Westminster Abbey. This attitude puzzled the French, who had suffered double the losses, but who saw the war as liberation and held victory parades.

At first, there were signs that the country's suffering might give birth to that optimistic new world. Class divisions, though far from wiped out by the war, were weakened forever. This was less the result of any feeling by the officer class that hard times had made them one with the men, and was more a recognition that ordinary men and women had given so much to save the country. In the absence of their menfolk, many more women had gone out to work – nearly a million in munitions factories alone. That gave politicians a face-saver. Those in power could never have been seen to reward the violent tactics of Emily Davison and her co-suffragettes; giving in to violence was not the English way. So at the end of the war, the Representation of the People Act, as we've seen, gave the vote to property-holding women over the age of 30, and to all men. In the same year, it was also decreed that women could serve on juries, become magistrates and work as lawyers. While these steps alone would not put an end to snobbish divisions of rank in English society, it did deliver a strong push towards greater equality. And once the 1928 Act had finally given all men and women the same voting rights, then real power was made available to the masses. The law no longer enshrined the supposed superiority of a privileged few.

The Great War – almost by accident – also helped to preserve something that the English had treasured ever since the Bloodless Revolution of 1688/89: political stability. With the end of the war, there was a proposal that all parliamentary constituencies should abandon the first-past-the-post system of choosing an MP, and instead adopt proportional representation, which enables smaller parties to be represented in the House of Commons. There was disagreement about its benefits among politicians, and in the torrent of business facing the government during the first post-war months, it all became too difficult to make the change. And so by default, the voting system was left as it was. The result is that the country has since then avoided the political turmoil and uncertainty that's afflicted other countries with a multi-party system.

***

The first flush of 'brave new world' optimism, however, was shortlived. Within little more than a decade, disillusionment set in. It became clear that the suffering of war had not created a better world, and the 'new England' envisioned by men like Geoffrey Kennedy faded. Economic depression swept the country. The 1920s saw strikes. My own grandfather was a local miners' leader in Nottinghamshire in 1926 protesting against a cut in pay. And soon came the rising threat of fascism in Europe. The war poets underwent a revival of popularity and were remembered not for their gallant patriotism but for the images they created of the hideous – and now unrewarded – suffering of millions of ordinary soldiers.

A century later, our overriding feelings about the First World War are ones of grief and futility. In the words of the twenty-first-century historian Robert Tombs, 'We cannot conceive of any political, ideological or military aim which could redeem the horror of the trenches.' So now we hold dear the memory of those we think died for nothing. The sombre, respectful atmosphere of the Imperial War Museum sums up that feeling.

This 'memory' of the Great War is peculiar to the English and to the other home nations we fought alongside. While I walked around the First World War galleries of the Imperial War Museum, I heard whispers of foreign accents, French, German, Scandinavian. I stopped several of these people as they were leaving the exhibition, and asked them if there was anything similar in their own countries. A French couple said, yes, there were several such museums, but they were mainly small local ones. A middle-aged German man and his son explained that they had a military museum, but it was more about the weaponry and tactics rather than what happened to common soldiers.

In terms of national identity, it doesn't matter that our memory of the Great War doesn't square exactly with the experience of those who lived through it or died in it. The memory we've built for ourselves over the decades is what has moulded our outlook not just on the Great War but war in general. It has allowed hatred of war to be respectable in England, something that doesn't label you a pacifist.

And there's something else more important. Our concentration on the lives and deaths of individual soldiers, sometimes our grandfathers or great-grandfathers, has brought back a humanity to the often dehumanised fatality statistics of mechanised warfare. Every single life lost in Iraq or Afghanistan in our own time was announced on the *Ten o'clock News*, and due tribute was paid. We recognise now that lives are not just numbers to be thrown at an enemy. Each one of them counts. That's the greatest legacy of the Great War.

***

It seems extraordinary that just twenty-one years after the armistice was signed to end the First World War, a Second World War should start. How did that happen? And how did that change the way the English think of themselves? To find out, we're going somewhere that couldn't be more different from the sombre galleries of London's Imperial War Museum. Somewhere bathed in sunlight, where big bands are playing jaunty melodies, families are having fun, and we're all staring up at the sky.

19

Duxford, Cambridgeshire

A People's War

THERE'LL ALWAYS BE AN ENGLAND,
AND ENGLAND SHALL BE FREE,
IF ENGLAND MEANS AS MUCH TO YOU
AS ENGLAND MEANS TO ME.

SUNG BY DAME VERA LYNN (1917–)

'Ai ai ai ai. Have you ever danced in the tropics? With that hazy, lazy, like kind of crazy, like South American way?'

Three young women, with exaggerated red lipstick, shining teeth, in a version of US service uniform with mid-thigh skirts and jauntily angled caps, are doing some lazy swaying themselves, as they sing, 'Ai ai ai ai. Have you ever kissed in the moonlight? In the grand and glorious, gay, notorious South American way?' They're accompanied by a swing band, a line of trumpets, a line of trombones, and a mass of tenor saxophones. Between verses, the band too does a bit of synchronised swaying, all aiming their instruments left, right, then up in the air. Two children, around six or seven years old, jump about in front of the stage, vaguely in time to the beat. A small crowd stands watching, a couple of mums jiggling infants on their hips along with the music. The singers sway to a climax – 'If you never kissed, who knows what you've missed, in the South American Way' – and then as they step forward with a deep bow, we all clap. All, that is, except for a man in a tracksuit top, and horn-rimmed specs, who carries on looking puzzled while chewing his burger.

We're not, as you might think, at a retro music festival or a Glen Miller tribute tour. We're at the world's biggest air show, at the old Second World War airbase of Duxford in Cambridgeshire. The Flying Legends – the Spitfires, Hurricanes, Lancaster Bombers, Bristol Blenheims and other aircraft that helped secure an Allied victory over Hitler in the Second World War – will take to the skies at two o'clock this afternoon. Meanwhile, the music is one of scores of side events keeping the 40,000 or so of us who have come to watch entertained.

We're spread out over a stretch of tarmac more than half a mile long. Many of us have brought canvas chairs and picnics, and have bagged our spots close to the barrier that separates us from the runway. Some have become 'Friends of Duxford', thus winning the right to set up camp in a privileged area 'Close to the Action!' But that still leaves thousands of us wandering about among the tented shops, and wondering if we need a 'Tactical Day Sack, £12.99', which – given that it's lurking in a sale of khaki trousers and taupe flying suits with map pockets at the leg bottom – I'm guessing is a variety of military backpack. Or maybe, we're tempted to go for a miniature Spitfire at Annants Model Store. They're on offer. Or then again, this is the perfect chance to buy a copy of *Haunted Second World War Airfields*, signed by the author. Other attractions are, well, less attractive. Inheritance Legal Services Ltd have wheeled in a mobile cosy office with sofas, where you're offered a can of orange juice along with 'FREE advice on Will Writing, Lasting Powers of Attorney & Estate Planning'. Nobody's taking them up. One of the biggest marquees belongs to Bremont, 'Award-winning British luxury watch company inspired by a love and passion for aviation, engineering & adventure'. Anyone who can make a wristwatch sound sexy deserves our attention, and a dozen or so of us are trying Bremonts for size and asking our partners what they reckon. Across the way, outside a small yellow tent urging 'Please sponsor a cat today', a small girl is pointing at a stuffed tabby kitten on the ground and demanding of her parents, 'Can we get it? Please!'

***

I feel the need to sample a flavour of the reasons why I've come here. I've seen that for £5 I can take a walk along the edge of the runway alongside many of the aircraft that will later be zooming around over our heads. So, after a klaxon startles me into dodging out of the way of an open-topped vintage car driven by Laurel and Hardy – who both raise their bowler hats to me in thanks – I head for the sign saying, 'Flight line walk. Entry.'

'Walk' turns out to be a misnomer. Several thousand folk, most with cameras, some with professional-looking long lenses, are standing this side of the grass – we don't step onto the grass, we've been asked not to – and are snapping away at all the propellers and cockpits, shining wings, vulnerable gun turrets, red-white-and-blue disks on glossy fuselages. And there are actors-for-the-day wandering about in front, dressed in wartime uniforms: Pilots with moustaches and peaked caps; WAAFs – members of the women's airforce – in thick stockings and heavy shoes, gas mask and tin mugs hanging from their shoulders; 'land girls' in baggy trousers and hair tied up in scarves, strolling along with RAF officers, all brass buttons and navy suits; a nurse, white from cap to shoes, who peers into a small mirror and reddens her lips.

The first dozen or so planes lined up along the grass are Spitfires. And I soon learn that a Spitfire is not just a Spitfire. There were twenty-four different models developed during the war, and many sub-classes too. This one – I overhear from one of my neighbours – is a Mark VIII, Merlin 63 engine with a two-stage, two-speed supercharger. And the next is an F.24 powered by a Griffon 85 engine driving a five-bladed Rotol propeller. Like all old things mechanical, vintage aircraft attract a certain kind of aficionado. I hear what sounds like an American accent. It's a young guy in his mid 20s. For some reason I assume he's an American airman off-duty and I ask him if he's based here.

'Oh, no, I'm Canadian,' he replies, 'from Alberta. I came over specially.'

'Do you mean just for the air show?'

'Sure,' he says. 'If you're an airplane geek, like me, Duxford is the best place on the planet. Folk come from all over the world for this event.'

Now this helps explain something that's been puzzling me from the moment I arrived at Duxford and heard that swinging, swaying

'Ai ai ai ai'. How is it that on the one hand we commemorate the First World War with all the sombre respect we saw at the Imperial War Museum, while here at Duxford we're all jolly and bright remembering the Second World War? There was suffering in both wars. Hundreds of thousands of our recent ancestors were killed in both. Of course, I can see from what the young Canadian guy told me that it's not entirely fair to compare the Duxford Airshow with the Imperial War Museum's First World War exhibition. Duxford isn't just about the war. It's also a day out for plane-spotters and for families too. But that said, the difference between the way the two places are presented – one dark and grieving, the other fun and bright – does say something about the English attitude to the two world wars. You can't imagine the trenches of the First World War being used as the backdrop for a jolly retail experience. We'll need to look into this contrast further.

***

Throughout the morning, we have heard, cutting in and out of the chatter and commotion of the crowds, announcements over the loudspeaker about how to find your lost child and where to go for pizzas and sausage sandwiches, and interviews with aviation experts. Now we're told there are only a few minutes before the Legends will be flying and 'The sky will be filled with the sights and sounds of glory.' So it's time we all took our places, on our foldable chairs, or – like me – leaning over a spare 18in of metal fencing. I'm lucky. I find myself close by one of the Spitfires. They're going to be on – I mean 'up' – first. It's now that the character of these extraordinary little machines strikes me. Without them, the war may well have been lost almost as soon as it had started. The one in front of me is only slightly longer than two family cars placed end-to-end, and not as wide. It balances on three wheels, the rear one little bigger than a dinner plate, which means the nose of the aircraft points upwards, eager to be off. I watch as the pilot clambers onto its wing and the whole contraption gives a bounce as though it might topple sideways. Then he shoehorns himself into the cockpit. If you've never heard and seen a Spitfire engine start up, your life has lacked a thrill. We all wait while the pilot adjusts his helmet and goggles, and checks his instruments. There are two sudden coughs of blue smoke from the exhausts on the side, and the propellers give a few slow, jerky turns. Then everything dies. For a second or two you think something has gone wrong and it won't be flying today. But there are more coughs of blue smoke. Flames spurt from the exhausts. Now you consider throwing yourself to the ground before it all explodes. The engine stutters for a second then gives a roar, and the propellers whirr, extinguishing the fire. She's ready. She turns, wobbling over the grass, like a toddler that's never done it before, and on to the runway.

Soon there are a dozen Spitfires in the sky. And it's clear this is their element. They're like a flock of swifts. They glide. They swoop. They turn and twist. But they also fly like swifts could never do. They climb straight up towards the clouds then bend back over themselves until they're upside down and swooping again, this time with frightening acceleration. Then at what seems the last possible safe moment they pull out of the descent, turn again and fly past, tipping their wings at an exact 45 degrees to salute us. We applaud: not riotous cheering and clapping – we're too breathless for that – just quiet, congratulatory approval. And before we have time to turn to our neighbours with a nod that says, 'That's something, huh?' they're coming around again. Now, one by one and without slackening their speed, in two precise, right-angled movements they turn upside down, before banking away and climbing to return, now darting here and there. Like swifts again, hunting flies.

***

In August 1940, these aircraft saved the country at the most dangerous and desperate point in the war. The Battle of France had been lost, and in the spring of that year hundreds of thousands of British, French, Belgian and Canadian troops were in retreat, heading to the beaches around Dunkirk on the French coast. Churchill called it a 'colossal military disaster'. But during ten days at the end of May and the beginning of June, hundreds of small fishing boats and pleasure craft from Dover and nearby ports on the south coast of England crossed the Channel and ferried almost 200,000 British and 140,000 Allied troops back to safety in Kent.

Churchill, proclaimed it a 'miracle of deliverance'. The English, in an echo of the Charge of the Light Brigade, had managed to salvage glory from the jaws of humiliation, though this time there were tangible benefits. Churchill used the Dunkirk evacuation to steady the nation's nerves for the desperate defence to come. In a speech to rival the stirring poetry of Shakespeare's *Henry V*, the Prime Minister told the House of Commons:

> We shall fight on the beaches, we shall fight on the landing grounds, we shall fight in the fields and in the streets, we shall fight in the hills; we shall never surrender.

Incidentally, every word in this famous piece of oratory has its origins in the Old English language of Anglo-Saxon times, with a single exception: the word 'surrender', which is French. The spirit of Dunkirk became embedded in the English character, to denote pulling together in times of adversity.

Hitler's Germany, now in control of France, faced the same problem that Napoleon had had in planning to invade England: how to cross the 22 miles of sea that separated his front line from the English coast. And Hitler faced an even greater challenge than Napoleon. He had much more equipment to ferry across, and any invasion force would be exposed to attack from the air. Before a full-scale invasion could be considered therefore, the Germans planned to overwhelm the RAF by attacking their air bases and radar stations in south-east England. What followed was christened by Churchill the Battle of Britain. It was more the Battle of South-East England, but that didn't have quite as much punch to it. It's still the only decisive battle anywhere in history to have been fought entirely in the air.

The Luftwaffe began with an advantage of technology. Radar was still primitive and had limited range. This meant that the RAF fighters on the ground had only a few minutes' warning of an attack. What's more, it then took thirteen minutes for a Spitfire to take to the air and reach 20,000 feet, the altitude of the approaching German aircraft. By this time, the enemy were already over, or close to, their targets. So the Spitfire pilots had to attack them at once. And while all that was happening, a second wave of German planes could be bombing the airfields below. But the RAF had their own advantages, chiefly in the sheer number of planes they could launch. Aircraft production was stepped up, to almost 300 a week. And whereas every Messerschmitt shot down over Kent was a permanent loss to the Luftwaffe, a Spitfire hit over the same area might sometimes limp back to base, to be repaired and sent back into action.

And just as we today at Duxford Airshow are watching the Spitfires darting above us like swifts chasing flies, so people living near the south-east coast would turn out to spectate the dogfights in the skies above them. BBC radio even provided commentaries, as though it were a sporting event – not to everyone's approval. 'A battle isn't a boat race,' complained one woman. The nation's opinion of fighter pilots changed. At the start of the war they had been despised as 'Brylcream Boys' for their oily hair and oily manners, and cinema audiences had even booed them when they appeared on newsreels. But now they were heroes. There were only around 3,000 of these pilots. Two thirds were volunteers. One in six was killed. On 20 August 1940, at the height of the battle, Churchill proclaimed, 'Never was so much owed by so many to so few.'

A Spitfire during the 2007 Battle of Britain Memorial Flight. (Ian Forshaw/MOD)

The pressure on the young Spitfire pilots, however, was enormous. More and more were needed. And at the height of the conflict, most of them went into their first dogfight with as little as five hours of training. Many were no older than 19 or 20, and – down on the ground – hadn't even passed their driving tests.

A new phase of the war began: the Blitz. Hitler turned the weight of his air attacks from fighter bases to the cities. After initial raids on Birmingham and Liverpool, Londoners – going about their daytime business on 7 September – heard a mighty drone of engines above them. 300 German bombers, escorted by 600 fighter aircraft, hit the East End. The blazing fires started by the falling bombs acted as a beacon for further nighttime raids. During the following days, it seemed the capital was undefended. But on the 15th a huge swarm of Spitfires intercepted the attackers. In one week, 175 German planes were shot down. Between July and October, the Luftwaffe lost a total of 1,300 aircraft over England; this compared with 790 RAF planes in the same period. Hitler had failed to establish supremacy in the skies, and he abandoned his planned invasion.

However, the German bombardment of England's cities continued, and so did the toll on young pilots. A friend of ours showed me a letter written to her mother in May 1941 by a 19-year old RAF volunteer. Len Chambers was training to be a pilot at a base near Leicester. It would be his job to defend that city against the Luftwaffe's bombs. He writes that a 'clear head and a cast-iron nerve is required … It's a case of "It all depends on me."' Much of his letter has the tone of a schoolboy away from home for the first time. He talks about walks in the countryside and birdwatching on his days off, and he explains that he's billeted with a family that has two teenage daughters. 'I know what you will immediately think,' he says, 'but, no, I'm here on business.' He tells how on an early solo flight he got lost somewhere over Leicestershire, and jokes that the training lectures are 'a bit of a farce'. Still, he says, 'It's great fun up in the air.' Less than two months later, Len was dead, killed in action, and our friend's mother was weeping at his funeral.

***

Over a period of seventy-six nights, 13,000 tons of high explosives and a million incendiary bombs were dropped on London. As well as hundreds of thousands of houses, several railways stations, factories and power stations, German bombs also hit the Houses of Parliament. The magnificent west front was partly shattered, and the statue of Richard the Lionheart knocked off its pedestal (the only permanent damage was a bent sword). A firebomb set the Chamber of the House of Commons alight. Buckingham Palace was hit three times. 'I'm glad we've been bombed,' commented the queen. 'It makes me feel we can look the East End in the face.' The king and queen didn't go into hiding somewhere safe miles away, but stayed and visited people in devastated areas of London, and in other cities too. In all 43,000 civilians were killed, 139,000 injured, and 2 million were made homeless.

Hitler's aims during these months were threefold: to destroy the aircraft factories; to disrupt the economy; and to smash the morale of the people. In all three, he was less than successful. The wartime economy had already slumped with so many workers pulled from factory floors and put into uniform, and the German raids didn't materially damage it further. And, as we've seen, aircraft manufacture in fact increased. The impact on morale was more complex. Of course, there were lots of reasons why people would become despondent. Thousands suffered personal losses, of their loved ones and their homes, and we should not romanticise their feelings. There was looting, a thriving black market that benefited crooks and 'spivs', and even strikes. But the events of 1940 and 1941, when many ordinary people of England found themselves on the front line in the war, brought out what's often today regarded as 'the best of the English'.

When at Duxford I took a break from being dazzled by the old fighter planes, I found myself, mug of tea in hand, sitting opposite two chaps of my age – that is, born in the generation after the war. We chatted and laughed together, and I asked them what they thought was the most obvious characteristic of the English.

'We don't give up,' said one without hesitation.

'That's right,' said the other. 'And we can even laugh about it when things go wrong.'

This cheerful stoicism in the English character shone through in the Second World War. When people suffering night after night of

German bombing were asked how they were, they'd often answer, 'Mustn't grumble.' An opinion poll carried out in early 1941 found that more Londoners complained about the weather than the bombs, but they appreciated being asked their views because – many respondents said – this was 'a people's war'. They were 'carrying on' (long before the comedy films were made), and liked to say they were 'doing their bit'. A diarist wrote that a woman he met who had spent her day with friends scrubbing floors in an air-raid shelter told him, 'Wish Hitler could see us now!' And there was a feeling that people were 'pulling together'. It was the spirit of Dunkirk. In an age when politicians claiming they're for 'one nation' provokes cynical head shaking in many of us, we still, when a group of people gets together to fight some local cause, say, 'just like in the Blitz'. It's a bit of a joke nowadays, but we also half-mean it.

Stoicism in England had its roots in the country's history. Even in the worst of times, England had never successfully been invaded, not by the Spanish Armada, Napoleon or the Kaiser, and people felt it wouldn't be now, however bad things seemed. It was the old English stiff upper lip softened and democratised: ordinary people pulling together and sticking two fingers up at the 'Nazzies', as Churchill called them, and singing with a smile on their faces, 'Who do you think you're kidding Mr Hitler, if you think we're on the run?'

But morale during the Second World War wasn't just left to tradition. The government stepped in to give it a mighty boost. The leaders of the wartime Conservative–Labour Coalition were astute enough to realise that the failure of the Great War to produce a better world for ordinary people could not be repeated this time. The sacrifice could not be for nothing. In November 1942, the economist William Beveridge produced a report identifying what he described as the five 'giant evils' in society: squalor, ignorance, want, idleness and disease, and he proposed a revolutionary system of state help for ordinary people at times of need. An opinion poll showed a massive 86 per cent in favour of Beveridge's recommendations, and Churchill committed the government to a post-war Four-Year Plan to implement a new 'cradle to grave' welfare system. It gave hope in the darkest days.

At the same time, people had a more practical view of what it was they were fighting for. Another wartime phrase commonly heard was 'just getting the job done.' And while that could indicate a modesty about an heroic struggle, it also reflected the idea that just getting back home to a normal way of life would be enough this time. English patriotism was now less about some nebulous idea of country, and more about loyalty to those around you. A young man from Wolverhampton called up to serve in the army wrote in a letter to be sent to his parents in the event of his death, 'England's a great little country, the best there is. But I cannot honestly say that it is "worth fighting for" ... No, Mum, my little world is centred around you and including Dad, everyone at home, and my friends ... That is worth fighting for, worth dying for too.'

Together, this new, more personal kind of patriotism and the belief that the more caring society proposed by Beveridge would be delivered this time go a long way to explaining why the country came through the war without the 'heroes slaughtered for nothing' regrets produced by the First World War. It was not as though the Second World War lacked casualty figures worthy of the term 'slaughter'. Plenty of families were left mourning, with 383,000 men and women killed fighting. Of those, 55,000 were aircrews and ground crews, which as a proportion of the total of those serving in the RAF was worse than the casualty rate suffered by the infantry in the trenches of the First World War. But the deaths in the Second War were regarded more as a worthwhile – though tragic – sacrifice. The English were fighting to save their own families from a dictatorial enemy who if victorious would wipe out their way of life, and they were fighting for a better post-war world for themselves and their loved ones.

***

So, what impact did the war have on the English view of who they were?

One result was heightened prestige in the popular mind for two ancient English institutions. The monarchy, because of the way the king and queen stuck out the Blitz along with their subjects, was seen as the embodiment of duty and togetherness. And Parliament, where most of Churchill's stirring words were delivered, became a symbol of pride and democratic freedom.

Once the war was over, other events followed to influence the national identity of the English. After the Allied victory in 1945, the way of life at home, and the role of the country abroad, would never be the same again.

Abroad, the Empire collapsed. The English could no longer see themselves as the rulers of half the globe, and – as we shall see – the idea gathered strength that England was a nation in decline.

On the home front, however, the war left more positive results. For a start, the English values which were seen to have won the war were not allowed to die in peacetime. During the 1950s, millions packed post-war cinemas to watch *The Wooden Horse*, *The Cockleshell Heroes* and *The Cruel Sea*. They portrayed small groups of men during the war staying loyal to each other and triumphing against the odds through the typically English qualities of doggedness, courage and ingenuity. And the late 1940s and the '50s saw the delivery of new institutions – rooted in the wartime promises of the Beveridge Report – that would change English society forever. In the first post-war general election, the people decided that a Labour government, rather than Churchill's Conservatives, would be more likely to deliver those promises.

First, there was a new three-level secondary education system – secondary modern, technical and grammar schools – which enabled more working-class children to move up into higher-earning professional jobs. Although the comradeship of both wars had brought some weakening of the rigidity of the English class system, the very fact that the country had been led to victory by a man who came from a family of dukes, showed that class divisions were far from dead by 1945. But the erosion of class differences in the following decades was dramatic. Many of my own grammar school classmates in the East Midlands during the 1950s and early '60s were the sons of coal miners. One became a headmaster, another a senior civil servant in local government, and a third a solicitor and Deputy Lord Lieutenant of Nottinghamshire. More than 50 per cent of children born at the end of the war ended up better educated and more prosperous than their parents. It has been called the Golden Age of social mobility in English history. During the last decades of the twentieth century, equality rather than 'knowing your place' became the guiding principle for governments, companies and individuals.

At the same time, the National Health Service was born, and a safety net of welfare payments was introduced for the most disadvantaged in society. We may sometimes complain today about the way that the welfare system and the NHS are run, but remember the opening ceremony of the 2012 Olympics in London, bragging to the world about the way we look after our sick. Fresh values became emphasised in the English character. Not only dogged in the face of adversity, but also now fair-mindedness and compassion. Of course, not everyone, all the time, in England displays these characteristics. That's not the nature of national identity. But they are qualities that we often believe we should aspire to, because – well, that's what being English should mean.

The greatest legacy of the Second World War, however, was not something new. It was a repeat performance. Yet again the English had pulled it off. Never mind that this time it was with massive help from the Scots, Welsh, Northern Irish, the Americans and the nations of the old Empire. The English, yet again, had emerged an undefeated, island race. Their identity – changed in part, reinforced in part – remained as ever distinct from that of their neighbours.

***

And so it's appropriate that the last stop on our journey through time and space is to the one place which – more than any other – has been responsible for that 950 years of independence. The English Channel. But I warn you, as often in the Channel, there's a fog swirling in. This time it's a fog of doubt. We English are wondering if we're quite as English as we used to be. Have we lost something? Is our Englishness being diluted? And it's not just the fog we've got to worry about. We're getting into uncharted waters too.

20

DOVER, KENT

THE LOCK AND KEY TO ENGLAND

I HAVE NOT A DROP OF ENGLISH
BLOOD IN ME BUT ENGLAND MADE ME.
ENGLISHNESS NOW IS MESSY, FUNNY,
IRRATIONAL AND WORKABLE. LET IT BE
EXPANSIVE, INVENTIVE, IMAGINATIVE. IT
IS OURS TO MAKE IN OUR OWN IMAGE.

SUZANNE MOORE, WRITING IN THE *GUARDIAN*
NEWSPAPER AFTER THE JUNE 2016 BREXIT VOTE.

Dover is the all-in-one vitamin pill of English national identity.

It strikes me, as I stand on the castle mound high above its historic port, that instead of travelling 3,500 miles criss-crossing England to visit twenty places, we could instead have swallowed the lot in one dose right here. That wouldn't have been so much fun of course. But it does seem that many of the key events that have moulded the English character over 1,600 years were in some way or other acted out in or around Dover and its white cliffs.

Before me is the finest Anglo-Saxon building in the county of Kent: the church of St Mary-in-Castro. And there's even a crumbling reminder here of those who ruled England before the English. At one end of the church, almost leaning on it for support,

On the highest point within Dover Castle, St Mary in Castro Saxon church –
undergoing restoration – dates from around the year AD 1000. The Roman light
house to the right was built in the second century AD.

is a weather-worn tower. It's a lighthouse built by the Romans. The
church itself with its hard, shining flint stone walls looks much as it
must have on the day the Saxon masons took down their wooden
scaffolding and packed away their trowels at the end of the tenth
century. I said 'looks *much as* it must have'. But not quite, and the
difference is telling. As I get closer to the church, I see that its stone
window frames and door arches are a bit too fresh. A Victorian
architect called William Butterfield got his hands on the church,
and neo-Gothicised bits of it – just as William Armstrong did at
Bamburgh. Today, there's twenty-first-century steel scaffolding
around the church's tower. English Heritage is carrying out a more
sensitive restoration than Mr Butterfield would have contemplated.

The church stands on its own hillock within the defensive walls
of Dover Castle. It would be hard to oversell the castle's brute
strength and sheer size. The harsh angles of this ancient fortification make dark silhouettes this morning against a stormy sky. Its
winding walls and four-square towers spread around the hilltop

before me, and far below, the modern cross-Channel ferry port looks little more than a child's plaything. The castle has had a long, bloody and, at times, heroic history. William the Conqueror hurried here in 1066 straight after his victory at Hastings. He knew Dover commanded the narrowest strait across the Channel to Normandy, just 22 miles away. It was where his reinforcements could be landed, and so he needed to control it. He did so by building a wooden fort near where I'm standing now. But much of what we see around us today was the brainchild of William's great-grandson, Henry II, in the later twelfth century. Henry tore down the wooden structure and replaced it with a massive stone keep, the Great Tower. It stands today – as it always has – at the highest point in the castle's grounds. You can see it from 15 miles away, on sea or land.

I clamber down grassy mounds to the huge curtain wall that Henry constructed to enclose the tower, and follow the footpath around. It's then I realise there's a second, wide and wandering belt of high stone masonry encircling Henry's inner wall. For a moment or two, I'm lost in a vast 3D maze where the walls, towers, mounds, barracks and barbicans straddle the hill. On my left – set into the outer curtain wall – is a dark, tunnelled archway beneath a cluster of circular towers with castellated tops. This, according to my guidebook, is the main entrance, the Constable's Gate. It was described by the thirteenth-century chronicler-monk Matthew Paris as the 'lock and key to the kingdom of England'. I need to turn right, and, after clattering across a wooden drawbridge, there before me is the Great Tower. In eight and a half centuries, it has never fallen to a foreign enemy. Nor has Dover. Nor has England.

***

The tower's courtyard is bustling and noisy this morning. It's half term, and Hallowe'en is a couple of days off, so lots of kids are rushing about with scary masks on, hiding round corners and popping out at their parents with ghostly wails. And I soon hear that plenty of my fellow visitors aren't English. There are people speaking French and German, as well as some Scandinavian languages I can't identify.

The Great Tower – the square castellated structure within the inner curtain wall of Dover Castle – has never fallen to a foreign enemy in its 850-year history.

A wide flight of steep stone steps leads into the tower, and at the top I find myself admiring a series of finely sculpted dog-tooth arches.

'Beauties, aren't they?' says a voice behind me. I turn and there's Keith – his name's on his English Heritage guide's badge. 'Exactly as they must have looked in Henry II's day,' he adds. 'No wind or weather to wear them down inside here.' And then he springs a surprise on me. 'Of course,' he says, (people about to tell you something they think you don't know often start 'Of course') '... Of course, this castle wasn't built as a military defence.'

'Really?' I say, with a shocked and questioning expression on my face.

'No, it was a piece of PR. It was the fashion for foreign kings and queens to go on pilgrimage to the shrine of St Thomas à Becket at Canterbury, and Dover was where they landed. Our king' (note the 'our') '... would then greet them here, and the size and beauty of this building – the Great Tower – was designed to impress them with the power of England.'

'But I thought it saw lots of fighting over the centuries,' I say.

'You're right, it did. It started out as a show palace, but then later it often had to serve as the guardian of England, and it got mixed up in domestic politics as well.'

Keith goes on to explain how in 1216, during the Magna Carta rebellion, the French prince who had been invited over by the barons twice laid siege to King John's garrison here and, although the French breached the outer wall, the Great Tower held out. Forty-seven years later, the castle did fall, though not to a foreign enemy. It was attacked and taken by Simon de Montfort – whom we know as the man responsible for forcing the king to summon England's first ever parliament. In the sixteenth century, Henry VIII strengthened and rebuilt the castle's walls. But his efforts were not enough to keep it safe for another king 100 years later. During the Civil War, the castle was a Royalist stronghold until one night Parliamentary supporters from the town below scaled the cliffs and took its defenders by surprise.

'At the end of the eighteenth century,' says Keith, 'we were expecting Napoleon to invade.' (Note again the 'we'. I'm always delighted by how we English identify so closely with our ancestors.) 'So the fortifications here were strengthened again, this time to withstand barrages from heavy artillery, and the underground tunnels that had first been dug out back in the reign of King John were extended even further under the white cliffs, so ammunition could be stored there, and they would be a safe haven for the soldiers barracked here. I recommend a visit to the tunnels,' adds Keith. 'They played a big part in two world wars.'

I thank him, am reminded how much we've learned from official guides on our journey, and decide to take his advice. This involves another test of my orienteering skills, through gatehouses, over bridges, skirting barrack blocks ('1745–56 incorporating medieval buildings', a plaque announces), artillery stores ('19th century – gunpowder for immediate use'), cannon and gun batteries ('Lower Flank – 1794–1805') till I reach the entry to the tunnels. Or not quite. There's a queue worthy of a wartime tea break in the NAAFI. It moves quickly, however, and I'm soon deep within the chalk rock beneath the castle's ramparts along with twenty-odd other visitors. Most of the tunnels we pass through over the next half hour are not crudely hacked out caverns like the ones we saw at Nottingham's Trip to Jerusalem. They're more like London Underground tunnels without the trains. This is because the walls were strengthened and made watertight during the twentieth century with steel rafters and corrugated aluminium plating. Dover in both world wars was in the front line. It was likely to be the first place in England that would have to meet an invasion by the Kaiser's or Hitler's troops.

We're shown a first-aid centre where wounds could be dressed, and a windowless room with white-sheeted beds along the walls. During the First World War the tunnels were used as a hospital and by local people as an air-raid shelter. The first aerial bomb to explode in England during the Great War fell close to Dover Castle. By the time of the Second World War, shells fired from German guns 22 miles away on the coast of France could – and did – hit Dover. Its tunnels again came into their own as protection for civilians and serving soldiers, and in 1940 they housed the operations station that oversaw the Dunkirk small ships evacuation. The last role for Dover's underground city came in the early 1960s. During the Cold War, these tunnels were equipped with generators and radio transmitters to become one of the country's twelve emergency Regional Seats of Government (RSGs). The drab, austere chambers of the RSG today have an eerie feel to them, shivering reminders that if they'd ever been brought into use much of England's population would have been wiped out in a Soviet nuclear attack, and we – this peaceful October morning – would not be here now.

***

Back in the thin misty light outside, I decide to take a look at what has made Dover so important in England's history: the English Channel, that barrier which ever since the Battle of Hastings no invader has crossed, leaving the English with nine and a half uninterrupted centuries to work out who they are. After a short drive from the castle (via Harold Road – as optimistic a piece of Anglo-Saxon patriotism as I ever saw), I'm standing on the clifftop footpath and taking in the eye-dazzling view. Three hundred feet below and to the left, tiny waves are rolling in on a pebbly beach. Black seaweed-stained stones at the water's edge fold around a white headland of sheer cliffs rising up to flat green fields on top. There's a distant fog on the horizon out at sea this morning, as there often is here. The Dover Strait can be dangerous. Over the centuries more than 2,000 vessels have been wrecked on the sandbanks that lie beneath the water. And it was right here on the stretch of sea before me that in 1588 Sir Francis Drake smashed the Spanish Armada and sent its ships scattering on their long disastrous retreat.

Today, through the mist, I count no fewer than fourteen vessels out there. There are two ferries, a cruise liner, several small boats and six giant container ships. The Dover Strait is the busiest shipping lane on the planet. In the twenty-first century, rather than a barrier separating England from the rest of the world, the Channel has become a passageway for the world's trade. And Dover itself has become England's gateway to Europe. Down below me to the right, scores of high-sided eighteen-wheeler lorries are weaving in a slow procession, nose-to-tail, around the docks and up a ramp onto a P&O ferry. Every day, cargoes of machine tools, electrical equipment, every kind of food and drink, not to mention millions of packets of cigarettes leave Dover destined for all the countries of Europe. And every day, many other lorries bring car components, vegetables, meat, clothing and more cigarettes back into the country.

Queues of lorries jamming east Kent roads have become the popular – and often unfair – image of Dover in the eyes of the rest of the country. In the summer of 2016, the Channel for a few days seemed to be slipping back into its historic role as a barrier. Lorries and holiday traffic were backed up for 20 miles on all roads leading to the port. Drivers and passengers had to sleep in their vehicles during a fourteen-hour wait. The cause was extra security checks and understaffing by French border officials. And the other image many of us have of this part of England is police pulling exhausted migrants from the back of trucks which have just arrived from Calais via the Channel Tunnel, 8 miles west of Dover.

Thousands of those refugees ended up close to where I am now. A few hundred yards from Dover Castle, on top of a stretch of white cliffs known as the Western Heights, is another series of forts, barbicans and ditches, these built two hundred years ago as a defence against the expected invasion by Napoleon. In 2002, this historic citadel was turned into an immigration detention centre. At any one time, some 300 adults whose applications for asylum had been turned down were held here until they could be removed from the country. The Dover Immigration Removal Centre was shut in 2015, because it was considered too old-fashioned and too far from any international airport.

On some days, you can see Calais from up here on top of the white cliffs. If it were clearer today, we might make out flames and smoke rising next to the French town. The 'Jungle' is being dismantled. The camp, where thousands of refugees from Syria, Somalia, Afghanistan and elsewhere have been living while they tried to hide in lorries bound for England, is being torn down by the French authorities. In protest, some of the Jungle's residents have set fire to their makeshift homes.

***

Mass immigration. European federalism. The globalisation of trade. These have all been blamed for watering down what it means to be English in the twenty-first century. And that leads to some tricky questions we have to face now at the end of our journey. Have the momentous changes in our world over the past sixty years somehow diluted English national identity? Are the English quite so different nowadays? And even if they are, what does it mean to be English today? Now we could hide behind the historian's traditional defence and say, 'It's too soon to tell.' But there is some evidence to guide us – though, when it comes down to it, you're going to have to make up your own mind on some of the knottier matters.

There can be little doubt that the English in recent years have found themselves taking a back seat. As we've seen, Victorian politicians, historians, writers and others often used to speak of 'England' and the 'English' when 'Great Britain' and the 'British' might have been more precise. Today it's a very different matter. In the twenty-first century, much in our daily lives – from British Airways, British Gas, and the British Library to the *Great British Bake Off* and the British Broadcasting Corporation – everywhere we look – seems to make clear now that we're British, not English. And politicians these days wouldn't dream of confusing 'English' and 'British'. They're always careful to talk about the

'United Kingdom.' They're worried – particularly with the rise of the Scottish National Party – that the Union, given a good shove, might start to break up, and that Scotland and England will be divided. The result has been that – in official circles, at least – English identity in the twenty-first century has tended to get submerged in a wider British identity.

But there's evidence that this is not the way many English people see themselves. An opinion survey, conducted by Ashcroft Polls on the day of the Brexit referendum in June 2016, asked 10,500 voters in England just how English they felt: 29 per cent described themselves as either 'English, not British' or 'More English than British', and a further 43 per cent saw themselves as 'Equally English and British'. So, despite the efforts of politicians, seven out of ten people in England still recognise their English identity. That said, do the English still think they're quite so special as they once did? Much has changed over the past seventy years. The end of the old Empire brought the first challenges. The Victorians saw England as the heart of the Empire. But following the Second World War and the granting of independence to all the former colonies, we began to feel that we were a nation in decline, or at least that we needed to reassert ourselves in order to recapture something of past glory. The phrase 'punching above our weight' was first applied to foreign policy in 1993 by the then Foreign Secretary, Douglas Hurd. A recent Open University teaching paper commented that this boxing metaphor suggests 'national pride is tinged with a suspicion that we don't quite deserve our place at the top table of world affairs.' We could argue that this suspicion that we're a nation of has-beens on the world stage has had at least one positive outcome. Perhaps the English these days are not as arrogant as they were in Victorian times. Being boastful when you've not got much to boast about risks being thought a clown.

***

So does Englishness today mean much? What has happened in the twenty-first century to much prized English characteristics such as tolerance, a respect for the law and parliamentary democracy, or the English sense of humour, for instance? Have they somehow been eroded or lost? And what has happened to the less attractive

qualities of the English, such as class division and snobbishness?
Who, exactly, in the twenty-first century, do the English now think
they are?

We're on safe ground in saying the English still value their
democracy. We may argue with each other about parliamentary
boundary changes or the powers of the House of Lords, but there's
no threat to the parliamentary system of lawmaking, and we still
feel proud that foreigners recognise Westminster as the 'mother
of parliaments'. The same goes for the rule of law itself. There's
heated debate about matters such as whether anti-terrorist legislation undermines basic legal rights, but it would still be unthinkable
to challenge the principles laid down 800 years ago, in that still-
revered English document Magna Carta, that those who govern us
are no different from the rest of us in a court of law and that arbitrary punishment is wrong. And the English by and large are still a
law-abiding nation. In 2015, there were 573 murders in the whole
of England and Wales, which is roughly the same as the number
of homicides in the city of Chicago alone during the first nine
months of 2016. And while every village police officer in countries
such as France, Spain and Italy – not to mention every small town
cop in the USA – has a pistol strapped to his or her belt, in England
the tradition of the unarmed bobby lives on. Eighty-two per cent
of English police officers don't carry guns, and firearms are only
seen on the streets where there's an exceptional threat – usually
these days from terrorism.

***

Much less straightforward is this question: what has happened in
the twenty-first century to English tolerance, born in the Glorious
Revolution of 1688/89 as a reaction against religious persecution, civil war and dictatorship? Are the English today tolerant, for
instance, of people from different religions, cultures and races? Or
is the sort of nationalistic arrogance we saw in the days of Empire
resurfacing? Some have claimed that this is what the Brexit vote
represented, that the desire to regain control of national borders is
born of an intolerance of foreigners settling in our country. Is that
so? Immigration was certainly cited as the main reason by many
of those who voted to leave the European Union.

The end of Empire brought a wave of immigrants from the new Commonwealth during the 1950s and '60s. Then in 1973, a new door was opened. Britain's joined the European Economic Community, and in 1992 the provision for the 'free movement of labour' among member states gave millions of European citizens the right to work and settle here. By 2014, three million people from other EU countries were living in the UK. And official statistics in August 2016 showed that one in eight of the UK's population had been born outside the country. How, then, have the English reacted to mass migration?

There are many different factors influencing the way we think about it. At one extreme, disapproval of immigration and of immigrants has led to discrimination, verbal abuse or physical attacks against people from ethnic minorities. In 2015, twice as many such 'hate crimes' were reported as in the year before, and there was a further spike after the Brexit vote. But we should not necessarily read into the actions of a few a shift for the worse in the values and behaviour of the English people as a whole.

Fortunately, we do have some solid evidence to tell us about the tolerance, or intolerance, of the majority of English people. The same Ashcroft Poll, on the day of the Brexit referendum, also asked people whether they thought immigration was a good or a bad thing – the question was as crude as that: 45 per cent didn't approve of it, while only 34.5 per cent were in favour. But when the same group were then asked what they thought about multiculturalism, the result was the other way around: 30 per cent gave it a thumbs down, while 47 per cent said that living in a society made up of different races and cultures was a 'good' thing. This result was borne out by a survey conducted in 2013 by a group of Swedish economists. They asked a cross-section of citizens in eighty countries worldwide a simple question: 'What sort of people would you *not* want to live next door to?' In Britain, only one person in twenty answered that they wouldn't want someone from a different race as a neighbour, and that put the country top of the international tolerance league. Incidentally, another survey in 2015 showed the Scottish and the English to be equally tolerant, so in effect both of them – and there's no reason to think the Welsh are any different – would tie for first place.

But we should also be clear what we mean by tolerance in the English character. It's never meant that the English will put up with anything. We tolerate people being different so long as their beliefs and actions don't undermine other fundamental principles that we hold dear. So you can be different, for instance in the colour of your skin or your religion, provided you accept the need for peaceful political debate, are willing to compromise, and avoid any form of extremism.

Today, while Germany, France and Austria are seeing the rise of popular far-right parties accompanied by outbursts of street violence, extreme right-wing parties here have never attracted much support. The only right-wing-ish party to do so in recent years was led by a man who likes nothing better than a fag and a pint down the pub, and who's often called – not a racist, nor a fascist – but that affectionate English name, a 'bloke'. Nigel Farage has a comfortable mateyness about him. What about the far left? Only two communist MPs have ever been elected to Westminster: in the 1920s and '30s, both for Scottish constituencies. And the English don't vote for extremist political leaders. Jeremy Corbyn, for instance, is hardly a revolutionary, and it's arguable that he did well in the 2017 election, less because of his hard-left views, and more because many voters liked his campaigning image as a decent, caring, tell-it-like-it-is chap. Violent revolutions or military coups are still certainly not the way the English do things.

***

However, political and social stability has had its downsides. As we've seen on our journey, the English preference for leaving things as they are has often in the past enabled the privileged at the top of society and the middle classes to hang onto power and keep the lower orders in their place. A preference for political stability has for much of England's history meant a rigid class system. And along with it, one of the worst English characteristics, snobbishness, a patronising contempt for those below you on the social ladder.

The job of dismantling class barriers didn't make much progress until well into the twentieth century. Granting a vote to all women and all men in 1928 saw the rise of the Labour Party representing the working classes at Westminster. And there's also been a transfer of power away from the House of Lords to the people's representatives in the Commons. At the same time, much of the inherited wealth of the upper classes was redistributed with the introduction of death duties. Then, the widening of educational opportunities after the Second World War enabled many working-class children to rise in business and the professions.

So, is class – in the sense of a strict, rigid social hierarchy – dead in the twenty-first century? The answer's not straightforward. The Office for National Statistics classifies 53 per cent of the population as working in managerial, administrative or professional jobs – in other words, what might be called middle-class occupations. And perhaps we should add the 21 per cent who are skilled manual workers to the middle-class tally too. So more of us are middle-class these days. But is it still hard for the remaining 26 per cent of us to climb the ladder?

Another way of looking at it is to ask: Does being born with a silver spoon in your mouth still give you an advantage? We could answer, 'No, it doesn't,' by pointing to the London Mayor, Sadiq Khan, elected in 2016. As well as being from an immigrant family, he's the son of a bus driver and was voted in with a healthy 14 per cent lead over his nearest rival, the Eton-educated son of a billionaire. On the other hand, Khan's predecessor as Mayor was an Etonian friend of an Etonian Prime Minister. And Boris Johnson and David Cameron were not alone. One in ten of all MPs in 2016 were educated at Eton. Half of all Conservative members – and what's more, 17 per cent of Labour MPs – had parents who could afford to give them a private education.

So, should we agree with the English sociologist Richard Hoggart, who said, 'Each decade we shiftily declare we have buried class; each decade the coffin stays empty'? Or do we think class in England has got both feet in the grave? And what about English snobbishness? Is that dying, or do we still look down our noses at those below us? A YouGov poll in 2014 showed that the 'toffs' at the top are not as toffee-nosed as they once were. Far from clinging to their top-drawer status, the upper classes may these days feel ashamed of it. Only 1 per cent of the survey's respondents described themselves as upper class. As we've seen, it used to be that your dress defined your class. But go into your local gastropub these days and there's no telling if that the young family at the next table – jeans and T-shirts the lot of them – are the lords of the manor, or plumber and hairdresser plus kids on a Friday night out.

So what's happened to make the titled and wealthy today so cagey about who they are? It's partly of course because equality, not privilege, has become the official mantra of life in England. But there's more to it than that. One man more than all others reflected the new attitude towards the 'idle rich'. Not Karl Marx, nor Leon Trotsky, nor some serious-minded social reformer. It was a comic writer, England's greatest, P.G. Wodehouse. His novels and short stories, written over several decades of the early and mid-twentieth century – and still madly popular today – showed the English upper classes, in the form of Bertie Wooster and Lord Emsworth of Blandings, as eccentric, delightfully funny and not as bright as their servants. And Wodehouse's tradition lives on. So, the last thing our family of 'nobs' (an almost extinct word) in the local gastropub want would be for their fellow diners to sneer at them for being stuck-up – or worse, to laugh at them for being old-fashioned, out of touch and rather silly by dressing differently. Far from being snobbish, members of the upper class know that flaunting their upper-classness might soon see them mocked in *Private Eye* or on the BBC's *Live at the Apollo*. How very English to bring down the ruling class not by violent revolution but by threatening to laugh at them. So, clearly, English humour isn't dead. We could all agree on that.

But hang on. Does our threat to ridicule anyone we think Woosterish mean the English love of eccentrics has faded? Are there fewer of them than there used to be? It would be a shame if that were so. You can only be an odd-ball in a free society where there are no secret police who might suspect your strange behaviour is subversive and lock you up. So we should pay tribute to one man from society's top drawer who still flaunts his class: the MP Jacob Rees-Mogg. With his double-breasted suit, carefully parted hair and unashamed clipped vowels, he looks and sounds like a Victorian hangover. He's even know in Parliament by the jokey title 'the honourable member for 1860'. But when you listen to him, you soon find that his words – stripped of the public-school accent – are designed to appeal to Brexiteers and like-minded Conservatives of any class. Rees-Mogg manages to be quite normal and eccentric at the same time. A very English piece of crazy logic in itself. And, of course, the House of Commons in the way it conducts its debates remains a fine specimen of collective eccentricity.

***

The decline – though perhaps not yet the demise – of class in England today is one example of how parts of our national identity can change. As we've often seen on our 1,600-year journey, the English have had to come to terms with many different pressures and influences, some from outside the country, others from within. The language you're reading on this page, for instance, is one long history of change. In the Middle Ages, the Anglo-Saxon tongue played a crucial role in developing English national identity. We managed – almost by a fluke – not to end up French-speaking and probably a French sub-nation. Old English changed by absorbing not only bits of Viking, Norman, French and Latin, but also Hebrew, Spanish, Hindu, Urdu, Malay, Afro-Caribbean, Chinese and many other scatterings of vocabulary including, recently, technospeak.

Ever since the Anglo-Saxons put down roots, the English have often had to adapt. At times the best course has been to hold the line and fight off the foreigner who threatened the foundations of Englishness. But sometimes the English have survived by absorbing the outsiders, just as the language has. Sometimes we've changed the way we do things and learned new tricks. Suffering decades of religious persecution and civil war made us start to be tolerant and to value social stability. When the world's horizons expanded to new far-away lands, the English made themselves sailors and colonisers. Technological revolution saw the English lead the world as enthusiastic inventors. When foreigners such as Napoleon, the Kaiser or Hitler threatened the English way of life, we've united with other foreigners as the best way to defend ourselves.

So we should add one more characteristic to the English list. The English can be flexible. Yes, they know when to dig their heels in. But the English also know when to do a deal, when to compromise. If circumstances change and something doesn't work, the English will use their ingenuity to fix it. If English identity were stuck in the past, no matter what happened in the world outside, then as a nation we would stagnate and lose touch. The English love of stability may make us slow off the mark sometimes, but we're strong finishers.

Not – as you'll appreciate – that I'm being in any way boastful, or arrogant.

***

Our 1,600-year journey has taken us from Hastings in the south to Bamburgh in the north, from Liverpool in the west to Cambridgeshire in the east, from the tiny village of Deerhurst in Gloucestershire to the centre of London, and we've arrived at the present day. It's true that English national identity has not emerged from its long – sometimes glorious, sometimes shameful – history intact, but then that's no bad thing. At the same time, core English values, such as our commitment to democracy, the rule of law and political stability, our sense of humour even, have managed to survive all the threats the modern world can fling at them.

Now, at the end of our journey, I look across towards the White Cliffs of Dover, and I see why they've come to symbolise the heart of Englishness. The sheer rock face has often signified the country's impregnability against an enemy and a timelessness that the works of mere humans can't match. But the white cliffs too have been a welcoming sight to friends and allies. And to English folk who've travelled the world and sail back up the Channel, they've said, 'You're home at last.' In times of war, the cliffs have been a promise, a promise of a return to normality – a peaceful English way of life again – once the fighting's done. 'There'll be bluebirds over / The White Cliffs of Dover,' Sang Dame Vera Lynn in 1942, 'Tomorrow, just you wait and see …'

So, what about the future? Was Brexit a mistake? Or will it turn out to have been a smart move? Will the English treasure their democracy, be law-abiding, independent minded, tolerant, happy in the middle ground, eccentric, funny, stiff upper lipped, inventive, outward-looking in 100 years' time? Or will their tendency to be snobbish, arrogant, brutal, patronising and self-righteous resurface? Or, yet again, will the English start to think and behave in ways we never could dream of? What's certain is that future generations will need that invaluable English quality of flexibility, of being able to adapt to a changing world.

Of course, we can't know what the English of tomorrow will look like. But whatever happens over the next twenty, fifty or 100 years, we'll still have our sixteen centuries of English history. Our children and grandchildren may not be the same as us, but so long as they learn about their country's past, they'll know what values have served the English people well.

They'll know where they came from. And that – in the end – is who we all are.

But now it's your turn. What do you think? Please tweet your thoughts #Englishidentity … And let's have a peaceful, English debate.

www.derekjtaylorbooks.com

Acknowledgements

My sincere thanks to Geoff Richards and Mike Morris for accompanying me on some of the research trips and for their invaluable guidance on the places and their history. And my thanks as well to Mervyn Allcock, Anne Archer, Chris Elton, Jan McCorquodale, Tim Norris, Colin Piper, Stephanie Robbins and Rosie St John Lowther for the help and information they provided. I'm grateful too to those named in the illustrations captions who kindly gave me permission to reproduce their photographs, and I thank all those official guides, often unpaid, who help so many of us understand our past.

In writing *Who Do The English Think They Are?* I consulted over fifty learned works on English history, one of which became my bible, always open on the desk with dozens of bookmarks poking out of its pages. So I'm much indebted to Professor Robert Tombs for his excellent book, *The English and their History*.

I thank Mark Beynon and Lauren Newby at The History Press, and my agent Robyn Drury at the Diane Banks Literary Agency for their encouragement and ever helpful comments.

Most of all, I'm grateful to my wife, Maggie, who was the first to read every chapter and who – as always – had an uncanny knack of spotting what needed changing. The book couldn't have been finished without her.

INDEX